AVOIDING CLAIMS

AVOIDING CLAIMS

A practical guide for the construction industry

M. Coombes Davies

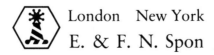

London   New York
E. & F. N. Spon

First published in 1989 by
E. & F. N. Spon Ltd
11 New Fetter Lane, London EC4P 4EE

© 1989 M. Coombes Davies

Typeset in 11/12 Sabon by
Scarborough Typesetting Services
Printed in Great Britain by
St. Edmundsbury Press Ltd, Bury St. Edmunds, Suffolk

ISBN 0 419 14620 2

British Library Cataloguing in Publication Data

Coombes Davies, M. (Mair), *1956–*
Avoiding claims: a practical guide to the
contruction industry.
1. Great Britain. Construction industries. Law
I. Title
344.103'78624

ISBN 0–419–14620–2

Contents

Preface

'How do I avoid claims?', asked the architect fearfully.

'Do not practice architecture', advised the barrister firmly.

'How do I stop getting claims from buildings I have built?', asked the contractor gruffly.

'Do not build them', proclaimed the barrister succinctly.

'How do we avoid spending thousands on professional indemnity insurance?', murmured the quantity surveyor and the engineer sotto voce.

'Never calculate, never advise, never be a quantity surveyor, never be an engineer', said the barrister loudly.

'That means that there would be no construction industry claims, no work for us', gasped the solicitor aghast.

'Exactly', replied the barrister sadly.

The reality of the problem is that it is extremely difficult to avoid claims in the construction industry. This is because of one very simple factor. It is human to err. However, it may be possible to limit claims not only by good practice but also on the basis that being forewarned is often forearmed.

The book covers both precontract liability in its many forms and also liability during and after a building contract. It points to some of the pitfalls which beset construction. In so doing, the book acts as a forewarning of those dangers: how is this done?

Common questions are asked. They are answered succinctly. The principles embodied within a series of questions and answers are illustrated by a cautionary tale. A cautionary tale is a case where someone got it wrong and having got it wrong what the courts then held to be their liability. It must be remembered that what is decided in one court one day may not be the same as is decided by a higher court the following day. Therefore, the cases are and can only be a snapshot of the law at a particular point in time.

It is possible to read and use the book in a number of ways. The first is to read the book from cover to cover to gain a broad appreciation of the subject. The second is to read only the cautionary tales on the basis of pure pleasure – the problems others have faced will never happen to me. Are you sure? It is too late to be wise after the event. The third way to use the book is to read only those sections which are appropriate to a current problem; in other words, to use it as a reference tool by turning first to the chapter which deals with the general area of the problem. For example, should the problem concern insurance then turn first to the chapter headed, 'What must I do to effectively limit my liability by insurance?' If the particular problem is to do with what can and cannot be left out of an insurance policy's questionnaire, read those questions and answers within the sections headed, 'Uberrimae fidei', and, 'Withholding information'.

ONE

What is the extent of

my liability?

The claims which can be made against any professional, be they architect, engineer or contractor, can be divided into two areas:

1. *Civil liability* – for claims arising in contract or tort;
2. *Criminal liability* – for claims arising from a breach of statute or common law.

1.1 CIVIL LIABILITY IN CONTRACT AND TORT

Q. How am I liable in contract?

Before any question of liability can arise, it must be established that a contract does in fact exist; and that the three elements of a simple contract (i.e. a contract not under seal) have been completed:

1. *An offer* – being a clear indication by one party to another of willingness to be bound by a contract, provided that certain specified terms are accepted (e.g. a contractor offers to build a house within a certain time, provided his client pays him £X);
2. *Acceptance* – being an absolute and unqualified acceptance of the precise terms of the offer (e.g. the client accepts the contractor's offer and agrees to pay him £X);
3. *Consideration* – being an act or counter-promise by one party made in return for another's promise (e.g. the price to be paid by the client for the contractor's promise to build a house); no consideration is required for a contract under seal.

The contract itself may take a number of forms, or combination of forms; it may be:

1. *Oral* – e.g. the client and builder, in the above example, simply discuss the type of house which the client has in mind, and the works which will be needed, and arrive at an acceptable price;
2. *Written* – e.g. an architect goes out on written tender to a number of contractors for the scheme; the architect having made a written recommendation for the selection of one contractor to the client, the client and that

---

The case of the overconfident young architect

A young student had passed the first part of his architectural examinations; these were in three parts, spread over a university course which lasted seven years. At the end of those seven years he would be eligible to register himself as an architect and become a member of the Royal Institute of British Architects (RIBA), and to use such letters after his name as the RIBA would grant him. He was confident that in the next few years he would pass the remaining examinations with success.

Meanwhile, in order to save time and get himself established, he began to build up a small but profitable architectural practice. He referred to himself as an architect with his clients. He placed an advertisement in the Yellow Pages; the advertisement described him as an architect, and after his name there appeared the letters 'ARIBA'.

One of his jobs was not successful. His client sued him.

He tried to escape liability by saying that he was simply a young and inexperienced architectural student. This did not help him. Because he had held himself out as a qualified architect, he was deemed to have the skills of an architect and would be judged against them. Furthermore, he had committed a statutory offence by using the title 'architect' to which he was not entitled. The title can be used only by someone who is registered with the Architects' Registration Council of the UK (ARCUK). He was fortunate, for he was only fined. However, the offence can lead on conviction not only to a fine, but also to imprisonment, or both.

There are similar facts in the case of *R. v. Breeze* [1973] 1 W.L.R. 582.

---

contractor then sign a Joint Contracts Tribunal (JCT) contract;
3. *Partly oral, partly written* – e.g. as in (1), except that the price which has been agreed has been written down;
4. *Express* – e.g. as in (2), where all the terms of a contract are set out in the written documents which together form that contract;
5. *Implied* – e.g. as in (1) or (3), where some or all of the contract terms are not in writing, but can nevertheless be implied, either because of a statutory requirement, for instance, to pay a reasonable price for work (*Supply of Goods and Services Act 1982*) or because, over a period of time, there has been a course of dealing between the two parties to the contract.

All contracts should be in writing whether they are made between professional architect or engineer, contractor and subcontractor, contractor and supplier or professional and client. In the case of a client commissioning an architect, the contract must be in writing. It is a breach of the RIBA Code of Professional Conduct if it is not. The responsibilities of each party must be clearly defined, particularly where certain aspects of a commission are to be excluded, as for instance, where part of the work is to be undertaken by others. Without a written contract, it may prove somewhat difficult later to rely upon any specific clause excluding or limiting liability.

Q. How am I liable in tort?

A tort is some wrongful act, such as negligence, which gives rise to a right of action.

There are essentially three elements to a tort, each of which must be present before liability can be established; they are as follows:

1. A duty of skill and care exists between yourself and the person who is claiming against you. The test which will be applied is whether the latter is your neighbour (a *neighbour* has been defined as 'persons who are so closely and directly affected by my act that I ought reasonably to have them in contemplation as being so affected when I directed my mind to the acts or omissions which are called in question': *Donoghue* v. *Stevenson* [1932] A.C. 562, 580, H.I.). Thus an engineer or architect owes a duty of skill and care to his client in designing a structure, so that it is fit for the purpose for which it is intended to be used;
2. The duty of skill and care has been broken. The test is objective; there will be a breach of duty, either:
   (a) by not doing something which a reasonable man would do in circumstances where a duty to act is owed, or
   (b) by doing something which a reasonable man would not do.
   The 'reasonable man', in this context, would be equated not so much with the man on top of the Clapham omnibus, but rather the competent professional architect, engineer or contractor who would exercise ordinary skill and care;
3. The person who is claiming against you, for example, the client, has suffered damage. The client would not have a claim until such time as the damage (e.g. to the structure) had manifested itself, nor would he have a claim if he could not show that but for your negligence, he would not have suffered damage. If in any event the damage would have occurred without a breach in the duty of skill and care, you will not be liable.

Q. Can I be liable both in contract and tort at the same time?

A statement of claim can be framed in such a way that it alleges both a breach of contract and tort as an alternative.

The distinction between contract and tort is important because of the different periods of limitation, that is the time in which a claim can be brought, in each case. However, where there is a contractual relationship between two parties, particularly a commercial relationship, their obligations in tort cannot be any greater than those found expressly or by necessary implication in contract.

Q. To whom am I liable?

(1) In contract
Only those parties to a contract can sue, and be sued, under the terms of a contract. A person who is not a party to it cannot, he is a stranger to the contract.

For example, a client has a contract with an architect when he retains him under the RIBA Memorandum of Appointment for the design and supervision of a scheme. Both client and architect may bring an action against the other for breach of contract under the terms of the Memorandum. However, the contractor is not a party to the Memorandum; he has no contract with the architect and, therefore, no cause of action under that contract against the architect.

(2) In tort
Regardless of whether or not a contract exists, the architect, engineer or contractor will be liable to any person, to whom

A cautionary tale about reading the small print – twice

A Canadian building contractor was one of the nine companies which submitted lump-sum tenders in response to a city council's request for contract bids. The form of tender stipulated that all tenders would be irrevocable once the tenders had been opened, until such time as the construction contract had been signed by the successful tenderer.

When the tenders were opened, the building contractor's proved to be the lowest. However, there was an error in it which was not apparent on the face of the tender. Before they were selected, the building contractor discovered the error and told the city council of it. The city council accepted the building contractor's explanation that a clerical error caused by an inadvertent transposition of numbers contained in the building contractor's original working papers had resulted in a substantial underestimate.

The city council would not allow the building contractor either to alter their tender or withdraw it. The building contractor refused to execute the contract. The contract was awarded to the second-lowest tenderer; and the city council began an action for the difference between the two tenders.

It was held that initially a contract had been formed when the city council made an offer by advertising for tenders which had been accepted by the building contractors when they submitted and did not withdraw their tender. At the time the tenders were opened, there was no mistake in the formation of that contract because the building contractor intended to submit the tender in the form in which it was submitted.

Under the terms of the initial contract, the city council had the right to select a tender obliging the selected party, namely the building contractor, to enter into a construction contract. By not doing so, the building contractor was in breach of the initial contract. Thus the city council was entitled to accept another tender and hold the building contractor responsible for the difference in value between the two tenders.

The city council's action under the initial contract was founded on what was described as a 'penalty clause'; nevertheless (even if it was so), the amount claimed by the city council was a fair estimate of damages. They had a duty to mitigate their loss, which they did by accepting the second-lowest tender. They could not be forced to accept the building contractor's corrected tender, even though it was still lower than any of the other tenders, as this would have changed the tendering system into an auction.

Calgary v. *Northern Construction Company Division of Morrison Knudsen Company Incorporated & Others* [1987], *Construction Law Journal*, 179.

he owes a duty of skill and care and whom he ought to have considered when committing a breach of that duty. For example, if he negligently designs or builds a structure which is later occupied by a tenant, the tenant will have a good claim against him if he can show that he has suffered loss as a result of that breach.

If one member of the building team has an action brought against him, he can join any other member of the team who either owed a duty of care to or was in breach of contract with the plaintiff, seeking an indemnity or contribution to any damages awarded against him.

Q. What are the remedies for a breach of contract and tort?

(1) *Damages* – one of the most common remedies sought not

only for breach of contract, but also for tort. However, in each case, the amount which will be awarded is assessed differently (this point is explained later).

(2) *Specific performance* – a court may order the party who has broken a contract actually to carry out or complete their obligations under the terms of the contract if damages would be an inadequate remedy.

(3) *Injunction* – the court may instruct a party to refrain from doing an act which infringes the rights of another.

(4) *Recission* – an equitable right to put an end to a contract and to have the status quo restored because of fraud, misrepresentation or mistake.

Q. How much will I be liable for, and how are damages assessed?

The principles which apply to the amount of damages awarded against you by a court depend upon whether the claim is made in contract or tort. The principles are:

In contract

1. Damages for breach of contract are to compensate the injured party for breach in performance; the amount of damages is assessed on the basis that they should be placed in the same position as if the contract had been performed;
2. Where there is some link between a breach of contract by one party and loss suffered by another, damages will be awarded, and if the loss is minimal, only nominal damages will be recovered;
3. The amount of damages recoverable is limited to damages which were within the reasonable contemplation of the parties at the time the contract was made; this is determined by reference to the actual or imputed knowledge of special circumstances giving rise to the damage.

In tort

1. The wrong for which an injured party is compensated in tort is the tortious act itself, and damages are assessed on the basis that he should be put in the same position as he would have been in had that act not been committed;
2. In any action for negligence the link between the negligent act or omission and the damage which is claimed must not be too remote; the kind of damage which is suffered must be reasonably foreseeable;
3. In claims for direct physical damage, once the test in (5) is satisfied, there is no need to go further, the injured party is entitled to recover the full extent of his loss; however, where pure economic loss is concerned (i.e. loss of profit), the extent of that loss must also be reasonably foreseeable; thus if the loss of profits are unusually high or are simply uncertain and speculative, they will not be recovered in damages.
4. Economic loss, or loss of profits, is recoverable as damages where it is the immediate consequence of physical damage.
5. 'Pure' economic loss is only recoverable where there is a very close proximity between the parties, and the injured party has relied upon the person who had committed the negligent act.

1.2 CRIMINAL LIABILITY

Q. When am I criminally liable?

Quite apart from the reasonably well-known aspects of criminal liability such as an engineer who accepts a bribe

The case of the runaway trolleys

An architectural practice approached a super-market chain with proposals for the develop-ment of a steeply sloping site which lay in the centre of a busy seaside town. The key to the commercial success of the new supermarket was that a large car-park was to be provided in order to attract customers. No other competi-tor offered such a facility.

The building works were successfully com-pleted. The site was cut and filled to form a car-park which, in some parts, had a gradient of 1 in 40; it was somewhat steep. Customers had difficulty in pushing to their cars trolleys loaded with groceries. When they reached the cars, the customers' trolleys had a tendency to roll back down the car-park towards the supermarket.

Turnover and profits for the new super-market were lower than expected. The supermarket chain believed the reason for their loss of profit was because customers were deterred from using the store by the steepness of the car-park which they had to negotiate.

The supermarket chain had a good chance of recovering damages in contract and tort for a number of reasons:

1. There was a contractual relationship be-tween the architects and the supermarket chain. It could be shown that it was in the reasonable contemplation of the architects that loss of profits would result from a defective car-park as they knew it was a vital part of the commercial development However, there was some uncertainty as to whether the architects had ever been instructed by their clients that the maxi-mum gradient of the car-park was to be 1 in 20; if they had, then they were in breach of an express contractual term;

2. The architects were in breach of two implied terms of the contract, which were that:
    (a) they would exercise the skill and care expected of a reasonably competent and prudent architectural firm in and about their performance of their con-tract of engagement
    (b) the architects would warn their clients of any adverse implications in their design upon the use of the car-park;

3. Upon reliability being established under (1) and (2), the architects would also be liable in tort for negligence.

Before starting proceedings against the archi-tects, the supermarket chain decided to call upon the services of an accountant. It was found that after the supermarket had opened, its profits peaked; later the profits fell rapidly to a level which was much lower than ex-pected.

One small but important point had been forgotten by the supermarket chain when they levelled the blame for their fall in profits against the architects' car-park design. The supermarket had been opened in the late spring: the profits were boosted by the fact that a large proportion of the supermarket's customers were visitors who had come to the seaside town on holiday during the summer months; and when they left, the super-market's profits fell. The smaller number of residents within the town continued to use the supermarket. They were prepared to put up with the inconvenience of a steep car-park because it was the only store in the town which had adequate car-parking. The super-market chain dropped its claim against the architects.

from a contractor, an architect who fraudulently signs false worksheets or corruption among the building team, there are others which are less well known – e.g. criminal liability under planning-control legislation. Indeed, it is a criminal offence to fail to comply with either an enforcement notice or a stop notice.

A local planning authority may serve an enforcement notice on the owner or occupier of land where development has been carried out in breach of planning control, for instance, where work has begun without planning permission, or where permission has been granted, a condition attaching to it has been ignored. There is a heavy obligation upon the owner to ensure that the steps set out in the notice are followed and completed within the specified time. A failure to do so will lead on summary conviction, that is where the case is heard before magistrates, to a fine not exceeding £2000; and on conviction on indictment, where the matter is brought before the Crown Court, to an unlimited fine.

Similar penalties apply to the contravention of a stop notice. The purpose of such a notice, which is served by the local planning authority after an enforcement notice has been issued, is to give effect almost immediately to that notice because the local planning authority consider it expedient to prevent the carrying out of any activity which is, or is included in, a matter alleged by the notice to constitute a breach of planning control.

The local planning authority, apart from displaying a site notice, may serve the stop notice on any person appearing to them to have an interest in the land, and on anyone, such as a contractor, who is engaged in any activity prohibited by the notice. Unlike an enforcement notice, criminal liability under a stop notice is not limited to the persons upon whom it has been served, but includes anyone who contravenes, or causes or permits the contravention of, the notice.

TWO

When will I start to be liable

for something, and how long

will I be liable for it?

Q. I am confused about when I will start to be liable for something, and how long I will be liable for it. Can you help?

Simply put, the earliest time at which an action can be brought is when there are at least two parties in existence:

1. One party, who is able to sue and present sufficient facts and suitable material which tends to uphold their case;
2. Another party, who can be sued and against whom the evidence can be placed.

The length of the time available in which an action can be brought varies. It depends on whether it is an action in contract or tort.

2.1 WHEN DOES TIME START TO RUN?

Q. When does time start to run against me in contract?

In an action for breach of contract time, or more precisely, the limitation period, then time starts to run at the date on which the contract was broken.

The limitation period is either:

1. 6 years for breach of a simple contract made either orally or in writing, or
2. 12 years if the contract is under seal.

The fact that the relevant limitation period has expired does not prevent a claim from being raised. Rather it offers the opportunity to say in defence that the claim should not succeed because it has been brought out of time.

Q. For how long will I be liable in contract?

A claim for breach of contract must be brought within the limitation period, otherwise it is statute barred, that is the time prescribed by statute in which the claim should have been brought has passed.

The limitation periods, which run from the date on which the contract was broken, are:

1. 6 years for breach of a simple contract made either orally or in writing;
2. 12 years if the contract is under seal – i.e. where it has been created by deed

The fact that the relevant limitation period has expired does not prevent a claim from being raised. Rather it offers the opportunity to say in defence that the claim should not succeed because it has been brought out of time.

Q. When does time start to run against me in tort?

In a tortious action for negligence time does not start to run against you until some damage has occurred. The basic limitation period is 6 years from the date of negligence.

However, damage to a building may not be apparent until some time after the date on which the duty of skill and care was broken. In other words, the damage is latent rather than patent.

The limitation period for latent damage, as set out in the *Latent Damage Act 1986*, is 3 years from the date of knowledge of certain material facts, namely:

1. The material facts of the damage which is sufficiently serious to justify bringing an action;
2. That the damage was caused by an act or omission alleged to constitute negligence;
3. The identity of the defendant.

Such knowledge may have been obtained in a number of ways, for example:

1. From facts which have been observed or ascertained by the plaintiff;
2. From facts ascertainable by him with the help of appropriate expert advice.

This is subject to a long-stop limitation period of 15 years from the breach of the duty of skill and care. It bars a right of action accruing if damage to a building appears after 15 years.

Q. If the ownership of a building changes, is the limitation period affected?

Should a building be damaged and has come into new ownership since 18 September 1986, the new owner who does not and could not know about the damage then acquires a right of action.

A limitation period of 3 years runs from the earliest date on which the new owner had both the right and the knowledge required to bring an action, that is knowledge of such facts about the damage as would lead a reasonable person who had suffered such damage to consider it sufficiently serious to justify commencing proceedings. If the previous owner of the property knew, or ought to have known, of the damage, then the limitation period begins to run from that date. It does *not*

The case of the missing damp-proof course

In 1962 the congregation of a church engaged a firm of architects to design and supervise the construction of a new church and hall, completed in 1970. The church was set over the hall which was partially below ground level. Staircases led down to the lower hall; they were built into its external walls.

Some time passed before it was discovered that there was no damp-proof course between the staircases and the walls. Water could penetrate the brickwork and cause damage to the internal plasterwork. This eventually happened. By the time the defect became apparent, an action in contract had become statute barred. Consequently, the church sued the architects in negligence.

The architects accepted liability for this defect. Indeed, one of their duties was to design the building such that it would be both suitable and adequate for its intended uses. However, the architects raised a limitation defence. The burden of proof on the limitation defence lay upon the church to prove that their cause of action accrued within the relevant period before the issue of the writ. In other words, they had to establish that on the balance of probability damp first reached the plaster by 1 February 1971; the church could not do so. Thus the architects' defence succeeded.

London Congregation Union Incorporated v. *Harris and Harris* [1987], *Construction Law Journal*, 37, C.A.

---

begin to run anew from the time the new owner first acquired his interest.

2.2 WHEN DOES THE CAUSE OF ACTION OCCUR?

Q. How is time in a limitation period calculated?

(1) *Time starts* – although time starts running against the person who has suffered loss, namely the plaintiff, on the day on which the cause of action arose, that day is excluded from calculating the precise length of the limitation period.

(2) *Time continues* – should a cause of action arise and before the claim is settled one party to the action dies, the time prescribed as the appropriate limitation period will continue to run either against the plaintiff's administrator or for the administrator, as the case may be. This is so even if there has been some delay between the date of the death and that when the Letters of Administration were granted.

(3) *Time stops* – time stops running against the plaintiff only when he brings legal proceedings against the defendant, provided that they are valid and regular.

This involves presenting to the correct court office, be it High Court or County Court, a writ of summons. Upon the appropriate fee being paid, the writ is endorsed with the official court seal recording the date on which it is issued. As it is a unilateral process in which only the plaintiff and court staff are involved, time stops running against the plaintiff immediately, though the writ still has to be served on the defendant.

As the first step in an action, the purpose of a writ of summons is simply to give the defendant notice of the claim made against him and to compel him to appear and answer it if he does not admit it.

A writ is not the only way of starting proceedings in the High Court or the County Court. An action may also be started, for example, by an originating summons. Whereas a writ is the normal mode of starting an action where damages

Table 2.1 Limitation periods

Course of action	Statute	Time starts from:	Years (Limitation period)														
			1	2	3	4	5	6	7	8	9	10	11	12	13	14	15
Latent damage	*Latent Damages Act 1986*, section 14(a)	Date of knowledge of material facts			3												
Personal injury	*Limitation Act 1980*, section 11	Date of cause of action or knowledge			3												
Fatal accident	*Limitation Act 1980*, section 12				3												
Tort	*Limitation Act 1980*, section 2	(a) If actionable *per se*, e.g. trespass, libel; date of commission of tort (b) If actionable only on proof of damage, e.g. nuisance; data damage occurred						6									
Contract not under seal	*Limitation Act 1980*, section 5	Date of the breach complained of						6									
Contract under seal	*Limitation Act 1980*, section 8	Date of the breach complained of												12			
Latent damage	*Latent Damages Act 1986*, section 14(b)																
	Limitation Act 1980	Date of alleged breach of duty															15

or specific performance are claimed, an originating summons may be used where there is no dispute of fact and there is no relief claimed – e.g. the only issue between the two parties is the meaning of a contract clause (Table 2.1).

A little history on the limitation of time

The term 'statutes of limitation' may be interpreted as those numerous acts which prescribe a certain time in which legal proceedings must be started otherwise the action will be barred. It was suggested in 1821 in *Murray* v. *East India Co.* (1821) 5B. & Ald. 204 that as the statutes were broadly similar, they should be construed in a similar manner, that is in a manner which was broad and generous rather than one which was strictly literal.

In their earliest form statutes of limitation were applicable only to these actions brought in common law. Yet, in some cases, the principle embodied within them was applied by analogy in courts of equity which developed the theories of laches and acquiescence. If it were shown that there had either been negligence or some unreasonable delay in bringing a claim before the courts, or that the plaintiff had appeared to waive his rights, he would be barred from claiming equitable relief. In 1767, Lord Camden, in *Smith* v. *Clay* (1767) 3 Bro. C.C. 639, remarked that a court of equity had always refused its aid to stale demands, where one party party had slept upon his rights and acquiesced for a great length of time, 'nothing can call forth this court into activity but conscience, good faith and reasonable diligence. Where these are wanting the court is passive and does nothing. Laches and neglect are always discountenanced and therefore, from the beginning of this jurisdiction, there was always a limitation to suits in this court.'

The doctrine of laches was not, and is not, an arbitrary or technical one. In the mid-nineteenth century it existed where it would be practically unjust to give a remedy, either because a party had by his conduct done that which might be fairly regarded as equivalent to a waiver of it or where by his conduct and neglect he had, though perhaps not waiving that remedy, yet put the other party in a situation in which it would be unreasonable to place him if the remedy were to be asserted afterwards. In both cases, then, lapse of time and delay are material. But if an argument against relief which otherwise would be just were founded merely on delay, that delay not amounting to a bar by a statute of limitations, the validity of that defence would be tried upon substantially equitable principles. Two circumstances which were always important in such cases were the length of the delay and the nature of the acts done during the interval, which might affect either party and cause a balance of justice or injustice in taking the one course or the other, so far as relates to the remedy.

In the twentieth century little had changed the doctrine of laches. The purposes of statutory limitation were summarized in the 1962 *Report of the Committee on Limitation of Actions in Cases of Personal Injury*:

1. Statutes of limitation protect defendants from the stale claims which by being dormant for some length of time when resurrected may possess more cruelty than justice;
2. They tend to act as an incentive, encouraging plaintiffs with good causes of action to start proceedings expeditiously and without unreasonable delay, thus enabling the case to be heard at a time when witnesses' memories may still be reasonably clear;
3. The limitation periods help to avoid the possibility that a person might have lost or destroyed evidence which could be used to disprove an old claim;
4. They allow a plaintiff to be secure in the knowledge that after a given period of time has passed, no claim may be made against him on an issue which might have given rise to him being held liable.

Inevitably, there is an arbitrary element in the number of years of any given limitation period. Indeed, there is little which makes a six-year period inherently better than, say, three years.

The *Limitation Act 1980*, together with the *Latent Damages Act 1986*, amended and consolidated the law in relation, among other things, to the limitation of actions. The former was largely based on what it termed 'the principal Act', namely the *Limitation Act 1939*. The 1939 Act had itself consolidated and amended earlier enactments on the limitation of actions. Section 2(1)(a) of the 1939 Act established that actions founded on simple contract or on tort could not be brought after the expiration of 6 years from the date on which the cause of the action accrued. Whereas an action based upon a speciality, a contract under seal may not be brought, under section 2(3) after 12 years, though this does not affect any action for which a shorter period of limitation is prescribed by the Act. An action cannot be brought upon any judgment after the expiration of 12 years from the date on which the judgment became enforceable and no areas of interest in respect of any judgment debt can be recovered after the expiration of 6 years from the date on which the interest became due. In the case of personal injuries, a claim may be statute barred after 3 years from the date on which the cause of action accrued or the date, if later, of the plaintiff's knowledge of facts relevant to his right of action. With certain exceptions, such as an owner's title to chattels and land extinguished after a stated number of years, the Limitation Acts do not extinguish a plaintiff's right, only the remedy by action or set-off. If a plaintiff has other means of recovering damages, in such circumstances, he may use those means.

The Limitation Acts do not apply in Scotland, but the *Prescription and Limitation (Scotland) Act 1973*, as amended by the 1984 Act of the same title, applies to time limits for bringing legal proceedings where damages are claimed, to establish the extinction of an obligation or claim corresponding to those in contract and tort of English law by a negative prescriptive period of 5 years subject to several exceptions and exclusions within an overall prescriptive period of 20 years. Section 6(1) of the 1973 Act states: 'if after the appropriate date, an obligation to which this section applies has subsisted for a continuous period of five years (a) without any relevant claim having been made in relation to the obligation and (b) without the subsistence of the obligation having been relevantly acknowledged then as from the expiration of that period the obligation shall be extinguished.' The section applies under schedule 1(g), 'to any obligation arising from or by reason of any breach of a contract or promise not being an obligation falling within

any other provision of this paragraph'. The obligation to pay damages or make 'reparation' is enforceable on the date when the loss, injury or damage occurred. However, if the damage occurs continuously, then the obligation arises on the date when it ceases; whereas if the 'creditor' or plaintiff was unaware that he had suffered, then time would start to run when he first became, or could with reasonable diligence have become, aware of his loss.

Q. Does someone still have a case against me if they serve a writ out of time?

Once a writ is issued, it must be served within 12 months on each and every defendant, otherwise it expires and may only be renewed by leave of the court.

Though a writ may be out of time, it does not become null and void simply because it has not been served within 12 months. It merely becomes irregular. It may not be set aside at a later date upon the suit of the defendant if he has already entered an unconditional appearance. By so doing, any objection he might have had to the irregular writ is assumed to have been waived.

2.3 EXTENSION OF LIMITATION PERIOD

Q. Can the limitation period be extended?

The general rule which prohibits bringing an action after a limitation period has lapsed is not absolute, but subject to certain exceptions, as follows:
(1) Because a certain procedure has to be undertaken within the court offices to stop time running against a plaintiff, the limitation period may be extended if it ends on a day when

The case of the brickie's mate

James Thompson was a bricklayer's mate. He worked for the Welsh building firm, Brown Construction Ltd. In March 1976 they were carrying out work at British Steel's plant in Ebbw Vale. Scaffolding had been erected for them by SGB Scaffolding (Great Britain) Ltd. The scaffolding collapsed under Mr Thompson and he was injured.

Through his trade union, Mr Thompson was put in touch with a firm of solicitors. He instructed them to bring an action in damages against the builders and scaffolders for personal injury caused by their negligence. Having been notified of the claim by the solicitors in April 1976, both the builders and the scaffolders referred it to their respective insurers. The scaffolders' insurers conducted negotiations for settling the claim as their clients were clearly liable to Mr Thompson. They wrote to the solicitors that they had completed their enquiries and were prepared to put forward an offer in settlement of the case after they had received details of Mr Thompson's earnings and medical report.

The solicitors were negligent. They allowed the 3-year limitation period to expire before issuing the writ. This was not only because they had experienced considerable delay in obtaining the medical report, but they had also mislaid and forgotten Mr Thompson's file. The file was not discovered until the spring of 1979. The solicitors then issued a writ in April, which was 37 days after the 3-year limitation period had expired. The scaffolders, in defence, pleaded that the action was out of time.

At the trial of the preliminary issue, of whether it would be equitable to allow Mr Thompson's action to proceed, it was held that he would not be prejudiced if the statutory limitation period continued to apply to his action as he had an incontestable case in negligence against his own solicitors, by which he could recover at least as much as he would have recovered against the scaffolders. Mr Thompson appealed to the House of Lords and his appeal was allowed. The limitation period was set aside.

Thompson v. Brown (Trading as George Albert Brown (Builders) & Co.) [1981] 1 W.L.R. 744.

the court offices are closed and no legal business can be transacted to the next day on which the offices are open; this covers Sundays, Good Friday, Christmas Day and Bank Holidays.

However, once time has started to run, it continues to run even though an action cannot be brought because the court office is closed for some unusual reason. In 1661 the 'unusual reason' of general rebellion led to the closure of the courts.

(2) In personal and fatal injury cases the courts have an unfettered discretion to override the limitation period if it appears equitable so to do, that is, if either the plaintiff or the defendant would be prejudiced by the limitation period. In deciding whether or not to allow an action, the court considers a number of points:

(a) The length of, and reasons for, the delay on the part of the plaintiff;

(b) The extent to which the delay would make the plaintiff or defendant's evidence less convincing or cogent;

(c) The conduct of the defendant after the cause of action arose, including the extent, if any, to which he responded to requests reasonably made by the plaintiff for information or inspection for the purpose of obtaining facts which were or might be relevant to the plaintiff's cause of action against the defendant;

(d) The duration of any disability of the plaintiff arising after the date of the accrual of the cause of action;

(e) The extent to which the plaintiff acted promptly and reasonably once he knew whether or not the act or

The case of the multi-coloured bricks

Mr Walker was a clerk of works employed by a local authority. As part of his sparetime occupation, he had an arrangement with George Alfred Woor, a builder, who had himself been a bricklayer and worked in the building industry for some thirty years. The arrangement was that Mr Walker would draw up plans for bungalows and the builder would prepare a specification. Mr Walker would then sell the plans to anyone interested in having a bungalow built. The buyer would be introduced by Mr Walker to a 'builder', namely Mr Woor.

In this way Mr and Mrs Clark learned from Mr Walker that a plot of land owned by Mr Woor was for sale. They entered into negotiations and bought the land. A contract was concluded in March 1953, whereby Mr Woor agreed to build a detached bungalow and garage for £2490 on or before 6 months from the date of completion of the sale of the land. The building work was to be carried out in a workmanlike manner to the reasonable satisfaction of Mr and Mrs Clark. It was to be in accordance with the plan prepared by Mr Walker and the specification drawn up by the builder. However, Mr and Mrs Clark were under the mistaken impression that Mr Walker would safeguard their interest by supervising the work. In effect, they were dependent entirely on the builder for the honest performance of the contract. The contract stated that multi-coloured Dorking facing bricks were to be used for the walls. However, knowing at the time the contract was made that he would be unable to complete the work in time as deliveries of Dorking bricks were subject to delay, the builder substituted them for best Ockley bricks without informing Mr and Mrs Clark. Although a considerable number of bricks were underbaked and of indifferent quality, the builder nevertheless built them into the walls of the bungalow.

Eight years later, in 1961, Mr and Mrs Clark noticed that some of the bricks were beginning to flake and found that they were not the specified Dorking bricks. They consulted an architect who discovered that 20–25% of the bricks were in poor condition. He recommended that the most economic course of action would be for all the bricks to be rendered over. The cost of the remedial work was estimated at £576 16s 11d.

In April 1962, Mr and Mrs Clark issued a writ against the builder, claiming damages for breach of contract. The builder, in denying breach of contract, claimed that the case was out of time as more than 6 years had elapsed from the date on which the cause of action accrued. Mr and Mrs Clark replied that their cause of action had been concealed from them by the builder's fraud.

It was held that the relationship between the parties was that of builder and building owner, and the circumstances were such that the builder knew perfectly well that the building owners were relying upon him to perform his contract and treat them in a decent and honest way. He also knew that nobody was supervising the work on their behalf and that they were dependent upon him for the honest performance of the contract. Despite this, the builder quite deliberately entered into the contract knowing that he could not perform it in accordance with the terms, and also finding himself with bad bricks on his hands, instead of discarding them and getting good bricks, he used them in the course of his building work. This was unconscionable behaviour and, in the circumstances, amounted to fraud.

Clark v. *Woor* [1965] 1 W.L.R. 650

A cautionary tale of fraud and the supervising team

The William Hill Organisation were clients for the building of an office block in Blackfriars Road, London. The work was to be carried out under the supervision of architects.

In March 1960 the client entered into a JCT form of building contract with the contractors Bernard Sunley & Son Ltd. The contract provided:

> . . . unless notice in writing of a dispute or difference shall have been given . . . before the final certificate has been issued the final certificate shall be conclusive evidence in any proceedings arising out of this contract . . . that the works have been properly carried out in accordance with the terms of the contract save in so far as it is proved in the said proceedings that any sum mentioned in the said certificate is erroneous by reason of
>
> (1) fraud, dishonesty or fraudulent concealment relating to the Works or any part thereof or to any matter dealt with in the said certificate, or
> (2) any defects (including any omission in the Works) which reasonable inspection or examination at any reasonable time during the course of the Works or before the issue of the said certificate would have not disclosed . . .
> (3) save as aforesaid no certificate of the architect shall of itself be conclusive evidence that any Works or instructions to which it relates are in accordance with the Contract

The office block was designed and built as a reinforced concrete frame structure. Externally the building was clad with Portland and reconstructed stone panels. The ground and first floor of the west elevation were clad in glass mosaic. The cladding was fixed between January and July 1961. A final certificate was issued by the architects in April 1963.

Between 1971 and 1972 the William Hill Organisation, being concerned at the external appearance of the office block, which had deteriorated, instructed the second firm of architects to inspect the building. A number of defects were found, especially in the cladding. The stone fixings had corroded, the specified phosphor-bronze fixings had been substituted for fixings of copper, brass or aluminium, and there was an absence of compression beds between the cladding panels. The architects took the view that these were merely isolated defects. However, in the summer of 1974 there were signs that the cladding was moving. On removing some of the cladding panels between 1974 and 1976, similar, equally dangerous, defects were revealed as had been uncovered earlier. As a result of these findings, the William Hill Organisation decided to have all the cladding removed and replaced. The cost of the remedial works was estimated at over £100 000.

In March 1975 the William Hill Organisation issued a writ for damages, claiming breach of contract and negligence on the part of the contractors. This the latter denied and pleaded that the client's claim was statute barred; 13 years had elapsed between the erection of the stone cladding and the decision to remove it, and 17 years had passed before the clients discovered that the mosaic was also unstable. Thus more than 12 years had passed since practical completion took place in 1962, and under the contract, the final certificate was conclusive evidence that the works were properly carried out.

The William Hill Organisation replied, in November 1978, alleging that the fixings were:

(1) fraudulently concealed by the contractors;
(2) the final certificate did not operate as a contractual bar;
(3) the defects first manifested themselves in 1972, and it was then that they first discovered or could reasonably have discovered them.

The trial judge held in dismissing the client's claim that the stone-cladding defects were not fraudulently concealed because the clients had failed to discharge the burden of proof that lay on them to show that their architects, in exercising reasonable care and skill, could not have been expected to have observed these defects. The Court of Appeal, in dismissing the client's appeal, held that they were wrong to argue that since the contractors were contractually obliged to provide their own supervision, the clients were entitled to rely upon the contractor's own supervising team and that that was sufficient to defeat a plea of fraudulent concealment.

William Hill Organisation Ltd. v. *Bernard Sunley & Sons Ltd.* [1982] 22 B.L.R. 1, C.A.

omission of the defendant to which the injury was attributable might be capable, at that time, of giving rise to an action for damages;

(f) The steps, if any, taken by the plaintiff to obtain medical, legal or other expert advice, and the nature of any such advice he may have received.

(3) The limitation period can also be postponed where:

(a) the action is for the relief from the consequences of a mistake;

(b) the plaintiff's right of action has been deliberately concealed from him by the defendant;

(c) there has been fraud on the part of the defendant. Fraud does not necessarily imply moral turpitude. It is enough if the act of the defendant, or his agent, is so unconscionable that it would be inequitable to allow him to rely on the limitation period, as where a builder carries out his works so badly that it is likely to give rise to trouble at a later date, but covers up his poor work so that it remains undiscovered for a number of years.

The limitation period does not begin to run until the mistake, concealment or fraud has been discovered by the plaintiff, or could with reasonable diligence have been discovered.

Q. Former clients for whom I had designed and supervised a building want to proceed against the contractors on the basis that they deliberately concealed defective work. In what way could they say I am liable too?

Where a building owner employs his own expert supervisors, be they architect, engineer or surveyor, and claims that defective work was concealed, he must establish that the work was carried out in such a manner that in exercising reasonable skill and care the supervisor could not have been expected to have observed the defects. At the same time, a question may also arise of whether or not the supervisor was himself negligent in carrying out his duties.

Fraudulent concealment does not result whenever a contractor does shoddy or incompetent work which is covered up as building works proceeds. Rather the question which must be answered is whether, in all the circumstances, the facts are such that the conscience of the defendant or of those for whose acts and omissions he is vicariously liable, should have been so affected that it was unconscionable to proceed with the work so as to cover up the defect without putting it right.

THREE

How do I organize my

practice to limit my

liability?

Q. What are the different ways in which I can practise to limit my liability?

It is a much-argued theory that if you set up practice in one form rather than another, then you will automatically reduce your liability.

The reality is that there is no particular way of practising in a profession, such as architecture or engineering, which if adopted would reduce your liability beyond that which you bear when carrying on business in a different form. Each has its advantages and disadvantages. Some of the different ways of carrying on a practice are as follows:

1. Single, self-employed, principal;
2. Partnership;
3. Limited partnership;
4. Private company;
5. Incorporated company;
6. Limited liability company.

Some would say that a co-operative should be included in this list. In effect, however, a co-operative is a partnership by another name, and it is regarded as such in law. For this reason, it has not been included here.

Q. I am an architect. Are there any limitations on the way I choose to run my practice?

Statutory limitations on architectural practice are contained in the *Architects (Registration) Act 1931*. The Act allows an architect to practise as:

1. An individual in his own right;
2. A partnership;
3. A company.

While anyone registered by the Architects' Registration Council of the UK (ARCUK) is entitled to use the name and title of 'Registered Architect', any person who is not registered is unable to practise under a name, title or style containing the words 'Registered Architect'. To do so is an offence.

Nothing in the Act prevents a body corporate, firm or partnership from carrying on business under the style or title of 'Registered Architect' under the following conditions:

1. The business of the body corporate, firm or partnership, so far as it relates to architecture, is under the control and management of a superintendent who is a registered person, and who does not at the same time in a similar capacity for any other body corporate, firm or partnership;
2. In every premises where such business is carried on and is not personally conducted by the superintendent, such business is bona fide, conducted under the direction of the superintendent by an assistant who is a registered person.

3.1 SINGLE PRINCIPLE

Q. What are the advantages and disadvantages of practising as a single, self-employed principal?

The advantages of practising as sole principal include the following:

1. Control over your own destiny;
2. Freedom and flexibility in your approach to commissions and clients;
3. Retaining the profits oneself;
4. Sole responsibility for everything that happens in the practice.

The disadvantages can be summarized as follows:

1. Who runs the practice if you are ill?
2. What happens if you have a work overload?
3. One cannot spread one's liability. You are liable for all mistakes as there is no one else to blame.

Q. What are the main liabilities of a sole practitioner?

(1) Contracts made by a sole practitioner (i.e. one who practises his profession on his own and not in association with a fellow professional) are his alone.
(2) Any obligations which arise during the course of his business are his alone.
(3) Generally the assets of a sole practitioner's practice may not be separated from his own personal assets.
(4) Any liabilities incurred by a person acting as a sole principal in his own practice may result in his being held personally liable to the full extent of his assets.

Q. What is the difference between a self-employed architect, or other professional, and one who is salaried?

In certain respects, the distinction between an architect who is salaried, an employee, and one who is self-employed, an independent contractor, is indistinct:

1. Both may be engaged on a limited basis to undertake a

particular project or provide help and part-time assist-ance. Equally, in both cases, the engagement may be permanent. Furthermore, the notion that only an archi-tect who is self-employed may exercise his own discretion as to the mode and time of carrying out a project, whereas a salaried architect cannot, is in many cases untrue.

2. In theory, a self-employed architect is not bound by his client's orders, yet neither, on occasion, is a salaried architect, and vice versa. For example, the former may feel obliged to accept all instructions from the client to ensure his financial stability by avoiding dismissal; while the latter may refuse to carry out his employer's instruc-tions to survey a building which appears to be dangerous.

3. The principle obligation of an independent contractor, the self-employed man, that he is bound to do only that which is in his contract of employment, similarly applies to the salaried architect.

One test is to answer the question of whether or not there is a contract of service or a contract for services; it is a question of mixed law and fact. The label by which the relationship is described by the parties to the contract may not necessarily be the same as that applied by the courts. For example, confusion can arise where an architect is initially retained as an independent contractor but on legal analysis it transpires that he was an employee. It may be helpful to identify the number of hours worked, the times at which they were worked and the rate to be paid for the work.

If it is found that an architect is an independent contractor, that he is self-employed and not a salaried architect, an employee, then, unlike the latter, he alone will normally be liable for his torts. As a general rule, a person is not responsible for the torts of an independent contractor; but in certain cases, the client is vicariously liable.

Q. What does the phrase 'client's vicarious liability' mean?

A client's vicarious liability arises because he warrants that due care and skill will be exercised by himself or by a professional whom he retains to perform his statutory or common law duty, for example, carrying out work to ensure the structural stability of dangerous premises.

The client does not fulfil the warranty merely by delegating the work to the professional. His warranty is broken if the the professional fails to use proper skill and care; however, if the employment of a professional in the capacity of an independent contractor sufficiently discharges the client's duty, then he will not be liable for any torts committed by that professional.

Q. I am self-employed and have my own practice which I run myself. To what extent will my clients be liable for my work?

A client who retains you as a self-employed architect, or indeed any other professional who holds himself to be competent to carry out the project he has in mind, is generally under no obligation to check your work. He may assume that it will be properly carried out with due care and skill. You will be responsible for any casual or collateral negligence you commit and liable to pay damages to any third party who has been injured.

However, this does not mean that vicarious liability will

not rest with the client if his personal duty, whether imposed by statute or common law, is called into question. This is because a person who causes something to be done and the doing of which casts on him a duty, cannot escape from the responsibility attached to him of seeing that that duty is performed by delegating it to a contractor.

A duty cannot be delegated, but its performance can be. The client, owing a duty, may not be liable for the architect's defaults where, for example, such delegation to an architect is sufficient to fulfil the client's duty.

Liability cannot be graded in this manner where an absolute duty is imposed by statute such as those contained in the Town and Country Planning Acts which require planning approval to be sought for any building unless it, or the company which is erecting it, has a specific waiver. For example, British Rail does not require planning permission for operational buildings on operational land.

The client will also be liable wherever the following apply:

1. An architect or contractor is retained to carry out extra-hazardous or dangerous operations; in other words, where the work by its very nature necessarily involves a degree of risk and has caused damage or loss to a third party, especially if the client has not imposed a duty overriding such loss;
2. There is vicarious responsibility for contractors in cases of nuisance; nuisance is commonly a continuing injury, and it is an inconvenience materially interfering with the ordinary physical comfort of human existence; nuisance may cover any act which wrongfully causes the escape of things which may cause damage or be deleterious to another person's property such as smoke, water, noise, heat, vibrations, electricity, disease, smell, fumes and gas, etc.

Q. Can a trust be an effective way of limiting liability?

Trusts as a method of limiting liability are a double-edged sword. In order to limit liability successfully, you must irrevocably part with your property. If the property is not got rid of absolutely, the settlement is totally ineffective and so does not limit liability.

Furthermore, as a general principle, you are not entitled to go into a hazardous business, and immediately before so doing, settle all your property voluntarily, the object being something like: 'If I succeed in business, I make a fortune for myself; if I fail, I leave my creditors unpaid – they will bear the loss.' In other words, a trust may often be an ineffective way of limiting liability. This is illustrated in the following cautionary tale of the inept businessman; the basic points apply as much to the practice of architecture, engineering and building as to that of the master baker with whom the case is concerned.

3.2 PARTNERSHIP

Q. What are the advantages and disadvantages of practising as a partnership?

The advantages of practising as a partnership may be summarized as:

1. Access to greater capital and resources;
2. Availability of expertise;
3. Distribution of responsibility;

A cautionary tale of the inept businessman

Charles Butterworth was a Manchester baker. Being quite prosperous, he invested some of his money on the purchases of several freehold houses. He also intended to purchase a grocery business.

To make himself safe and to screen his wife and children from the risks of the venture by saving his property for them, he made a voluntary settlement on 8 August 1878 which was about a month before he purchased the business. The settlement conveyed the houses and assigned the household furniture and goods to trustees upon certain trusts for the benefit of his family.

The deed contained a recital, that 'the settlor is now in a solvent position and capable of paying his debts as they become due'. When he consulted his solicitor about making the settlement, the solicitor told him that it would be good for nothing unless he was able to pay the debts which he then owed independently of the property which was to be included in the settlement. He then drew up a statement of his affairs, showing that he had sufficient assets to enable him to pay his debts irrespective of that property.

In September 1878, Butterworth bought the grocer's business and carried it on for about six months though he lost money by it. He then sold it for the same price that he had given for it and carried on the baker's business alone.

Three years later, in July 1881, he filed a liquidation petition. His liabilities exceeded his assets. The debts which he owed at the date of the settlement had all been paid. The trustee in the liquidation applied to Salford County Court for an order declaring the settlement void as against them, either under section 91 of the *Bankruptcy Act 1869* or under the Act 13 Eliz.c.5.

The first Act stated:

Any settlement of property made by a trader not being a settlement of property made by a trader not being a settlement made before and in consideration of marriage, or made in favour of a purchaser or encumbrancer in good faith and for valuable consideration of a settlement made on or for the wife or children of the settlor of property which has accrued to the settlor after marriage in right of his wife, shall, if he becomes bankrupt within two years after the date of such settlement be void as against the trustee of the bankrupt approved under this Act, and shall, if the settlor becomes bankrupt at any subsequent time within ten years after the date of such settlement unless the parties claiming under such settlement can prove that the settlor was at the time of making the settlement able to pay all his debts without the aid of the property comprised in such settlement, be void against such trustee.

Although it was shown that not all the debts and assets had been shown on the statement of affairs when the settlement was drawn up, it was nevertheless found by the judge that the settlor was at that time able to pay his debts without the aid of the settled property, in as much as he was entitled to assume that his trade debts, though due, were not in the ordinary course of business, then payable as it was the custom of his creditors to allow him a month's credit.

Though no opinion was given on whether the deed was void under section 91 of the *Bankruptcy Act 1869*, it was held that it was void under the statute of Elizabeth, because the settlor withdrew from his creditors the only means whereby he could have carried on the grocer's business, so that the creditors should not lose if the business was unsuccessful.

The judge of the County Court setting aside the settlement appealed to the chief judge who discharged the order of the County Court. The trustees in the liquidation appealed. The Court of Appeal held that the trustees of the settlement ought to have been satisfied with the decision of the County Court and that they must bear their own costs of both appeals and must pay the trustee in the liquidation of both appeals. The Court of Appeal also held that independently of the question of whether Butterworth was solvent at the date of settlement, the settlement was void against the trustee in the liquidation, under section 91 of the *Bankruptcy Act 1869* and under statute 13 Eliz.c.5, because it was evidently executed with the view of putting the settlor's property out of reach of his creditors in case he should fail in a speculation on which he was about to enter.

Ex parte Russell. In *re Butterworth* [1882] 19 Ch.D.588.

4. Larger commissions may be obtained and carried out;
5. A partnership may sue and be sued in the partnership name.

The disadvantages include:

1. Liability, both jointly and severally, for acts or omissions of another partner;
2. Personal assets can be claimed to settle a partnership debt.

A little history on partnerships

A partnership is the relationship which exists between persons carrying on business in common with a view to profit. The development of the word 'partnership' is closely linked to the meaning which is attached to the term 'a firm'.

In its older and less usual sense it meant the 'style' or name under which the business of a commercial house was transacted. This meaning was derived from the still earlier usage in which a 'firm' was a signature which confirmed a document and used in such phrases as: '. . . Whereas the person or persons named in the Schedule herein carrying on business under the firm and style stated in the said Schedule.' From that use the word came to mean a partnership of two or more persons carrying on a business. Hence 'firm' has become a collective noun, denoting the partners in a business.

Section 4 of the *Partnership Act 1890* gives the meaning of a firm in the following:

1. Persons who have entered into partnership with one another are for the purposes of this Act called collectively a firm, and the name under which their business is carried on is called the firm-name;
2. In Scotland a firm is a legal person distinct from the partners of whom it is composed but an individual partner may be charged on a decree of diligence directed against the firm, and on payment of the debts is entitled to relief pro rata from the firm and its other members.

Q. When does a partnership exist?

Such things as the common ownership of property or the sharing of gross returns do not of themselves create a partnership. Whereas the receipt of a share of the profits of a business is prima facie evidence that a person is a partner in that business.

Section 43(a) of the *Companies Act 1948* provides that a firm should usually be limited to no more than 20 partners, though section 120(2) of the *Companies Act 1967* permits the Department of Trade and Industry (formerly the Board of Trade) to grant exemptions to this rule by way of the Partnerships (Unrestricted Size) Regulations to various trades or professions, including architects. Where no fixed term has been agreed for the duration of the partnership, then any partner may determine it, at any time, on giving notice of his intention so to do to all the other partners. On the other hand, if a partnership has been entered into for a fixed term but is continued after that date without an express new agreement, the rights and duties of the partners remain the same so far as consistent with the incidents of a partnership at will.

A partnership will exist where there is:

1. A written agreement between the partners to practise in such a manner;
2. An oral agreement to the same effect;
3. The conduct of the members implies that they are practising as a partnership.

Q. What are the liabilities of a partner?

With the exception of Scottish partnerships, a partnership is not a legal entity which is separate and distinct from the constituent partners. Each partner may have unlimited liability for both the partnership debts and contractual obligations which arise because of the transactions of a fellow partner. In other words, every partner is liable jointly with the other partners, and in Scotland severally also, for all debts and obligations of the partnership incurred while he is partner; and where, after the death of one of the partners, his estate is also severally liable in due course of administration for such debts and obligations, so far as they remain unsatisfied but subject in England or Ireland to the prior payment of his separate debts.

Each partner is jointly and severally liable with his co-partners for any wrongful act or omission of another partner, including the misapplication of money or property in the custody of the partnership which results in loss or injury to someone who is not a partner. By common law, every member of an ordinary partnership is liable to the last vestige of his property for debts and engagements of the partnership. The law, ignoring the partnership as anything distinct from the persons composing it, treats the debts and engagements of the partnership as the debts and engagements of the partners and holds each partner liable for them accordingly. If judgment is obtained against parties for a joint debt, the judgment creditor is under no obligation to levy execution against the property of the partnership before having recourse to the separate property of the partners, nor is he under any obligation to levy execution upon him or them until the judgment is satisfied, leaving all questions of contribution to be settled afterwards between the partners themselves.

In effect, every partner is an agent of the partnership and the other partners for the purpose of the business of the partnership; and the acts of each partner who does any act for carrying on in the usual way business of the kind carried on by the partnership of which he is a member binds the partnership and the partners. A partner who is salaried, or an associate, may have the same liabilities as any other partner unless he is given an indemnity by the partnership as to the extent of his liability.

Q. Will I be liable if one of my partners commits a fraud?

The simple answer is 'yes'. As between the partners of an ordinary partnership and the outside world, each partner is the unlimited agent of every other in every matter connected with the partnership business. Thus a partner who may not have left a penny of capital may take moneys or assets of his partnership to the value of millions, may bind the partnership by contracts to any amount, may give the partnership acceptance for any amount and may even involve his innocent partners in unlimited amounts for frauds which he has carefully concealed from them.

Q. What happens if one of my partners does work outside my partnership agreement?

As a partner knowing nothing of your fellow partner's wrongful action, you are nevertheless vicariously liable for any wrong done by him, though it may fall outside the agreed sphere of work which you as the innocent partner undertook within the partnership.

A cautionary tale of the right hand knowing what the left hand is doing – always

Sidney Colin Clode and David Lynn Thomas were both working partners in a firm selling cars. For their own convenience, they decided that Mr Thomas would be responsible for dealing with customers, while Mr Clode was responsible for the administration. Both functions were exclusive. In January 1972, Mr D.L. Thomas, while selling a car to Mr Richard Thomas, wrongly told him that it had a new engine and had done no more than 2000–3000 miles. Mr Thomas's partner (Mr Clode) was working in the office. He had no idea that an unauthorized representation had been made which was false (though even if he had been aware of what had been said, he would not have known that it was untrue).

A case was brought by Mr Oswald Weston Barnes, the Chief Inspector of Weights and Measures for the City of Cardiff, jointly against the two partners whom it was claimed had contravened section I of the *Trades Descriptions Act 1968*; section 1 states:

any person who in the course of a trade or business
(a) applies a false trade description to any goods; or
(b) supplies or offers to supply goods to which a false trade description is applied;

shall . . . be guilty of an offence.

Both were convicted by the Cardiff Justices, and the decision was upheld in the Crown Court. Mr Clode appealed. In dismissing the appeal, it was held that although he did not himself apply the false description, his partnership with a person who had was sufficient to justify his conviction.

Clode v. *Barnes* [1974] W.L.R. 544.

A similar principle also applies to statements. For example, a partner in a building and repair business is present when his co-partner makes a false statement concerning a process to be applied to a customer's roof. He does not correct that statement, though both of them act together equally in the firm. The first partner will be held to have committed an offence. However, if the partner was acting on his own account and for his own benefit, he alone will be responsible for the consequences of his actions.

The theory behind this is that a partner makes a promise as agent for the other partners and for himself as principal. If he really had authority to subscribe the promise for all, they are all liable. If he did not, then he is personally liable – at all events, for misrepresentation. At this point, it is worth noting that any action taken by a partner may not be binding on the partnership if it were done maliciously.

Q. What is the effect of a term limiting liability in the partnership deed?

Where A, B and C are in partnerships together, they may stipulate among themselves that each will not be liable for more than £1000. Yet if the partnership incurs a debt of £10 000, each partner would be liable for it, notwithstanding the stipulation.

This principle does not depend upon the partnership's client having notice of the stipulation. Indeed, any notice would be quite immaterial, for a client or a creditor would not normally know what agreement the partners had made between themselves. Their rights are wholly extrinsic to such agreements.

Even if the partnership deed containing the stipulation

were hung up in the office, it would make no difference, for how could a person dealing with the partnership tell whether or not each partner would be liable to him. They might have incurred debts with other persons to the extent provided; it would not, then, be possible for him to ascertain the limit of their liability.

However, there is nothing to prevent partners reaching an agreement whereby the authority of one or more of them is limited by a term in the partnership deed; for example:

1. A restriction is placed on the power of one or more of the partners to bind the firm;
2. Certain activities are prohibited.

If express notice of this is given to persons dealing with the partnership, then no act done, in respect to them, which is in contravention of the agreement, is binding on the partnership. Here the crucial point is that you must establish that the person in question did have notice.

Q. Are there any circumstances in which our partnership will not be liable for the actions of an individual?

Your partnership may not be liable for the actions of one of the partners, even though they fall within the ordinary course of the partnership business, if a client decides to deal with that partner alone as principal in certain transactions. Thus, where A knowing B and C to be partners refuses to contract with them jointly and insists on contracting with B alone, he cannot afterwards treat C as liable.

A person who is admitted as a partner into an existing partnership does not thereby become liable to the creditors of the partnership for anything done before he became a partner. However, a partner who retires does not cease to be liable for those partnership debts or obligations which were incurred before he retired. Nevertheless, a retiring partner can be discharged from existing liabilities by an agreement to that effect between himself and members of the partnership as newly constituted and the creditors. This agreement may be either express or inferred as a fact from the course of dealing between the creditors and the firm as newly constituted.

Q. What is the position if one of our partners specializes in a particular field?

Where there is only one partner who can competently undertake work in a particular sphere, for example, mechanical engineering, it may be of benefit for the partnership to permit him so to do.

This, then, merely enlarges the potential scope of the practice. It does not alter the nature or character of the practice, the profession of the partners or give the specialist partner any special qualification outside or beyond his normal and necessary professional qualifications. Indeed, there is nothing which implies that co-partners cannot give authority to one of their number to perform, as a partner, acts which they themselves are not legally qualified to perform.

If such authority is given, and certainly where the actions authorized are in themselves within the lawful competence of the partner so authorized, and if the authority is acted on as a result of a wrongful act or omission in the course of carrying out what was authorized loss or injury is caused to a third

A cautionary tale of the malicious architect

Mr Meekins brought an action against three architects. They practised together under the name of Sir John Brown, A.E. Henson & Partners. The three partners were Colonel Henson, who was at that time President of the Incorporated Association of Architects and Surveyors (IAAS), Wilfred Valder and John Edward Southgate Sayers. Damages were claimed by Mr Meekins for defamations which arose both in the sphere of the IAAS's domestic affairs and also in the course of the partnership activities of Mr Meekins's firm and the architects. The defamations were contained in several letters which formed part of an acrimonious correspondence between the two firms. It concerned the question of who was to blame for the belated agreement of certain accounts which Wood Green Borough Council needed to have determined for them. Mr Meekins's firm had during January 1960 complained in a letter that the architects had delayed conducting the correspondence between them. A copy of the letter was sent to the borough council. The defamatory words were contained in a letter from the architects replying to Mr Meekins's complaint; it stated: 'We have been careful to confine our correspondence to facts and avoid provocative statements, as letters requested from us by you in the past have been misrepresented to our clients when applying for fees.' The letter was signed 'p.p. Sir John Brown, A.E. Henson and Partners, J.E.S. Sayers'. The partnership was entitled to publish these words by reason of qualified privilege, provided that they entertained no malice. A copy of the letter was sent to the Borough Treasurer. It was found by the trial jury that the publication of the libel had been actuated by the malice of Colonel Henson alone; neither of the other partners had acted maliciously. A motion was put on behalf of the architects to arrest judgment on the grounds that, under section 10 of the *Partnership Act 1890*, none of the partners were liable since no tort could be established against Mr Sayers.

Section 10 of the 1890 Act states: 'Where, by any wrongful act or omission of any partner acting in the ordinary course of the business of the firm, or with the authority of his co-partners, loss or injury is caused to any person not being a partner in the firm . . . the firm is liable therefore to the same extent as the partner so acting or omitting to act.' Counsel for the architects submitted that the provision that the firm (i.e. the other partners) were 'to be liable to the same extent as the partner so acting' meant that no partner other than the partner acting wrongfully and thereby causing injury could, in law, be liable to a greater extent than the partner acting, from which it would follow that if the partner acting were not liable in law, the others could not be liable at all.

It was held that in order to establish liability arising from a duty owed by a partner personally, or from an act in which he was actively involved, it was not necessary for the person damaged to rely on section 10 of the *Partnership Act 1890*, albeit the act was done by the hand of another partner. Furthermore, each of the three architects had his personal, separate privilege with regard to the publication of the copy letter, which must in the circumstances be regarded as a publication by each partner. Accordingly, liability attached to Colonel Henson alone, malice having been established only against him.

Meekins v. *Henson & Others* [1964] 1 Q.B. 472.

---

party, then vicarious liability is imposed for that injury upon the partners of the firm. Should a partner without the consent of the other partners carry on any business of the same nature as, and competing with, that of the partnership, he must account for and pay over to the partnership all profits made by him in that business.

Q. What is our partnership's liability if one of our partners borrows money?

The borrowing and handling of money on behalf of partnerships by one of its partners is one of the most important

The case of the group of five

Five chartered accountants formed a partnership in 1957. The partnership continued until it was dissolved in May 1967. The name of the firm was Harie Cuthbertson & Co. One of the partners was qualified or 'approved' by the Treasury under its statutory power to audit the accounts of industrial and provident societies. His name alone appeared on the Treasury list of persons appointed as official auditors; neither the name of the firm, nor the names of his other partners, were listed. Under the terms of the *Industrial and Provident Societies Act 1893*, and *1913* and revised by the *1965* Act of the same name, the accounts of all industrial and provident societies were to be submitted annually for audit by one or more persons selected from the Treasury list. The Kirkintilloch Equitable Co-operative Society Ltd were such a society registered under the Act. They appointed that particular partner whose name appeared on the list as their

official auditor from 1952. He was re-appointed thereafter yearly, until he resigned in February 1967. When auditing the Society's accounts, the partner was assisted by employees of the partnership. The audit fee was paid by the Society to the partnership and received by them as a fee due to the partnership. The Kirkintilloch Society found that they had suffered substantial losses between 1963 and 1966 which they claimed were the result of bookkeeping errors. The Society sued its secretary, the executrix of its general manager, the official auditor for professional negligence and his then partners.

The four partners said that the case made against them was irrelevant and should be dismissed because their fifth partner, the official auditor, had been acting as an individual and not as a partner in the firm. They claimed that the only person who had been entitled to act as auditor to the plaintiffs was

the fifth partner. A partnership could not be appointed an official auditor; they could not give him authority to do the acts complained of since the Treasury was the only body who could authorize him to act as an official auditor. Therefore, they claimed they could not be liable as he – when acting in this capacity – was not acting in the ordinary course of the business of the partnership since it was not legally entitled to undertake such acts, nor had he been authorized to do so by his partners. However, it was held that there was a case to be answered by the members of the partnership because the partner was acting in the ordinary course of the business of the partnership.

Kirkintilloch Equitable Co-operative Society v. *Livingstone* [1972] S.L.T. 154.

duties which a partner may be authorized to undertake. Any liability which arises as a result of a partner's handling of such a duty may be attributed to the partnership as a whole only if it can be shown that the partner was acting under some clear authority or that his actions were ratified. In such a case, a debt which is accepted by one partner in the name of the partnership, and in the normal course of the firm's business, is binding upon all members of a partnership.

The use to which borrowed money was put, even if it were for the benefit of the partnership, does not alter a contract of loan between the lender and the partner if he borrowed it without the authority of his fellow partners. The partnership may not be obliged to reimburse the lender unless the latter can bring himself within a doctrine of equity. This doctrine is founded partly on the right of the lender to stand in equity in the place of those creditors of the firm whose claims have been paid off by his money; and partly on the right of the borrowing partner to be indemnified by the firm against liabilities bona fide incurred by him for the legitimate purpose of relieving the firm from its debts or of carrying on its business.

For example, a partner may be prohibited from borrowing money on behalf of the partnership unless he is authorized so to do. Without that authority, he nevertheless borrows money from a second firm and uses it to discharge existing debts which are owed by his own partnership. The second firm know when the advance is made that the partner's authority to borrow is limited. Despite this knowledge, they may be entitled to repayment.

The position might be somewhat different where a debt is incurred through borrowing money as capital to found a partnership. Originally each partner would have to bring in his proportion of the capital, and it would be very unjust to let the acceptance of one for the capital bind all the others; no authority of that nature can be implied, nor does it arise by operation of law, the debt not being a partnership debt.

Q. What happens if a partner does not make it clear that he is a member of a partnership?

A partnership may be held liable for the payment of goods ordered only verbally by one partner, even though no mention was made of the other partners.

If a person contracting with another delivers an invoice made out to a partnership and nothing is said as to the person composing the partnership, he takes his chance on who the partners are. In other words, he makes the contract personally with the individual with whom he deals but takes his chance as to which of the persons constituting the partnership are liable to him.

If the person with whom he is dealing represents himself as the only person composing the firm, an action may be brought against him alone. Similarly, if on being asked as to who his partners are he refuses to say, that may be sufficient to indicate that he holds himself out as being solely liable. But a person may not succeed against one of several partners simply because he supposes him alone to be liable. It must be shown that either the partner is in point of fact solely liable, or that he has clearly represented himself to be so.

Anyone who, by spoken or written words or by conduct represents himself or knowingly allows himself to be represented as a partner in a particular partnership, is liable as a partner to anyone who has given credit to the partnership on the basis of such representation. This may be so, whether or not the representation has been made or communicated to the person, so giving credit by or with the knowledge of the apparent partner making the representation or suffering it to be made.

Q. What is the general effect on my liability of a contract which my partner has entered into?

As has already been indicated, a partner is liable for the actions of his fellow partner when he has authority to carry them out as part of the usual business of the partnership. He may be bound by the contracts made and varied by his partner, though he may not be bound by one which is illegal, especially where the other party to the contract knows that it is a fraud on him.

In respect of fraudulent misrepresentation, false description of the character or solvency, for instance, of a person given in writing and signed by one partner on behalf of the partnership, while binding on that partner, it may not be binding on his co-partners; whereas if it were signed by all of them, then it might be binding on the partnership as a whole.

A partnership may be regarded as having committed a fraudulent misrepresentation if a partner innocently makes a false statement when the truth is known to another partner who either does nothing to correct it, or that statement is actually authorized by him.

An admission or representation made by any partner concerning the partnership affairs and in the ordinary course of its business is evidence against the firm. However, such a representation or statement might not be held against the co-partners of a firm unless they had the opportunity of contradicting it. Furthermore, it may not act against the partnership if the statement itself had been made by a person before he became a partner, or otherwise, it might merely act as an estoppel.

There is no way in which the innocent acts or intentions of members of a partnership when acting as principal and agent, whatever detrimental effect they may have on the third party, could amount to a fraudulent misrepresentation upon which a third party could bring an action in deceit.

Q. I have been offered a partnership in a well-established practice. What will be my liability for partnership debts?

A change in the make up of a firm by a new partner coming into it may give rise to a number of questions concerning the relative liability of the firm's members.

Unless a new partner has clearly entered into an agreement with the firm to accept its liabilities which existed before he joined them, he may not be liable for anything done by the firm before he became a partner. Even where such an agreement has been entered into, to the benefit of a third party, it may not be sufficient to confirm an actionable right upon that party to proceed against a new partner for the firm's old liabilities. Where a partnership has undertaken a continuing or long-running contract and a new partner enters the firm after it has been made but before the contract is completed, then he may be liable for any new debts which arise from it.

Q. I am about to retire from a partnership. What points regarding my liability should I be aware of?

(1) As a partner retiring from a firm, you cannot relieve yourself of any of the contractual liabilities which have been incurred while you were with the partnership, unless both the person with whom the contract has been entered into and the remaining partners agree to discharge you from such liability. The agreement need not be express, but depending upon the circumstances, it would be sufficient if it could be inferred from the conduct of the parties.

If, for example, a partnership consists of A, B and C who enter into a contract with D, but before its completion, A with the knowledge of D retires from the firm, B and C undertaking to indemnify him from all liabilities, then A nevertheless remains liable to D even after his retirement for acts properly done under the contract by B and C. However, should the contract be varied in any way by D, A's liability may be discharged if he is considered to be in the position of a surety.

(2) Where someone deals with a partnership after a change in its constitution, he is entitled to treat all apparent members of the old firm as members of the partnership still, until he has notice of the change. Where the principal place of business of

A cautionary tale of a partner's innocent state of mind

Mr and Mrs Armstrong bought a bungalow through James Abbott, a firm of estate agents whose partners were Skinner and Allcoat. They had been commissioned to find a purchaser for the bungalow by Strain, its owner. Strain was himself a partner with Uren in another firm of estate agents in Scotland. Though Strain became an estate agent in 1933, he devoted much of his time not to real property, but to the auctioneering of chattels. In October 1935 he had decided to move from Scotland and carry on business from a private house in Rayleigh, Essex. The two firms of estate agents arranged to share the commission on the sale of the bungalow.

Mr and Mrs Armstrong paid a deposit of £30 on 6 May 1949 after they had been told by Skinner that he had seen the bungalow and that any building society would lend £1200 on it as it represented a small percentage. Strain did not authorize Skinner to make such representations, nor did he know that they had been made. However, Strain did not know of

facts which rendered it untrue.

The contract of sale was executed on 19 May, and completion was effected a month later on 16 June 1949. The price paid was £2400, £1100 of which had been advanced by a building society.

When Mr and Mrs Armstrong had bought the bungalow, it had just been repaired and redecorated. However, soon after they had moved in, cracks appeared as the building began to settle. Later investigations showed that there had been settlement on four previous occasions.

Expert evidence called at the trial on behalf of Mr and Mrs Armstrong that the bungalow could not be regarded as a fit security for a loan went unchallenged. Allcoat, a partner of Skinner, said that with knowledge of the previous history of the bungalow, he would have advised a building society to have nothing to do with it and would have sent no applicant to see it.

Mr and Mrs Armstrong brought an action for

damages for fraudulent misrepresentation against Strain and Skinner. The trial judge found that neither were guilty of fraud and gave judgment to them. Mr and Mrs Armstrong appealed, contending that the representations made by Skinner being untrue to the knowledge of Strain (though not to the knowledge of Skinner), and as principal and agent were one in law, fraud was thereby established. The Court of Appeal held that this was not so as there was no way of combining an innocent principle and agent so as to produce dishonesty.

Birkett, L.J. cited the judgment of Devlin, J. in this case, and said: 'You may add knowledge to knowledge, or . . . state of mind to state of mind. But you cannot add an innocent state of mind to an innocent state of mind and get as a result a dishonest state of mind.'

Armstrong & Another v. *Strain & Others* [1952] 1 K.B. 232, C.A.

a firm is in England or Wales, it would be sufficient if an advertisement were placed in the *London Gazette*, or the *Edinburgh Gazette* if the business is in Scotland; and if the firm is in Ireland, it is necessary to place a notice in the *Belfast Gazette* or *Dublin Gazette*.

(3) It is possible that a partner who has retired from a firm may leave himself open to a liability claim, if he holds himself out as still being a partner of that firm. Holding out oneself to

the world as a partner, as contra-distinguished from the actual relationship or partnership, imparts at least the voluntary act of the party so holding himself out. It implies the lending of his name to the partnership and is altogether incompatible with the want of authority that his name has been so used. Thus in ordinary instances of this occurrence where a person allows his name to remain in a firm, either exposed to the public over the office door or used on printed invoices and letters, or published in advertisements, the knowledge of the party that his name is used and his assent thereto is the ground upon which he is estopped from disputing his liability as a partner. It would therefore be wise, in order to limit your liability, to ensure that your name is deleted from documents used in the partnership on the day you retire.

(4) What happens when no notice of your retirement has been given to the clients of the partnership? Consider this sequence of events: A and B were in partnership, and the firm's name was different from their own; A later retired and C came into the firm as a new partner. A client who had a claim against the partnership, and dealt continuously with it, was not informed of the revised nature of the firm. Then the client can elect which group of partners to sue: those who formed the partnership before it was reconstituted, or those who were partners afterwards.

Q. One of our partners recently died. Only his wife is now alive, and she is worried about the estate's liability to pay any partnership debts. What is the clarification of our position?

Where after a partner's death a partnership business is continued in the old partnership's name, the continued use of that name, or of the deceased partner's name as, part of it, does not of itself make his executors' or administrators' estate or effects liable for any partnership debts contracted after his death.

The estate of a deceased partner may be liable for the debts which have been contracted by the partnership before his death, for example, where the debts were joint debts and the surviving partner becomes bankrupt. However, it would be wrong to conclude that every debt owed jointly by a partnership should be settled from the assets of a partner who has died.

A creditor need not be under an obligation to institute proceedings first against the surviving members of a partnership before proceeding against a deceased partner's estate. If he elects to do the latter, he need not show that the surviving partner is insolvent or that the assets of the partnership are not enough to cover the debts which are owed by the firm. On the other hand, should a creditor proceed against the surviving partner first, and be successful in this claim, he may nevertheless still press his original claim against a deceased partner's estate.

Q. What happens to partners' liability when a partnership is dissolved?

After the dissolution of a partnership, the authority of each partner to bind the firm, and the other rights and obligations of the partners continue notwithstanding the dissolution so far as may be necessary to wind up the affairs of the partnership and to complete transactions begun but unfinished at the time of the dissolution but not otherwise.

Should a continuing obligation on a particular scheme which was accepted before a partnership was dissolved be negligently handled afterwards, all partners may be held liable for such negligence. Where a partnership is dissolved on the death of one of the partners, the surviving partners have the right and duty to complete all unfinished operations necessary to fulfil contracts of the partnership which are still in force when the partnership is dissolved. Such an obligation involves an implication that it will be discharged with reasonable care and skill.

An old, but still cautionary, tale of the dying partners

An indenture dated 20 May 1801 had been given to the executor of William Sumner, a partner in a firm who had died in 1797. It was agreed that the executor would make certain payments to the partnership and discharge the existing partners from all claims and demands which he might have against them as the executor of their deceased partner; it stated:

> In consideration of this each partner . . . did release, acquit, and forever discharge the executor . . . his executors and administrators, and all and singular the estate and effects of the said William Sumner, of and from all claims and demands whatsoever, which they . . . or any of them might have against executor by reason or upon account of the said William Sumner having been a partner with them.

At the time of William Sumner's death, the partnership was liable for a breach of trust as one of the partners, unknown to the others, sold stock, known as the Cookson settlement, in their care and used the proceeds in the banking business of the partnership.

In 1802 one partner, Powell (the elder), died; a year later, another partner, Wilson, quitted the partnership and died in 1805. In 1804 the two remaining partners, Castell and Powell (the younger), became bankrupt.

A bill was successfully filed in 1806 by interested parties under the Cookson settlement to make good their loss against the surviving trustee of that settlement, the two bankrupt partners and their assignees and the representatives of all the deceased partners. The executor then brought a bill, insisting that by virtue of the deed of indemnity dated 20 May 1801, he was entitled to be repaid out of the estates of Wilson and of the two Powells. (Powell the younger had become bankrupt a second time but no assignment of his estate and effects had yet been executed, while Castell had died an uncertified bankrupt.)

The question which was considered by the Master of the Rolls, Sir William Grant, concerned the liability of Wilson's estate under the covenant in the deed of indemnity because the executors of Wilson alleged that although the name of the testator appeared in the partnership, he never was a partner in it and had not participated in its profits or losses. It was therefore claimed that his estate was not subject or liable to repay the executor what he had paid in pursuance of the decree. It was agreed that the deed constituted an obligation which, though only joint at law, might be considered several as well as joint in equity. However, it was held that it was not a principle of equity that every joint covenant should be considered as if it were joint and several. It could not be extended in equity beyond its legal operation as there was no ground on which to infer a mistake in the nature of the instrument, and no previous equity entitling the covenantee to a several indemnity from each of the covenantors.

Sir William Grant said that he found,

> no such general proposition anywhere laid down. When the obligation exists only by virtue of the covenant, its extent can be measured only be the words in which it is conceived. A partnership debt has been treated in equity as the several debt of each partner, though, at law, it is only the joint debt of all. But, there, all have had a benefit from the money advanced or the credit given and the obligation to pay exists independently of any instrument by which the debt may have been secured. So, where a joint bond has, in equity, been considered as several, there has been a credit previously given to the different persons who have entered into the obligation. It was not the bond that first created the liability to pay. But, in this case, the covenant is purely a matter of arbitrary convention, growing out of no antecedent liability in all, or any, of the covenanters to do what they have hereby undertaken.

George Holme Sumner v. *Whitson Powell, Sarah Powell, George Wilkinson & Susannah Blackmore* (1816) 2 Mer.30, 36 per Sir William Grant, M.R.

A cautionary tale of liability after death (of a partnership)

In January 1966 clients instructed partners in a firm of solicitors practising under the name of Bryson and Davie, Writers to the Signet, to act on their behalf in a claim for damages suffered as a result of a road accident in September 1965. Although the clients' instructions were accepted, no steps were taken by the partnership to pursue the claim and court action became time barred on 20 September 1968.

The partnership was later dissolved, though before this occurred, two of the partners, Craxton and Macari, withdrew from the partnership on 30 September 1967 and 28 February 1968 respectively. The clients brought a claim against all those who were partners in the partnership in January 1966, claiming damages in respect of the loss which they had suffered because of the partnership's negligence in failing to pursue their claim.

Craxton and Macari said that they were not liable for any actions of the partnership after they had withdrawn from it as the clients' cause of action arose only when the injury was suffered, that is when proceedings became time barred, at which point neither of them were partners. In referring to section 17(2) of the *Partnership Act 1890*, which provides that a partner who retires from a firm does not thereby cease to be liable for partnership debts and obligations incurred before his retirement, it was held that the obligation to prosecute the clients' claim from January 1966 (when the partnership was instructed) was a continuing obligation on each and all of the partners, and that all were liable for the negligent omission to raise an action, even though the partnership had been dissolved in the meantime.

Lord Stott noted that it was trite law that a partnership was dissolved by the retrial of any of its partners. There was no reason why those of the former partners who continued to style themselves 'Bryson and Davie' should be held bound any more than another partner to carry out the obligations undertaken by the partnership prior to dissolution. Where none of the ex-partners of the partnership had done anything to see that an action was raised, it would seem to follow from their argument that since the partnership had meanwhile been dissolved by resignation of one or more of the partners, no one could be held liable to the pursuers for the negligence involved in that omission. Furthermore, in the case of Craxton, it was averred that following the dissolution of the partnership on the 30 September 1967, the partnership's notepaper was altered by the deletion of his name from the letter-heading. It was argued that in view of section 18(1) of the *Registration of Business Names Act 1916*, the terms of which the pursuers must be presumed to have known, they would be bound on seeing the letter-heading to realize that Craxton was no longer in the partnership. Lord Stott, however, did not think that that was an inference that the pursuers were bound to draw, nor indeed that it was a necessary inference of fact, particularly in the light of an averment by Craxton himself that he was never registered as a member of the partnership in the register of business names; in any event, the omission of his name from the letter-head seemed, to Lord Stott, to fall short of what would be required to give notice to the pursuers that he had ceased his association with the partnership and that he was no longer to be taken as concerning himself with the pursuers' business.

Welsh & Another v. *Knarston & Others* [1972] S.L.T. 96, 97 per Lord Stott.

Q. Our partnership has a sleeping partner, what are his and our liabilities?

Generally a sleeping partner is bound by the acts of any of the ordinary partners which are carried out in the name of the partnership. This is so even if the sleeping partner does not know of them.

An ordinary partner may bind the partnership under a penalty to observe a contract which he is authorized to enter into on its behalf. It may apply to a sleeping partner who chooses to give an implied authority to the ostensible partners to contract for him – in which case, it will not be able to say that he has given any such authority.

It is to be noted that the mutual rights and duties of partners may be varied by the consent of all the partners. Such consent may be either express or inferred from a course of dealing.

For example, A, B and C trade under the name of A & B in an electrical business. C takes no active part in the business and is not known to the world as a partner in it. A and B also trade, as partners alone, under the same name in a mechanical heating business in which C was never interested. In this latter business, A and B become indebted to D. They give him their acceptance, but they are unable to take it up when it becomes due. In order to provide for it, they endorse in the common name of A and B a bill of exchange to D which they had received in the electrical business in which C is interested. The endorsement is unknown to C. Moreover, C himself is unknown to D, the endorsee. The bill is not honoured, and A and B become bankrupt. The endorsement in a name common to both partners of a bill received by A and B in the electrical business binds C, their sleeping partner, in that business. Consequently, C is liable to be sued by D.

3.3 LIMITED PARTNERSHIP

Q. I have heard that the liabilities of a limited partner are less than those of a general partner. Is this true?

Within a partnership liability may be limited if a partner is a limited partner rather than a general partner, provided that the firm is registered as a limited partnership otherwise, the benefits attached to a limited partner will cease and he will be considered a general partner.

However, it should be noted that an ordinary partnership is not a legal entity like a limited company, and although the *Limited Partnership Act 1907* recognizes a limited partnership and requires it to be registered and gives liberty to inspect the register, it does not create it a legal entity. It is merely a combination of persons for the purpose of carrying on a particular trade or trades.

Q. What is a limited partnership, and what are the differences between limited and general partners?

A limited partnership is one which may consist generally of no more than 20 persons, of whom one or more must be general partners.

A general partner will be liable for all the debts and obligations of the partnership and, in this respect, his liability is the same as if the partnership were an ordinary partnership. A general partner, if he so chooses and with agreement

A cautionary tale of the dangers of being a sleeping partner

Houston and Strong were partners in the firm of John Houston & Co. They arranged that the conduct of the business should be left to Houston, Strong being a sleeping partner. One of Houston's duties was to obtain by legitimate means information about tenders submitted for contracts by competitors' firms. The more secret were these matters, the greater the value of the information to the partnership.

Mr Hamlyn was one of John Houston, & Co.'s competitors. Houston bribed My Hamlyn's clerk to give him information about the names of Mr Hamlyn's customers, and the contracts which he had made, together with those for which he tendered. He also induced the clerk to give him possession of one of Mr Hamlyn's books containing entries concerning contracts. This was done in total disregard of the fact that it was one of the terms of the clerk's employment that he should not divulge the business secrets of his employer.

Mr Hamlyn brought an action to recover damages from both Houston and his partner Strong in respect of the former's actions. It was held that the two partners were responsible to Mr Hamlyn for the action of one of them because it was within the general scope of the authority given to him as a partner to conduct the business of the firm. This was because if the act done by an agent was within the general scope of the authority given to him, it mattered not that it was directly contrary to the instructions of his principal, or even that it might have been an offence against society itself.

Hamlyn v. *John Houston & Co.* [1903] 1.K.B.81.

---

of his fellow partners, may alter the liability which he may carry in future within the partnership by becoming a limited partner. The new arrangement must be advertised in the Gazette and registered at the Register Office in that part of the UK in which the partnership is registered.

A limited partnership may consist of one or more persons who are limited partners. Such a partner when entering a partnership must at that time contribute to it a sum, or sums, as capital or property valued at a stated amount. A limited partner will not be liable for the debts or obligations of the firm beyond the amount which he has contributed, provided that he takes no part in the management of the firm, though he may offer advice on the partnership business. However, should he draw out or receive back any part of his contribution either directly or indirectly during the life of the partnership, then that limited partner will be liable for the debts and obligations of the partnership up to that amount. Moreover, if a limited partner takes part in the management of the partnership business, he will be liable for all debts and obligations of the partnership incurred while he so takes part in the management as though he were a general partner.

A limited partner has no power to bind the partnership, though should he act on behalf of the partnership, this might give rise to a breach of warranty of authority for which he might be liable in damages. However, if the other party to a contract knows or is aware that the limited partner with whom he deals has no power to bind his partnership in that contract, then the limited partner may incur no liability. In contrast, a partner in an ordinary partnership may act on behalf of the partnership and his co-partners to the extent of either suing or entering an appearance for all the partners if a case is brought by or against them individually or in the partnership's name. A limited partner may not be entitled to decide any differences which may arise in the ordinary course of the partnership business. This is to be done by a majority of the general partners.

3.4 PRIVATE AND INCORPORATED COMPANIES

A little history on the birth of companies

At first, a company existed under the favour of the Crown, which gave them charters of incorporation. Nobody ever supposed that the holders of stock in the Bank of England or the East India Company had anything to do with the law of partnership, or were partners. But there were large societies which did not enjoy royal or legislative favour. The aim of many of these associates was to make their particular society as like a corporation as possible with:

1. Continuous existence;
2. Transferable stock;
3. Without any individual rights in any associate to bind the other associates or to deal with the assets of the association.

Legislation was passed to protect the unwary who were trapped in numerous enterprises which were often 'bubble' schemes. To provide some security against the impositions being practised, it was declared unlawful for any persons to form themselves into a company or to receive subscriptions without at once registering themselves so as to give public notice of the object they were engaged in. They might then receive subscriptions, and after complying with certain prerequisites, proceed to complete registration and prosecute their scheme under the sanction of the law.

In 1854, Lord Cranworth, the Lord Chancellor stated:

these companies being consonant with the wants of a growing and wealthy community have forced their way into existence, whether fostered by the law or opposed to it; they have not, however, proceeded to the extent of enabling their members to enter into arrangements absolving themselves from liabilities without the circle of their own deed, that is, from liabilities to third persons.

Q. What is the difference between a partnership, a company and a private company?

The distinction between partnerships and companies is often merely of machinery, not of function, with the most obvious advantage of the latter being that the property of a company is clearly distinguished from that of its members. Furthermore, a company escapes the consequence attached to partnerships, for in theory the death of a partner brings the partnership to an end. But death of a member leaves the company unmoved. Members may come and go but the company may go on for ever.

A company may be defined as one which is 'existing' or one which has been formed by two or more persons subscribing their names to a memorandum of association, which has been registered. Each member has the right of assigning his shares to any other person, subject to the regulations of the company.

In comparison, a private company, which may be formed by no more than two people, is a company which not only restricts the right to transfer its shares, but also prohibits any invitation to the public to subscribe for any shares or debentures of the company. The articles of a private company must limit the number of its members to 50, excluding

---

A cautionary tale of the dubious advantages of a limited partnership

A limited partnership was registered under the names of W.H. Barnard, Metal Broker, 24 Lime Street, on 4 October 1928. The partnership term was seven years from 25 September, terminable at Barnard's death. Barnard was the sole general partner and there was one £100 limited partner.

On 17 May 1929 another limited partnership was registered under the name of the Scrap Metal Co., 24 Lime Street. It was an accepting-house conducting financial operations in connection with the business of the metal broker. The partnership term was seven years from 14 May, terminable at Barnard's death. Again, Barnard was the sole general partner, and there were three other £100 limited partners.

Between 12 March and 12 May 1931, five bills of exchange were drawn up by Moss Isaacs Ltd on the Scrap Metal Co. by Barnard as managing partner. The bills of exchange were then held by Martins Bank.

On the petition of Barnard, a receiving order was made in June 1931 against the firm of W.H. Barnard, and later in July against the Scrap Metal Co. In each case, Barnard was adjudicated bankrupt.

On 1 October, Martins Bank, having withdrawn a proof in the second bankruptcy of the Scrap Metal Co., lodged a proof for their £9869 in the first bankruptcy of W.H. Barnard. On 23 October the trustee rejected this proof on the ground that, 'the bankrupt is not a party to the bills upon which the proof is made'. In November the bank moved that this decision might be reversed and the proof admitted.

Subsections 6(2) and (3) of the *Limited Partnership Act 1907* were considered, among others, by the court. They state that a limited partnership is not dissolved by the death and bankruptcy of a limited partner and his lunacy is not a ground for dissolution unless his share cannot otherwise be ascertained and realized. Furthermore, in the event of dissolution of a limited partnership, its affairs shall be wound up by the general partner unless the court orders otherwise.

It was held that the bank was entitled to prove that in the firm of W.H. Barnard and the Scrap Metal Co. there was no joint liability. The assets of the firm, W.H. Barnard, should first be applied in payment of that firm's debts and the surplus in repaying the limited partner his contribution. The balance would form part of Barnard's separate estate applicable to payment of his own private debts and any other debts incurred by him on behalf of other limited partnerships. The assets of the Scrap Metal Co. should be applied in a similar way.

Farwell, J. said,

The principal provision for the purpose of this motion is in section 4, subsection 2, by which the liability for all debts and obligations of the firm is cast on the general partners. In this case, Barnard, the sole general partner, is personally liable for the firm's debts. The limited partners are not so liable unless they have taken some active part in the management, which is not so here. The result is that Barnard is now personally liable for £9869 debt to Martins Bank. It is a debt for which he alone can be made liable at law.

In re Barnard, *Martins Bank* v. *Trustee* [1932] 1 Ch.269, 272 per Farwell, J.

---

those who are or have been employed by the company and have remained members of it after their employment has been terminated.

Every company which has been registered on or after 1 November 1929 must have at least two directors, apart from a private company, which may have only one.

Q. I have sometimes heard a director being referred to as a trustee. What is the effect of this?

While the appointment and power of a director are governed by a company's articles of association, the acts of a director shall be valid notwithstanding any defect that may afterwards be discovered in his appointment or qualification. On numerous occasions the acts of a director have been referred to as those of a trustee.

Although directors are not, properly speaking, trustees, they have always been considered and treated as trustees of that money which comes into their hands or which is actually under their control. For example, directors have been held liable to make good moneys which they have misapplied upon the same footing as if they were trustees. Directors are only trustees because of the particular property which is put into their hands or under their control, and which they have applied in a manner which is beyond the powers of the company. *Qua* such fund they are constructive trustees or trustees by implication of the law.

They are bound to use reasonable diligence having regard to their position. It is probable that an ordinary director who only attends at the board occasionally cannot be expected to devote as much time and attention to the business as the sole managing partner of an ordinary partnership, but they are bound to use fair and reasonable diligence in the management of their company's affairs and to act honestly.

But where without fraud and without dishonesty the directors have omitted to get in a debt due to the company by not suing within time, or because the man was solvent at one moment and became insolvent the next, by no means does it follow, as it might in the case of ordinary trustees of trust funds or of a trust debt, that they are to be made liable. Traders have a discretion as to whether they shall sue their customers or clients, and a discretion which is not vested in the trustees of a debt under a settlement. In fact the clients of a company often are allowed time, because the directors may think that if they do not allow them time, they will drive the clients into bankruptcy and so suffer a greater loss. Indeed, often they will not only give them time, but lend them money or sell them goods, in the hope that better times may come and enable them to pay their debts!

Q. What are the duties of a director?

The duties of a director may vary considerably depending on the size of the company. In order to ascertain the duties that a person appointed to the board of an established company undertakes to perform, it is necessary to consider not only the nature of the company's business, but also the manner in which the work of the company is in fact distributed between the directors and the other officials of the company, provided always that this distribution is:

1. A reasonable one in the circumstances;
2. Not inconsistent with any express provisions of the articles of association.

In discharging the duties of his position, a director must of course act honestly, but he must also exercise some degree both of skill and diligence. To the question of what is the particular degree of skill and diligence required of him, the authorities do not give any clear answer. So long as a director acts honestly, he cannot be made responsible in damages unless guilty of gross or culpable negligence in a business sense – but one cannot say whether a man has been guilty of negligence, gross or otherwise, unless one can also determine

A cautionary tale of the grasping directors

In 1905 the Toronto Construction Co. was formed. G.S. Deeks and G.M. Deeks were partners under the name of Deeks & Deeks. They had just completed a subway at Winnipeg under the track of the Canadian Pacific Railway, for the railway company. In 1905, Deeks & Deeks tendered for, and won, a contract from Canadian Pacific Railway to build their Toronto Sudbury line from Bolton to Parry Sound. Before Deeks & Deeks had tendered, they made an arrangement with the firm of Winters, Parsons & Boomer that if their tender was accepted, the latter would take an interest in the contract to the extent of one-half. Meanwhile Mr Winters had assumed certain obligations which rendered him unwilling to accept his full share of responsibility. Therefore, he introduced Messrs Cook and Hinds to Deeks & Deeks, in order to supplement his obligation. The result was that all the parties agreed to share the contract in the following proportions, Deeks & Deeks were to take three-eighths, Cook and Hinds to take three-eighths, and Winters, Parsons and Boomer one-quarter. To place these relationships upon a fixed footing and to define their interests better, the Toronto Construction Co. was formed, and its share capital distributed in the proportions mentioned, with the company taking over and carrying out the work under the contract.

In 1906, Winters and Boomer withdrew from the company. The stock they had held was divided equally among the remaining parties, so that Cook, Hinds and G.S. and G.M. Deeks held one-quarter of the entire capital of the company, with the exception of four shares held by Mrs Deeks, the wife of G.S. Deeks, whose introduction as a shareholder, brought the total number to five. The board of directors was G.M. Deeks, who was also president of the company; G.S. Deeks; Mr Hinds, who also served as secretary and treasurer; and Mr Cook, who was also the general manager.

The company carried out the work of laying the Toronto Sudbury line to the entire satisfaction of the Canadian Pacific Railway. Afterwards they continued to tender and won a considerable number of valuable contracts from the Canadian Pacific Railway. Though the construction company undertook no other work apart from these contracts, nevertheless, Cook, Hinds and Deeks and Deeks were associated in other similar enterprises in Montana and in the west. In 1907 they disagreed, and the different firms formed between them, which were all partnerships at will, were dissolved. They refused to enter into any further voluntary arrangements between themselves.

Subsequently, in 1909, the Canadian Pacific Railway invited tenders for the important Seaboard No.2 Contract, which involved the continuation of a line already laid by the Toronto Construction Co. The company entered into competitive tender for the contract. Their tender price, however, was not the lowest, but because the company had previously built the line known as Seaboard No.1, the company was given the contract on 14 May 1910. Seaboard No.3 was again taken up on behalf of the Toronto Construction Co., and the negotiations for it were conducted by Hinds and Hicks. Another contract was won for the Gulf Junction and Hamilton branch. As this contract was nearing completion, Hinds instructed the manager of the Toronto Construction Co. to get the work done as quickly as possible as other work was coming up, namely the South Shore contract. That contract led to the final dispute between the parties.

In 1911, Messrs Deeks and Hinds quarrelled with Mr Cook. They settled that they would no longer continue business relationships with Cook. There was nothing to compel them either legally or morally to work with or for Cook. They were, however, involved with him in various reciprocal duties because of their relationship in connection with the Toronto Construction Co. If they desired freedom to act without regard to the restrictions that that relationship imposed, it was necessary that they should terminate their positions as directors and shareholders in the company and place it in dissolution. Nevertheless, while still retaining their positions as directors and managers of the Toronto Construction Co. their duties to the company in

(continued)

which Cook was a shareholder entirely unchanged, they entered into negotiations with the Canadian Pacific Railway for the contract to build the South Shore line. Though the negotiations (which were unknown to Cook) were conducted in exactly the same manner as they had always been when the Messrs Deeks and Hicks were acting for the company, they were now in reality negotiating on their own behalf.

The negotiations for the South Shore line contract were opened by a telephone message sent through to Hinds at the Toronto Construction Co.'s office. On receipt of that message, certain units of price were prepared in the company's office, and the prices being ultimately fixed, Hinds was informed by a representative of the railway company that although the prices had been agreed to, the contract would not be let immediately as it was necessary that there should be an appropriation of the necessary cash made to authorize the contract by the Canadian Pacific Railway Co.

During the whole of these discussions the representatives of the Canadian Pacific Co. were not told that the contract would in any way be different from the others that had been negotiated in the same manner on behalf of the Toronto Construction Co. It was only after discussions had been concluded, that Hinds remarked to the railway's representative, 'Remember if we get this contract, it is to be Deeks and I and not the Toronto Construction Co'.

On 12 March 1912, Messrs Deeks were informed that the Canadian Pacific Railway Co. had made the necessary appropriation for the contract and work was to start at once, though the formal contract was not to be signed until 1 April 1912. Messrs Deeks and Hicks being certain of their position, in that they had obtained the contract for themselves informed Cook of what had happened for the first time. He protested without result. The Dominion Construction Co. was formed by Messrs Deeks and Hind to take over the contract, carry out the work and receive the profits from the job.

On 20 March 1912 there was a meeting of the directors of the Toronto Construction Co. It was resolved that another shareholders' meeting be held to consider the question of the voluntary liquidation of the company.

On 26 April 1913, owing to the defendants' voting power, resolutions were passed approving the sale of part of the company's plant to the Dominion Construction Co. and a declaration was made that the company had no interest in the South Shore line contract and that the directors were authorized to defend this action which in the meantime had been instituted.

Their lordships found that, in the circumstances, they were guilty of a distinct breech of duty in the course they took to secure the contract. Even supposing that it were not *ultra vires* for a company to make a present to its directors, it appeared quite certain that directors holding a majority of votes could not be permitted to make a present to themselves. That would be to allow a majority to oppress the minority. They could not retain the benefit of such a contract for themselves, but must be regarded as holding it on behalf of the company. In other words, while entrusted with the conduct of the affairs of the company, they deliberately designed to exclude, and use their influence and position to exclude, the company whose interests it was their first duty to protect.

It was noted that it was quite right to point out the importance of avoiding the establishment of rules as to directors' duties which would impose upon them burdens so heavy and responsibilities so great that men of good position would hesitate to accept the office. But on the other hand, men who assume the complete control of a company's business must remember that they are not at liberty to sacrifice the interests which they are bound to protect, and while ostensibly acting for the company, divert in their own favour business which should properly belong to the company they represent.

Cook v. *G.S. Deeks & Others* [1916] 1 A.C.554, P.C.

what is the extent of the duty which he is alleged to have neglected.

In general terms, the duties of a director are as follows:

1. A director need not exhibit in the performance of his duties a greater degree of skill than may reasonably be expected from a person of his knowledge and experience. Thus a director may not be liable for mere errors of judgement. If he acts honestly for the benefit of the· company he represents, he discharges his equitable, as well as legal, duty to the company;
2. A director is not bound to give continuous attention to the affairs of his company. His duties are of an intermittent nature to be performed at periodical board meetings, and at meetings of any committee of the board upon which he happens to be placed. He is not bound to attend all such meetings, although he ought to attend whenever in the circumstances he is reasonably able to do so.
3. In respect of all duties (having regard to the exigencies of business and the articles of association) which may properly be left to some other official, a director is, in the absence of grounds for suspicion, justified in trusting that official to perform such duties honestly.

Q. What are a director's duties and liabilities in relation to contracts?

Where directors of a company obtain a contract in their own names to the exclusion of the company, the contract is obtained under circumstances which amount to a breach of trust by the directors and constitute them trustees of its benefits on behalf of the company.

The directors cannot validly use any majority voting power they may have to vest the contract in themselves by subsequently passing a resolution declaring that the company had no interest in the contract.

Q. I am one of the directors of a company which is about to become insolvent. What are the general liabilities of myself and co-directors?

The prime effect of liability upon the company's insolvency is to prevent you and your directors from being involved in the management of another company for not less than 2 years if it is established that:

1. A person has been a director of a company which has at any time become insolvent either during his term of directorship or subsequently;
2. Their conduct, including that in relation to any other company, makes them unfit to be concerned in the management of a company.

You, or anyone else, who was a director or shadow director in the 12 months before the company became insolvent, may not for 5 years become a director of, or involved in the formation or management of, any other company of the same name, or similar name such that it suggests an association with the insolvent company.

If you knew, or should have known, that there was no reasonable prospect of avoiding the insolvent liquidation of the company, you may be liable to contribute personally to the company's debts; the test which will be applied is that of a 'reasonably diligent person', having both of the following attributes.

1. The skill and knowledge reasonably expected of a person in your position;

2. The actual skill and knowledge of yourself.

Where your company is being wound up, either the official receiver under the direction of the Secretary of State, or the latter alone, may make an application to the High Court within 2 years of the company becoming insolvent to disqualify a director; the Secretary of State may call for the following:

1. Information about a director's conduct;
2. Producing and permitting inspection of documents to decide whether or not to proceed against a director.

Q. What is the general effect of a term limiting liability within the partnership deed?

Lord Granworth, Lord Chancellor stated the principle that every person engaged in a partnership is liable, 'solidarily as they say upon the Continent', for everything, in terms which he believed could be disputed. For example, A, B and C, who are in partnership together, may stipulate among themselves that one of them shall not be liable for more than £1000, yet if in the conduct of their business they incur a debt to the extent of £10 000, every one of them will be liable for it notwithstanding the stipulation.

That doctrine does not depend upon the persons dealing with the partners having notice, and any notice may be immaterial, for creditors would not normally know what agreement the partners had made between themselves. The rights of creditors are wholly extrinsic of any such agreements. It would not be possible for a creditor to ascertain the limit of their liability.

If express notice were given to a third party that certain activities were prohibited, or that the authority of a partner was limited by reason of a term within the partnership deed, such a notice may be effective to those whom it reaches. Thus, if it has been agreed between the partners that any restrictions shall be placed on the power of any one or more of them to bind the partnership, no act done in contravention of the agreement is binding on the partnership with respect to persons having notice of the agreement.

3.5 LIMITED LIABILITY COMPANIES

Q. What are the advantages and disadvantages of a limited liability company?

The advantages of a limited liability company include the following:

1. Among the principle reasons which induce people to form limited liability companies is the desire to avoid the risk of bankruptcy; a profession can be carried on with limited liability and without exposing those interested in it in the event of failure to the harsh provisions of the bankruptcy law;
2. Increased facility afforded for borrowing money; a company can raise money on a floating charge which an ordinary trader cannot do;
3. Any member of a company acting in good faith is as much entitled to take and hold the company's debentures as any outside creditor;
4. The personal wealth of the shareholders is immune from claims made against the company.

The disadvantage in a limited liability company is that every creditor is entitled to get and to hold the best security the law allows him to take.

Q. Who may use the term 'limited', and what is its effect?

An incorporated company may be formed with or without limited liability. If no limit has been placed on the liability of its members, it may be known as an 'unlimited company'. A company cannot be formed in such a manner that its members are completely free from liability. Liability may only be 'limited', in which case the word must appear after the company name, either by itself where the company is one which is private or where it is not in the formula 'public limited company'.

It is an offence for anyone other than a limited company to use the term after its name, or for a public company to give the impression that it is merely a private company.

A company may either have the liability of its members limited by the memorandum to the amount, if any, unpaid on the shares respectively held by them, in which case it may be known as a company 'limited by shares'. Alternatively, the liability of a company's members may be limited to such amount as those members respectively undertake to contribute to the assets of the company in the event of its being wound up, in which case it is termed a company 'limited by guarantee'.

An exception to the general rule regarding limited liability is that if at any time the number of members of a company are reduced, in the case of a private company below two members, and in the case of any other company also below two, and it carries on business for more than six months while the number is so reduced, every person who is a member of the company during the time that it carried on business after those six months and is aware of the fact that it is carrying on business with fewer than two members, shall be severally liable for the payment of the whole debts of the company contracted during that time and may be sued therefore. A limited company, if so authorized by its articles, may by special resolution alter its memorandum so as to render unlimited the liability of its directors, managers or managing director.

Q. Are there any particular requirements for a contract with a limited company?

There is a certain form in which contracts may be made on behalf of a company and are binding on it and its successors. A contract made between two private persons, by law, would be required in writing, and if made according to English law to be under seal, and may also be made on behalf of the company in writing under the common seal of the company. A written contract may be signed on behalf of a company by anybody acting under its express or implied authority.

A contract made between private persons would, by law, be valid though made orally, and not reduced into writing and may likewise be made orally on behalf of the company by anyone acting under its authority.

In identifying a company which is an artificial person, the name is naturally of importance, but should it not be given correctly in a contract, the company may nevertheless enforce the contract if it can be identified in another way.

Q. What is the general effect on our liability if we change our practice from a partnership to a limited liability company?

An architectural practice, or indeed any other practice which

The curious question of whether or not a contract made on a Sunday between 2 limited liabilities is enforceable?

It was argued before Mocatta, J., in *Rolloswain Investments Ltd.* v. *Chromolit Portugal Catelarias E. Produtos Metalicos S.A.R.L*, that the *Sunday Observance Act 1677* was applicable to the case.

Section 1(3) of the Act states:

all and every person and persons whatsoever shall on every Lord's day apply themselves to the observation of the same by exercising themselves thereon in the duties of piety and true religion publicly and privately (4) and that no tradesman, artificer, workman, labourer or other person whatsoever, shall do or exercise any worldly labour, business or work of their ordinary callings upon the Lord's day or any part thereof (works of necessity and charity only excepted), and that every person being of the age of fourteen years or upwards, offending in the premises shall for every such offence forfeit the sum of five shillings (6) and that no person or persons whatsoever shall publicly cry, show forth, or expose to sale any wares, merchandises, fruit, herbs, goods or chattels whatsoever, upon the Lord's day, or any part thereof, upon pain that every person so offending shall forfeit the same goods so cried or showed forth or exposed to sale.

It was contended by the defendants that by virtue of section 2(1) of the *Interpretation Act 1889* the statute might apply to a modern company incorporated under the *Companies Act 1862*.

Mocatta, J. remarked that the social background of today was very different in relation to Sunday observance from what it was in 1677, when no doubt there was a political motive for the statute, quite apart from a religious one. In 1677, although there were certain moves afoot in the direction of what has subsequently become the limited liability company, 'that creature of the law as we now know it just did not exist'. A limited company is incapable of public worship or repairing to a church or exercising itself in the duties of piety and true religion, either publicly or privately, on any day of the week. It was therefore held that the *Sunday Observance Act 1677* had no application to contracts made on a Sunday between limited liability companies and such contracts were therefore enforceable. The case was heard on 3–4 February 1970. The court did not know that the 1677 Act had been recently repealed by the *Statute Law (Repeals) Act 1969*.

Rolloswain Investments Ltd. v. *Chromolit Portugal Catelarias E. Produtos Metalicos S.A.R.L.* [1970] 1 W.L.R.912.

operates as a partnership, may if its partners so wish be reconstituted into a limited liability company in order to afford some protection for its members as a whole against claims for damages.

However, an architect or member of a company may not escape personal liability in tort where he owes a duty of care independently of the company's contractural obligations. This may especially occur where an architect can be clearly identified by the plaintiff as being responsible for a particular scheme which has given rise to a claim in damages, and in such case he may be held liable for them.

Likewise a single principal may reconstitute his practice in order to limit his liability and obtain the preference of a debenture-holder over other creditors, selling his business to a limited company consisting only of himself and his family, the business being solvent all the terms of sale being known to and approved by the shareholders and all the requirements of the Act being complied with.

A cautionary tale of a limited liability company which fell on hard times

Mr Aron Salomon had been a wealthy man with a thriving business in July 1892. He had been for thirty years a leather merchant and wholesale boot and shoe manufacture, trading on his own account under the name of 'A. Salomon & Co.' in High Street, Whitechapel, where he had extensive warehouses and a large establishment.

He had a wife and a family consisting of five sons and a daughter. Four of the sons worked for their father, the eldest, who was about 30, was practically speaking the manager. The sons, not being partners in the business, were dissatisifed with their position and pressed their father to give them a share in the concern. 'They troubled me', said Mr Salomon, 'all the while.' At length, he decided to make provision for his family and extend his business by turning it into a limited company which was to consist exclusively of himself, his wife, his daughter and four of his sons. From the first, the intention was that it should be a private company, no prospectus was issued and no invitation was ever addressed to the public to take shares. All the requirements of the *Companies Act 1862* were observed.

On 20 July 1892 he entered into a preliminary agreement with Adolph Anholt as trustee for the future company; settling the terms upon which the transfer was to be made by him. One of the conditions was that part-payment might be made to him in debentures of the company. A memorandum of association was executed by Mr Salomon and the six members of his family, each of whom subscribed for one share. The stated object for which the company was formed was to adopt and carry into effect, with such agreed modifications as necessary, the agreement of 20 July. Its effect was to incorporate the company under the name of 'Aron Salomon & Co. Ltd', with liability limited by shares and having a nominal capital of £40 000 divided into shares of £1 each. The first directors were to be nominated by a majority of subscribers to the memorandum of association. The directors, when appointed, were authorized to exercise all such powers of the company as were not by statute or by the articles required to be exercised in a general meeting. There was express power given to the directors to borrow on debentures with the limitation that the borrowing was not to exceed £10 000 without the sanction of a general meeting.

On 2nd August 1892 the agreement of 20 July was adopted and the business was taken over by the company, as from 1 June 1892. The price fixed by the contract for the business was duly paid. The price on paper was somewhat extravagant as it amounted to over £39 000 and represented the sanguine expectations of a fond owner rather than anything that could have been called a businesslike or reasonable estimate of value.

As money came in, sums amounting in all to £30 000 were paid to Mr Salomon and then immediately returned to the company in exchange for fully paid shares. The sum of £10 000 was paid in debentures for the like amount. The balance with the exception of about £1000 which Mr Salomon received and retained went in discharging the debts and liabilities of the business at the time of the transfer, which were thus entirely wiped out. Mr Salomon received for his business about £1000 in cash and £10 000 in debentures, together with half the nominal capital of the company in fully paid-up shares. In September 1892, Mr Salomon applied for and obtained 20 000 shares, he thus held 20 001 in all. No other shares were issued except the shares taken by the subscribers to the memorandum who, knowing all the circumstances, had no grounds for complaining of overvaluation.

The company had a brief career. Shortly after it was started, there was a depression in the boot and shoe trade. Because of the danger of strikes, contracts with public bodies were split up and divided between different firms. These contracts had been the principal source of Mr Salomon's profit. Both Mr and Mrs Salomon lent the company money. Mr Salomon also got his debentures cancelled and re-issued to Mr Broderip, who advanced him £5000 which was immediately handed over to the company on loan. Mr Broderip's interest was not paid on his debentures when it became due. Therefore, in September 1893 he instituted an action in order to enforce his security (as the debentures were secured) against the assets of the company. A liquidation order was made and a receiver appointed. The forced sale of the company's assets realized enough to pay Mr Broderip, but not enough to pay the debentures in full, the unsecured creditors or the ordinary creditors. The receiver met Mr Broderip's claim by a counter-claim to which he made Mr Salomon a defendant. He disputed the validity of the debentures on the ground of fraud and claimed rescission of the agreement for the transfer of the business, cancellation of

(continued)

the debentures and repayment by Mr Salomon of the balance of the purchase money. Alternatively, he claimed payment of £20 000 on Mr Salomon's shares, alleging that nothing had been paid on them.

When the trial came on before Vaughan Williams, J., the validity of Mr Broderip's claim was admitted and it was not disputed that the 20 000 shares were fully paid up. The case presented by the receiver broke down but the learned judge suggested that the company had a right of indemnity against Mr Salomon. The signatories of the memorandum of association were nominees of Mr Salomon — mere dummies. The company was an alias. Mr Salomon employed it as his agent. Therefore the company was entitled to an indemnity against its principal, namely, Mr Salomon.

An appeal was lodged by both parties. It was dismissed by the Court of Appeal, who declining to make any order on the original counter-claim. They were of the opinion that the formation of the company, the agreement of August 1892 and the issue of debentures to the appellant pursuant to such agreement were merely a scheme to enable him to carry on business in the name of the company with limited liability contrary to the true intent and meaning of the *Companies Act 1862*, and further to enable him to obtain a preference over other creditors of the company by procuring a first charge on the assets of the company by means of such debentures. Mr Broderip was paid.

Mr Salomon appealed and the company brought a cross-appeal against so much of the judgment of the court below as declined to make any order upon the original counter-claim. The House of Lords, in reversing the decisions of Vaughan Williams, J. and the Court of Appeal, held that the proceedings were not contrary to the true intent and meaning of the *Companies Act 1862*; that the company was duly formed and registered and was not the mere 'alias' or agent of or trustee for the vendor; that he was not liable to indemnify the company against the creditors' claims; that there was no fraud upon creditors or shareholders; and that the company (or the receiver suing in the name of the company) was not entitled to rescission of the contract for purchase.

To Lord Halsbury, L.C. it seemed impossible to dispute that once a company is legally incorporated, it must be treated like any other independent person with its rights and liabilities appropriate to itself, and that the motives of those who took part in the promotion of the company are absolutely irrelevant in discussing what those rights and liabilities are. Lord Watson pointed out that any person who holds a preponderating share in the stock of a limited company has necessarily the intention of taking the lion's share of its profits without any risk beyond loss of the money which he has paid for or is liable to pay upon his shares. The fact of his acquiring and holding debentures secured upon the assets of the company does not diminish the risk of that loss.

Lord Herschell said that many industrial and banking concerns of the highest standing and credit have, in recent years, been converted into joint-stock companies, and often into what are called 'private' companies where the whole of the shares are held by the former partners. It appeared to him that all these might be called 'schemes to enable them to carry on business in the name of the company with limited liability'. The profits of the concern carried on by the company will go to the persons whose business it was before the transfer and in the same proportions as before. The only difference being that the liability of those who take the profits will no longer be unlimited. The very object of the creation of the company and the transfer to it of the business is that whereas the liability of the partners for debts incurred was without limit, the liability of the members for the debts incurred by the company shall be limited. In no other respect is it intended that there should be any difference. The conduct of the business and the division of the profits are intended to be the same as before. The memorandum must state the amount of the capital of the company and the number of shares into which it is divided, and no subscriber is to take less than one share. The shares may, however, be of as small a nominal value as those who form the company please, the *Companies Act 1862* prescribe no minimum. Although there must be 7 shareholders, it is enough that each of them holds one share, whatever its denomination. Therefore, the legislature sanctions a scheme by which all the shares except 6 are owned by a single individual, and these 6 are of little more than nominal value. Though it should not be forgotten, as Lord Macnaghten remarked, that in almost every company that is formed the statutory number of shareholders is eked out by clerks or friends who sign their names at the request of the promoter, or promoters, without intending to take any further part or interest in the matter. Lord Herschell concluded: 'it must be remembered that no one need trust a limited liability company unless he so please.'

Broderip v. *Salomon* [1895] 2 Ch.322, C.A.

3.6 EMPLOYEES

Q. I am a salaried architect. What are my liabilities in comparison with those of my employer?

The real question is: are you worth suing? Will you be able to pay substantial damages? If you cannot, then you probably will not be sued because it would be too expensive to set in motion the necessary legal machinery.

However, returning to the original question, a salaried architect is frequently to all intents and purposes 'his own master', carrying out all things necessary to achieve the satisfactory completion of a project from the inception of a design through to a final completion of a building with little direction from his employer. Nevertheless, the employer will usually be liable for all the architect's actions, whether express instructions have been given or not, provided that what has been done falls within the course of the architect's employment be it done negligently, fraudulently or mistakenly. If it does not, the employer is not vicariously liable.

For example, the Royal Institute of British Architects (RIBA) in its Code of Professional Conduct directs a member who employs architects to permit the 'architects he employs to engage in sparetime practice'. Such practice is not infrequently carried out in the offices of the employer. Any work produced at that time by the architect which contains mistakes amounting to negligence will be the responsibility of the architect. The employer will not be vicariously liable for the negligence of a salaried architect while that architect is doing private work for his own profit, permitted by the employer. It constitutes work which the employer has not retained the architect to carry out. If it is a different

interpretation as to the employer's, vicarious liability may be implied.

Q. What is my position if I do something wrong after I have been 'loaned' to a practice?

Occasionally a salaried architect or engineer may be 'loaned' by the practice for which he works to another, where for example the latter has entered a competition and requires help to complete the submission by a set deadline.

Thus, the salaried architect having 'two masters', should he then be responsible for committing a tort, the employer to whom he had been 'loaned', and for whom he was working when the wrong was done, would be vicariously liable, even if the tort was committed against a fellow employee and not a stranger as the distinction is irrelevant.

Q. What is the liability of a company architect?

Where the employer is a limited liability company, which does not have a 'soul' all members of the company being employees including its directors, though regarded as 'superior' for the manner in which they appoint and direct or supervise other members of the company, the company, in the form of its directors, will not be responsible for the actions of its employees. The salaried architect is liable. He is liable for the tort from the moment when he commits it. Vicarious liability cannot be placed on his apparent employers, the directors of the company, for they too are employees.

This proposition was prior to the *Law Reform (Married Women and Tortfeasors) Act 1935* and the case of *Wah Tat Bank Ltd* v. *Chan Cheng Kum* [1975] A.C. 507. It was the common law rule that 'anyone who suffered damage by reason of a tort jointly committed by a number of persons was deemed to have but one cause of action'. Once final judgment had been received against any tortfeasor, a plaintiff was barred from recovering damages against any other joint tortfeasor responsible for that tort at a later date. Because of the highly unsatisfactory nature of this common law rule, the Privy Council in considering the 1935 Act in the Wah Tat Bank Ltd case concluded that it had been abolished.

An architect who is an officer of a company, be he chairman or managing director, may himself find that he is sued as a joint tortfeasor with the company itself if he instructed the salaried architect who committed the tort.

Q. What are the duties of a salaried architect?

A salaried architect is under a duty, whether or not it is expressly stated in his contract of employment, to take reasonable care both in the manner in which he carries out his work and in the way in which he uses any equipment or other property with which he is entrusted by his employer. Should that equipment or property be damaged or lost, or the architect's work be negligent, so that a third party is injured and constitutes a breach of his implied contractual duty, his employer, vicariously responsible as he is for his employees' acts, may recover such damages which consequently arise from the architect, provided they are not too remote a consequence of the breach.

Q. To what extent must I exercise reasonable care in doing my job?

The implied contractual duty of a salaried professional, whether they be architect, engineer or surveyor, to exercise reasonable care is of particular importance when carrying out work which is or might be dangerous. The risk represented by surveying or inspecting old buildings is 'a necessary incident of employment'. Where such danger is virtually impossible to eliminate or reduce by anything which the employer might do, then it may be referred to as a risk which the employee is paid to take. If you know that what you are doing is dangerous yet are also aware of what precautions should be taken to avert it (e.g. wearing protective clothing) but do nothing and are injured, you may be guilty of primary negligence and be liable to bear some proportion of the damages. On the other hand, it would be with some hesitation that blame would be attributed to a man skilled in his profession if he decides to follow a dangerous course of conduct not for the sake of saving himself trouble, but primarily in order to get on with his employer's business.

Nevertheless, if you do not guard against such normal risks which occur while carrying out on-site work or at the premises of a third party, or you are not well protected and are injured, and the occupier of those premises is then sued, or the employer by yourself for breach of their common duty of care, they may plead that they are entitled to expect a skilled man such as yourself to be well protected knowing the normal risks. On the other hand, an employer owes a common law duty to his employees to ensure that reasonable care is taken to prevent his employees being subjected to unnecessary risk during the course of their employment by providing and maintaining proper equipment. This does not mean that such equipment should be of the latest design. What it does mean is that it obliges the employer to make reasonable provision for avoiding or mitigating the foreseeable consequences of injury. There is a common law duty on the employers to take care of their employees. The care they must take depends upon all circumstances of the case which include the age and experience of that employee.

Q. Is there a test which indicates when someone will be considered either as an employee or self-employed?

An employee can be defined as one whom the employer cannot only instruct as to what work is to be done, but can state quite specifically in what manner it is to be done and closely supervise its execution. In other words, an employee may be defined as any person employed by another to do work for him on the terms that he, the employee, is to be subject to the control and directions of his employer in respect of the manner in which his work is to be done. However, it is questionable whether the degree of control exercised by an employer is actually a decisive factor in determining whether or not one is an employee.

The control test is somewhat unrealistic in the case of a salaried architect or engineer, who are both professional people with a refined skill and particular experience. Frequently the only control exerted by a principal of a practice is to hand to them the broad outlines of a brief which requires an intensely personal development before a satisfactory scheme, let alone a building or structure, can reach fruition. There can be little question of the employer telling him how to do that work.

A different test may be to consider whether or not the person employed is an integral part of the business. Yet this does not suffice. The services of an architect, whether he is salaried, self-employed or acting in the capacity of an agent, can be vital to the satisfactory administration of a contract and an integral part of the entire scheme.

The definition given by the *Employment Protection (Consolidation) Act 1978* of an employee is: 'an individual who has entered into or works under a contract of employment.'

Here 'contract of employment' means a contract of service or apprenticeship, whether express or implied; and if it is express, whether it is oral or in writing.

The test of establishing whether or not there is a contract of service may be found by asking the question: 'is the person who has engaged himself to perform these services, performing them as a person on his own account?' If the answer to the question is 'yes', then the contract is a contract *for services*. If the answer is 'no', then the contract is a contract *of service*. The distinction is of great importance not only in relation to the legislation governing tax, National Insurance contributions, unfair dismissal, etc., but also to the doctrine of vicarious liability.

As a salaried professional has been put into a position by his employer of being able to do 'a class of acts' which, theoretically, is done under the supervision and direction of the employer, the latter employer is answerable for anything he does in the process of performing any one of those 'class of acts' during the course of his employment, and however he chooses to do it, regardless of whether or not the employer receives any benefit.

Sir John Holt, C. J. gave the principle of vicarious liability, in *Hern* v. *Nichols* [1701] Holt K. B. 462, as follows: 'seeing somebody must be a loser by this deceit, it is more reason that he, that employs and puts a confidence in the deceiver, should be a loser than a stranger.' The principle may have been given added weight by the promise that the employer is often financially better able to bear the cost of any damages arising out of a tort committed by his employee. The cost is now infrequently borne by the employer's insurance cover, but this does not prevent the insurance company from claiming back its loss from the salaried architect or engineer if a waiver of subrogation has not been agreed upon between him and his employer. Therefore, always make sure that your conditions of employment include a term waiving subrogation.

Q. In a nutshell, what are the options open to me to limit my liability by practising in one way rather than another?

In terms of the actual practice of architecture, members of an ordinary partnership, like a sole practitioner, carry unlimited liability. Yet the consequences of being held liable for a particular breach of duty may be limited to a certain extent. A clear and unambigious agreement may be reached between the partnership and the other parties to a contract that the financial liability of the former will be restricted to a certain sum. If liability is established against the firm, a claim will not be made against it which exceeds this prearrănged sum.

The alternative is to form a limited partnership where at least one partner agrees personally to accept the entire liability of the firm's business ventures, while the remaining members of the firm become limited partners. Such a proposition may prove less attractive than simply forming an ordinary partnership where financial liability is limited on each and every scheme by a separate contract to that effect. This is not merely because of the burden placed on the person who is obliged to bear liability in all the partnership's dealings, but also because the scope of a limited partner's actions are severely restricted. Indeed, they may be limited to merely giving advice without taking part in the management of the firm, which at times may prove somewhat difficult. However, if such restrictions are accepted, a limited partnership could prove a most effective way of practising.

This may be compared with practising in a limited liability company which does not impose the same restrictions on its members as are imposed within a limited partnership. Financial liability, so far as it arises in contract, may be most effectively limited by carrying on a business in such a company. However, it is a fallacy to suggest that by so doing, you may escape from all other personal liability, especially that which arises in tort and where you or more members of a company can clearly be associated with the scheme that has given rise to that particular claim. There is no particular way of practising a profession which, if adopted, would clearly reduce your liability beyond that which you would bear if carrying on business in a different form.

Furthermore, it is somewhat unreasonable, professionally unethical and irresponsible to put forward the notion that where a claim of liability for professional negligence is justified, its consequences can and should be wholly avoided. What is perhaps more reasonable and acceptable is to attempt to limit the amount of damages claimed, and the time in which they should be claimed, to a reasonable level which is acceptable to both parties to a contract and has been agreed before the contract has been signed. Each alternative for limiting liability, whether it is by the use of a protective clause, by time or by insurance cover, should not be used alone and independently of any other, but rather used together to form what may be considered a series of defences, the sum of which offers a greater degree of protection than any one of the constitutent parts alone.

FOUR

Sometimes I am referred to

as an 'agent' –

what does this mean?

Q. If my client or employer calls me his 'agent', is he correct?

The question of defining what is the legal relationship created between an architect or other professional and the client has given rise to numerous attempts by the courts to establish a clear and concise yet comprehensive answer.

The architect or engineer may be the agent of the building owner for achieving those objects for which he is normally employed, for example, preparing drawings for the building or structural works in contemplation and the superintendence of their construction. However, to this clear definition a rider must be added – it is dependent on the terms of the contract.

In other words, an architect may be engaged as the agent of the owner of the building for whom the building is being erected, and his function is to make sure that when the work has been completed the owner will have a building properly constructed and in accordance with the contract, plans, specification, drawings and any supplementary instructions which the architect might give.

However, Salmon, J. considered that while it may be true that for some purposes, such as the ordering of materials, that an architect is the agent of the building owner judged, nevertheless, an architect to be clearly an independent contractor, the building owner having no control over the manner in which the architect does his work. Likewise, in *A.M.F. International Ltd.* v. *Magnet Bowling Ltd.* [1968] 1.W.L.R.1028, an architect was regarded, when acting in a professional position, as in independent contractor. A proposition, which was echoed in the case of *W.H.P.T Housing Association Ltd.* v. *Secretary of State for Social Services*, [1981] I.C.R.737, where Mr Peter Frederick Lowe, an architect, accepting work initially on a freelance basis from the housing association yet was required to work in its offices under the direct supervision of a chief architect, his obligations to his employer constituted a contract for services and not a contract of service. The former being to provide his services for the use of the employer whereas in the latter it was to provide himself as an employee to service. It was a decision which upheld the findings of an industrial tribunal that the architect was self-employed, an independent contractor, but reversed that of the Secretary of State for Social Services, who held that he was an employee, placing him in the same position as other architects who worked for the housing association and who were regarded by the association as employees.

Such is the wide divergence of opinions which holds an architect or other professional to be an agent, an independent contractor and an employee. Their significance lies in the various degrees of liability, particularly vicarious liability, which each is said and has been found to have embodied in it. The measure of liability fluctuates with time and is by no means stable.

Q. What does the term 'agent' mean?

An 'agent' or 'agency' can be explained in philosophical terms, that is by agency the individual's legal personality is multiplied in space.

Attempts to refine such a definition have also multiplied, but in confusion. This confusion was apparent in the nineteenth century and continues today. No word is, perhaps, more commonly and constantly abused than the word 'agent'. A person may be spoken of as an 'agent' and, no doubt, in the popular sense of the word may properly be said to be one, though when it is attempted to suggest that he is an agent under such circumstances as create the legal obligations attaching to agency, this use of the word is only misleading.

Generally an 'agent' is a person who is employed not merely to act on behalf of another (a common application of the term), but has the authority to create legal relations by contract between his principal and a third party, provided that authority is a mirror image, which if necesary can be reduced, of the personal authority of that principal. An agent can do nothing which his client cannot. His own contract with a client is, in its simplest form, a transference of legal powers. Once an agent has brought his principal into contractual relations with another, he drops out and his principal sues or is sued on the contract. Thus an architect may act as agent under the RIBA Conditions of Appointment to employ consultants on behalf of the client.

The client will be vicariously liable for a tort committed by an architect or any other professional in like position in the course of his agency, provided that it comes within the scope of his authority. The client's liability may not be mitigated by the fact that it was a reasonable discharge of his obligations to employ an architect as agent, unlike the case of the architect who is retained as an independent contractor.

It is wise for the appointment or retention of any professional to be recorded in writing. Indeed, it is recommended by the RIBA that an architect's appointment be in writing, preferably on its Memorandum of Agreement and Schedule of Services and Fees, setting out and defining clearly the extent of the architect's authority. It is a point of reference which will determine whether or not an architect contracting as agent has gone beyond his terms of reference and thus incurred personal liability. In the case of oral contracts, the personal liability of an agent is a question of inference; whether or not the agent himself intended to incur personal liability may be deduced or inferred from the surrounding circumstances.

Q. When will I be considered an agent?

It is a question of fact whether there is an agency. Equally, it is a question of fact when any other relationship exists. But it is a question of law what the legal mind will interpret that as being. There need be no reference to any type of legal relationship in any contract of employment; nor needs there to be a written contract, only a verbal one. As a matter of principle, any legal relationship is determined by the legal interpretation of the facts and not by the label which the parties choose to put on them. The contract of employment need not be found to be a 'sham' if the statement of the relationship set out there is not the same as the court might find. Though in truth it is perhaps a mere fiction or façade hiding the reality of the situation.

The 'label' which is attached to the contract – i.e. a contract of service or a contract for services – by the client and the professional is not a conclusive factor in deciding what the true nature of it is. Thus where A acts as agent, P (the principal) becomes liable to T (a third party) not only where A is an employee, but also where he is an independent contractor, for in the law of agency P's liability does not depend on A's precise employee status. P can be liable whether A is employed or self-employed, provided that he is an agent.

The label which you and your client choose to use to describe your relationship cannot alter or decide your true relationship, although in deciding what is that relationship the expression by you or your true intention is relevant but not conclusive. The legal relations between you are classified not by appearance, but reality. However, if your relationship is ambiguous and is capable of being one or the other, then you can remove that ambiguity by the very agreement itself which you make one with the other; it then becomes the best material from which to gather the true legal relationship between you and your client.

4.1 CREATION OF AN AGENCY

Q. How is an agency created?

The creation of an agency is generally a matter of consent between the client, on the one hand, and the professional, on the other. The client must agree to the latter acting as his agent to create a binding contract between himself and another as in, for example, engaging specialized consultants for a project. Equally, the professional must agree to act thus. The consent of the agent may be inferred from his acting on behalf of the principal.

In the case of an architect, should circumstances arise inconsistent with the architect's professional obligations and integrity and particularly in maintaining confidentiality between clients, apart from declaring those circumstances and obtaining the agreement of the parties concerned to the continuance of his engagement, then he is required by the RIBA Code of Professional Conduct to remove the source of conflict or to withdraw from the situation.

In order to establish clearly that a party entered into a contract as agent for a principal, there should be a previously existing agreement between the alleged agent and the principal, that the alleged agent should contract on behalf of the principal. As a matter of good practice, to avoid creating uncertainties it is recommended that a comprehensive contract of employment between architect and client be exchanged either by using an institute's own forms (to which a professional belongs) or by letters of agreement, provided that the services, responsibilities and fees basis are fully defined.

The architect, engineer or other professional may be given authority to act in the capacity of agent for his client without that relationship being recorded in writing. Indeed, it is not necessary in the eyes of the law that it should be. Furthermore, in some circumstances an agency relationship may exist, even though no consent may be found on the part of the principal to the existence of any such relationship, for the purpose of imposing liabilities on one party.

Although part of the services offered by an architect includes acting as agent on behalf of the client, nevertheless the architect in private practice has no implied power or authority *per se* to make a contract, and apart from one that has already been agreed by introducing variation clauses e.g. an architect simply superintending the construction of a building does not have the implied power to agree with the adjoining owners to vary the works in such a way as to affect the rights of his client. If the architect does so, and consequently causes loss to the adjoining owner with whom he has contracted, he may be liable for an action of deceit being held against him.

Such liability in tort for deceit may not be held against you if you mistakenly (though innocently) believe that you possess such authority. For example, a Borough Surveyor may act within the scope of his authority in negotiating the terms of a contract and within the scope of his ostensible authority in agreeing those terms with the contractor. He could therefore make an agreement to vary the terms of a contract which was then binding on the council.

4.2 AUTHORITY OF AN AGENT

Q. If I am an agent of my client, what is the extent of my authority and my liability?

Generally an agent's authority must of necessity be confined within the limits of the principal's own powers. In other words, when acting as agent for your client, you may do nothing which your client may not. Agency is essentially a transfer of power of authority from one to another. Your authority is a mirror image of your client's. It is no greater. It can certainly be less where it is so limited by the client in your terms of reference or contract of employment. Thus you will not be liable if your client 'had the right to do the act', as long as you 'acted with authority'.

Where your authority is limited to a specific act, such as the employment of a single consultant or civil engineer, but you go beyond that to employ both a civil engineer and a mechanical and electrical engineer, you need not necessarily be liable for any loss that your client has suffered by the employment of the additional consultant. Although not bound by the second contract, because you entered into it without his authorization, the client at a later date can adopt or ratify it.

At the turn of the century it was believed that an agent possessed neither contractual rights nor liabilities towards third parties. By the late 1960s it was said that the rights of the agent were subordinate to those of the principal. Now both the agent and client may be held jointly and severally liable for any tort which the former commits in the course of his agency. The person who has been injured financially or physically may sue at his choice either the agent or the client, or both, to recover his loss; either one can be sued first, then another action be brought against the one not originally sued.

A similar principle applies if you are retained as the agent of the Crown, for the *Crown Proceedings Act 1947* provides that the Crown shall be subject 'to all those liabilities to which if it were a private person, of full age and capacity it would be subject in respect of any breach of duty or torts committed by its agent'. However, any one who contracts on behalf of the Crown cannot be sued on the contract made by him, or be made liable for a breach of warranty of authority, unless it can be inferred from the circumstances that there was an intention that he be personally liable, or he expressly pledges his own credit.

Q. How does my client give me authority to act as his agent?

You may have authority from your client to contract as agent in a number of ways. The authority may be actual, either express or implied; or it may be ostensible or apparent.

Actual authority may be defined as a legal relationship between principal and agent operated by consensual agreement to which they alone are parties. Its scope is to be ascertained by applying ordinary principles of construction of contracts, including any proper implications from the express words used, the usages of the trade or the course of business between the parties.

Actual authority may be 'express' when it is given to you by express words in your contract of employment, or 'implied'. Implied authority may be inferred from the conduct both of the client and yourself, as well as from the circumstances of each case. For example in a large architectural practice the directors appoint one of their number to act as managing director, thereby impliedly authorizing him to do all such things as fall within the usual scope of that office. While agency must ultimately derive from consent, the consent need not necessarily be to the relationship of principal and agent itself, indeed the existence of it may be to state a fact upon which the law imposes the consequences which result from agency.

Ostensible or apparent authority is the authority of an agent as it appears to others. It often coincides with actual authority but, on occasion, it may exceed it, as for instance where an engineer has been given authority to order materials by his client, but that authority is limited to materials below a certain sum. To a third party not knowing of this limitation to the engineer's actual authority, it may appear to him that the engineer ostensibly buys materials to any value.

Where an agent acts with actual authority, whether express or implied, or ostensible authority, the client will be bound by such acts. The liability of the client will rest in either tort or contract, depending not only on the authority the agent purported to have when he was responsible for committing the wrong, but also on all the circumstances of the case.

In other words, a principal is only responsible to contract for those things done within the actual or ostensible authority of the agent, but he is responsible in tort for all wrongs done by the agent in the course of his employment, whether within his actual or ostensible authority or not. The presence of actual authority is decisive to show that his conduct is within the course of his employment, however, the absence of it is not decisive the other way.

Q. Can the actions of an agent be later ratified by a client, and if so what is the effect of such ratification?

As a general principle, neither an engineer nor an architect acting in the capacity of an agent, under their normal professional authority are empowered to accept tenders, enter into a contract without the knowledge of their client or to promise that conditions contained in a contract will be varied or waived. Where either exceeds his authority, the client is not responsible for his acts. The architect or engineer alone is liable for the consequences which arise from them.

Such abuses of authority without the knowledge of the client, and the liabilities which stem from them, can be amended if the client is prepared to forgo the fact that he did not have prior knowledge and ratify the agent's actions; thus the client becomes responsible for them just as if he had given prior authority for their commission. The only qualification to this is that the architect or engineer's actions must have been done on his behalf, for no man can ratify an act which was done not on his own behalf, but on the behalf of the doer himself.

A contract is not binding on a client or a third party if the architect or engineer makes it subject to the ratification of his client. Until such ratification is forthcoming, the position between the two parties is in a state of flux. It is possible for either party to withdraw usually without obligation to the other.

Ratification of the contract by the client may be implied if he does nothing, though knowing that work has been ordered by the architect or engineer and is being carried out. He will be liable to honour any invoice which places a reasonable price on the work. Furthermore, where an architect or engineer has contracted beyond his authority the client can yet ratify his actions, so justifying that contract, provided that the client is still in a position of being able to authorize lawfully the particular contract and the actions which led to its formation.

Q. What is my liability when I am contracting as agent?

Agency forms an important basis of liability. One of the most fundamental principles which stems from this must be that when contracting as an agent, you must retain the confidentiality of your position with a particular client. You may not divulge any information you have been given directly by the client or have acquired during the course of designing a scheme, at any time, for example, the manufacturing process of a new product, which knowledge would be of great advantage to competitors and if divulged adversely affect the commercial stability of a company.

You may not place yourself in such a position as agent of one party as to be open to criticism from the other. Here the classic example is that of the architect being paid by both the builder and the client; it is considered a sufficiently distasteful practice as to be in complete violation of the architect's contract to warrant that the client is not liable to pay him anything for his services.

The rule of confidentiality may be summarized as: you shall avoid all actions and situations inconsistent with your professional obligations or likely to raise doubts about your integrity. The great weight attached to this rule by the courts was emphasized in 1874 by Lord Cairns, L.C. in the case of *Parker* v. *McKenna*, (1874) L.R.10 Ch. 96, 118, 'Now the rule of this court as to agents is not a technical or arbitrary rule. It is founded on the highest and truest principles of morality. No man in this court, acting as agent be allowed to put himself into a position in which his interest and his duty will be in conflict.' If you are in breach of such a duty to retain confidentiality between one client and another, even if the information was divulged inadvertently, you may be liable for an action by your client to recover damages.

Should the situation arise that you, having been asked to act as agent of a prospective client, know that your interests either in respect of another client's or in another field of business will conflict, you should declare them to the client before you are engaged by him. Your liability may be waived if the client chooses to retain you after having been made fully aware of the circumstances, and similarly, if the client continues to employ you without protest after he has discovered circumstances which places a conflict between your duty as his agent and his interest. A corollary of this is that you must act with all necessary speed and diligence when contracting on behalf of your client, generally keeping him as fully informed as possible, particularly where you cannot or have failed to carry out the client's instruction.

Q. What is the position if I delegate my authority?

An architect, or indeed any other person, undertakes the service of agency in an atmosphere of mutual trust between himself and the client. It would be an abuse of the confidence placed in him if that authority were delegated.

The liability of an architect in delegating authority may be negated if it is shown that the client expressly or impliedly allowed the appointment; for example, a client may appoint a practice to carry out a scheme, his initial dealings being with the principal of that practice, yet the scheme itself may be delegated to a job architect. Normally this is an acceptable course of action. In so doing, the authority of an agent is delegated where the job architect places orders for materials on behalf of the client.

4.3 AGENT FOR AN UNNAMED CLIENT

Q. What is my liability if I act for an unnamed client?

As a general principle, although a client is not named in an authorized contract made by his agent, he can subsequently ratify it.

There is no reason if commercial necessity demands it why you should disclose the name of the client for whom you are acting as agent to the other contracting party. The question which arises is whether or not it was intended that you should be personally liable. It is a question which can only be answered by looking at the facts as they appear in the particular case, or where there is a written contract considering its true construction.

Where you sign a contract or letter of agreement retaining a consultant for a project but do not mention or give any indication that that signature is given purely in your capacity as agent, the circumstances may be such as to support the inference that you are personally liable to honour the contract, that is to pay the consultant's fees yourself. Should the signature be qualified by such phrases as 'on account of', 'for and on behalf of' or 'as agent', etc., your personal liability as agent will be negated, otherwise something very strong on the face of the contract is needed to exclude your personal liability.

In a nutshell, the question to be answered is whether you contracted purely as an agent, without personal liability being attached to yourself as a result of the contract, or whether the opposite is true because you contracted as a principal. For example, a client and an engineer may agree upon any terms of employment connected with the engineer's agency, or indeed any other matter, which will be legally binding on both provided it does not fall within the purlieu of the *Unfair Contract Terms Act 1977* or any other relevant legislation which would negate it. They can by an express contract provide that the agent shall be the person liable either concurrently with or to the exclusion of the principal, or that the agent shall be the party to sue either concurrently or to the exclusion of the principal. Furthermore, the agent may act as surety for his client or enter into a collateral agreement with its own terms. However, the fraud of the client in inducing a contract whereby an onerous liability is placed on the agent is a defence for the latter when sued on the contract.

4.4 AGENT FOR AN UNFORMED COMPANY

Q. What is my liability if I act as an agent of an unformed company?

If you enter a contract for the directors of a company which is to be formed but as yet does not exist, that is it has not been incorporated (e.g. you order materials for the new building into which the company will move), you will be personally liable for any loss suffered by a third party unless there is some agreement to the contrary.

The case of *Kelner* v. *Baxter* [1866] L.R.2C.P.174 gives rise to a series of distinctions to the effect that the agent no liability if a formula such as 'agent for X Company' or 'for and on behalf of X Company' were asked to sign the contract. That distinction was obliterated by section 9(2) of the *European Communities Act 1972*: 'Where a contract entered into by the person purporting to act for the company or as agent for it, and he shall be personally liable on the contract accordingly.' Thus to exclude personal liability the agreement to the contrary may not be inferred by the fact that the contract was signed by a person acting as agent, whatever the phrase used might be. Rather there has to be some clear exclusion of the agent's personal liability if he were in some measure to avoid the consequences of acting for an unformed company.

Where the agent of the company is an established architectural practice with retired partners, those partners will be liable equally with the active partners for damages which arise as a result of them having acted for an unformed company, unless public notification of the retirement has been given. In other words, where the principal is a member of a partnership who retires without notifying the public he will be bound by contracts made by the remaining partners with persons who had previously had dealings with the firm or who were aware of his membership, provided of course that they had no notice of his retirement.

4.5 AGENT FOR A FOREIGN CLIENT

Q. My practice acts for a number of foreign clients, how does this affect my liability?

The personal liability which you incur when contracting as the agent of a foreign client has undergone a change since 1932 when the eighth edition of William Bowstead's digest *Law of Agency* was published. Bowstead stated that an agent of a foreign principal was prima facie presumed to contract personally and was therefore liable for any actions which arose from it. Thus the foreign principal could not sue, or be sued, on contracts made by a home agent unless the agent 'had authority to establish privity of contract between the principal and the other contracting party, and it clearly appears from the terms of the contract or from the surrounding circumstances that it was the intention of the agent and of the contracting party to establish such privity of contract'. This view found support in the mid-1950s when an agent who contracted on behalf of a foreign principal was presumed to incur a personal liability unless a contrary intention appeared.

In 1968 the Court of Appeal found the presumption no longer exists due to changes which have taken place in commerce. In other words, when an architect, engineer or contractor acts as agent for a British or foreign client the personal liability he shoulders in making a contract for either will generally be similar, depending on the circumstances surrounding each case. Nevertheless, the fact that the principal is foreign is a factor to be taken into account in determining whether or not the other party to the contract was willing, or led the agent to believe that he was willing, to treat as a party to the contract the agent's principal, and if he was so willing, whether the mutual intention of the other party and the agent was that the agent should be personally entitled to sue or liable to be sued on the contract as well as his principal.

FIVE

What is the extent of my

liability as an agent,

and how can I limit it?

5.1 WARRANTY OF AUTHORITY, RATIFICATION AND FRAUD

Q. What is the effect of a warranty of authority?

An architect, engineer or other professional may be liable if he makes representations to another either negligently or fraudulently that he has the authority of his client, when in fact he does not, to enter into contract on his behalf. If that other person P, subsequently relies on the good faith of the professional, A, and A's truth in warranting his authority, and the P suffers physical or financial damage, P may be entitled to reimbursement from A. For example, if an architect provides a builder with quantities and assures him that they are correct, but the architect has no authority to bind his client in this manner, then the client may not be liable to the builder for errors in the quantities, but the architect may be.

It is of no consequence that the architect might have been the agent of a client and have previously, but no longer, had the authority to act in the way he did, that he did not know that the authority had been rescinded due to the death of his client or for any other reason, or had no means of finding out that such was the case. Where such circumstances are known by the architect and the third party, and also that the former's representation of authority was merely a question of law, the architect may not be liable for any loss suffered; nor will an action against him succeed if it is shown that the third party knew he had no authority from his client to act in a particular manner.

Q. When and how may I be liable for fraud?

If you make a statement in the process of arranging a contract which is a complete falsehood, unbeknownst to yourself, and the remark being made innocently with the intention that it should be acted upon, then you may not be liable if any damages result, provided that you had not spoken negligently or acted without due care. Neither will your client be liable if he too were innocent, there being no intention to commit a fraud or to obtain an unfair and wrongful advantage over the other party to the contract. In other words, you cannot add an innocent state of mind to an innocent state of mind and get as a result a dishonest state of mind.

Conversely, where you act fraudulently, you are personally liable for damages, even though you were acting as your client's agent and for his benefit. An agent cannot plead authority of his principal in defence, even though he did not know that what he was doing was tortious e.g. the infringement of copyright in a design. In other words, you cannot use your position as an excuse. All persons directly concerned in the commission of a fraud are to be treated as principals. No party can be permitted to excuse himself on the ground that he acted as agent of another. The reason for this is that a contract of agency or of service cannot impose any obligation on the agent or servant to commit or assist in the committing of a fraud.

Where the client has suffered loss because you acted fraudulently within the scope of your employment, as when you come to an agreement with the builder over what work is and is not to be included in the contract, you yourself receiving some 'token of gratitude' from the builder, the client may not only recover damages from you and the builder for such an act, but also dismiss you and rescind the contract he has with the builder as it is so fundamental a breach of it. Furthermore, the client may recover any money paid as a bribe or secret commission to yourself.

You will not be liable if your client acts in a fraudulent manner; there is no doctrine of 'respondent inferior'. Neither will you be personally liable for fraud if you innocently made a misstatement, even though your client or another agent knew that it was false. Nevertheless, if the client does not intervene to correct the fault, he will be liable, for the party with the guilty knowledge can himself be treated as being guilty of fraud.

5.2 THE CLIENT'S INSTRUCTIONS

Q. What is the extent of my duty in carrying out my client's instructions?

One of the first principles of any professional code of practice is to carry out faithfully the duties which you undertake.

An architect, for example, contracting as an agent is under a professional as well as an implied contractual duty to carry out any express instructions given to him by his client to the best of his ability, with all necessary skill and care and within a reasonable time. If he cannot or fails in trying to carry out the instructions, he must inform his client of the fact within a reasonable time. An agent who fails, whether deliberately or negligently, to carry out his principal's instructions has no right to remuneration because in such a case he has not earned it.

The duty to carry out the instructions of your client holds true even if you may reasonably believe that it would be in his best interests not to follow them, and the client later believes that he has acted without due care. Take as an illustration the architect who has been instructed to 'build down to a price'. His duty of care may be limited to the context of a house to be built down to a price. Although the architect in such circumstances may not be in breach of any duty to his client in this respect, i.e. to follow instructions, he may be liable to a third party, particularly if the person was injured as a result of the defective condition of the structure 'built down to a price'.

Generally you are under a duty to inform your client of any information which comes to your attention during the course of your agency which may influence the client's judgment. If you do not divulge such information, you may be liable for your failure to do so, even though it concerned a matter on which you were not specifically instructed.

Where the client's instructions are ambiguous and are capable of having two or more meanings, you may not in certain circumstances incur any liability if you reasonably interpret them in the sense not intended by the client. Nevertheless, it is usually the agent's duty to seek clarification.

5.3 FEES, SECRET PROFITS AND ACCOUNTS

Q. Can I (and at what point) be liable for any profit which I make on a scheme?

Whether you are an architect, engineer, surveyor or other professional, when you act as an agent for a client you are under a heavy equitable obligation not to make any profit for yourself which is unknown to your client and without his approval.

This fundamental obligation may be put in the following way. Any surreptitious dealing between one princpal and an agent of another principal is a fraud on such other principal cognizable by the court. The defrauded principal, if he comes in time, is entitled at his option to have the contract rescinded, or if he elects not to have it rescinded, to have some other adequate relief as the court may think it right to give him. That 'adequate relief' can involve you in being directed to relinquish to your client not only what profit you have made by such dealings, but also the interest on it as well.

The argument that the client did not suffer any injury when the money was acquired, say, by the architect perpetrating a fraud against a third party to whom he is liable or that the architect had put himself to some degree of risk in order to gain the money, is irrelevant. Indeed, such action making a secret profit, goes against one of the three principles of the RIBA code of professional conduct that the architect 'shall avoid actions and situations inconsistent with his professional obligations or likely to raise doubt about his integrity'. Moreover, it is specifically prohibited for a member of the RIBA to take discounts, commissions or gifts as an inducement to show favour to any person or body.

A court may hear no evidence of a custom to pay secret commissions. It being a presumption, that if such commissions were paid, then it follows as a matter of course that the professional was being improperly influenced and therefore he is liable. This essence of your liability remains the same, the amount of damages which you are responsible for may be reduced if the client knew that you would receive a commission and did not object to it. In other words, no element of secrecy surrounded the transaction.

Q. What are my liabilities if my client asks me literally to handle the money side of a project?

Occasionally an architect, engineer or other professional may be instructed to run a project in the following way. The client will pay into an account sufficient moneys for it to be kept in credit while the architect himself withdraws cheques from it in settlement of any accounts, including the honouring, on behalf of the client, of any interim certificates or valuations, the aim of the client being to have as little to do with the building as possible when it is under construction. In

A cautionary tale of not making your client your father confessor

An architect had arranged for his client to enter into a JCT minor works contract, June 1968, February 1977 revision, for extending a drycleaning business. The architect failed to perform his duties with reasonable care and skill, as follows:

1. He did not use his best endeavours to obtain planning permission and other necessary consents with expedition and to notify his client of his failures to obtain such permission;
2. He failed to warn his client adequately that work undertaken without planning permission or other necessary consents may involve additional expense and possible demolition; the architect had allowed the work to commence and to be completed before planning permission had been obtained, and indeed it was refused on several occasions and only granted following partial demolition and modification;
3. He failed to advise his client as to the nature of the JCT minor works contract and misled the contractor as to his responsibility for selected subcontractors.

The total fees claimed amounted to more than £15 000. There was no total failure of consideration and therefore the architect was entitled to his fees subject to a set-off in respect of the losses caused by his negligence. To disallow the architect his fees and, at the same time, to make him pay damages in respect of his negligence would be to penalize him twice. In other words, provided the architect's work was of some significant benefit to the client, he will be entitled in principle to his fees, but subject to any successful claim against the architect by the client.

Terry Pincoth v. *Fur & Textile Care Ltd. and Others*, [1986] unreported.

such a situation, the architect is confronted with a wider spectrum of liabilities.

The *Bill of Exchange Act 1882* allows for the signing of a cheque by an agent. The agent will not be personally liable for the cheque unless his name appears on it, though he would not be liable if he added such words to his signature indicating that he signs for or on behalf of the client, or in a representative capacity. Indeed, in the earlier case of *Leadbitter* v. *Farrow* [1816] 5 M. & S. 345 the court was led to the conclusion that an 'agent signing his name will therefore be personally liable unless he states upon the face of the bill that he subscribes it for another or by procuration of another'. So be warned!

For example, where you pay from your own money the prescribed fees for planning and building regulation approval, the client is immediately placed under an obligation to reimburse you, either by way of an express term within the contract of employment or otherwise by one which will be implied. He is bound to indemnify you against such losses and liabilities as you suffer in the course of your employment, provided that they are not the result of your own negligence or breach of duty.

The broad principle is that where A has been compelled by law to pay, or being compellable by law has paid money which B was ultimately liable to pay, so that the latter obtains the benefit of the payment by the discharge of his liability, then under such circumstances B is held indebted to A in that amount. You, acting as agent, may enforce this by the exercise of a lien which you may have on the client's property, or money in your possession, or by way of set-off.

A cautionary tale of fees or no fees

An architect had, through a quantity surveyor brought in by him, estimated that the cost of refurbishing a mansion including the installation of a swimming-pool would be about £240 000. Following the client's approval of this estimate, the architect undertook a considerable amount of work and claimed fees of £15 000.

After the architect had done much of the work but before a contract for the refurbishment had been let, the client was made aware by the architect that there had been an underestimate. The client decided not to proceed with the scheme and refused to pay the fees, as he could afford only about £250 000.

The architect had neither built into the estimate a sum for inflation between the dates on which the estimate was given and the anticipated date of completion of the work (about 2–2½ years); nor as an alternative, had he warned the client that the estimate was based on current prices.

The client thought the estimate of £240 000 was for the cost of the work including an inflationary element. In truth, the revised estimate including an element for inflation was in excess of £400 000. The judge found that the architect had been negligent, and this was so even though he had used a quantity surveyor; he said:

In my view the principle that an architect cannot, without his client's consent, delegate his duties, applies to an architect's duty of giving estimates. But on certain matters the best way of performing his duties as to estimates may well be the taking of advice from a quantity surveyor.

Even so, in this case the architect should have realized the need to warn his client of inflation just as much as a quantity surveyor should'

In addition, the architect was found to have been negligent in removing from the estimate the figure inserted by the quantity surveyor for contingencies, especially as the nature of the work, namely refurbishment of an old mansion, was of a type for which a contingency should normally be included.

It was conceded that if an architect does work which is completely useless to his client, the architect is not entitled to fees after the date of the negligence. The client acted reasonably in deciding to cancel the scheme; he would not have gone ahead with it in the first place had the proper estimate been given to him at the outset. Accordingly, the architect was not entitled to recover his fees.

The work done by the architect was of no use to his client because the scheme was cancelled. If the work was of some use, even though there had been negligence on the part of the architect, then he would not lose his entitlement to fees – but the damage caused to the client due to the negligence would be set against this.

Nye Saunders & Partners v. *Alan E. Bristow* [1986], unreported.

If you do administer an account on behalf of a client in the manner described above, it is essential not only that correct accounts be kept, but also that the money is kept separate from that of the practice by being placed in a separate, easily identifiable bank account. If you do not, everything is presumed against you. Where an agent mixes his principal's property with his own, the principal can exert a charge on the whole mixture.

Generally you will be bound by your own accounts and must hold them open together with all other documents connected with any matters with which you deal in the capacity of an agent for your client's examination. Where the account has already been settled but is later found to be wrong because there is some mistake in it, the client may be given leave to surcharge and falsify. The unauthorized items of expenditure, such as the employment of specialized consultants without the client's consent, will be disallowed together with the consultant's fees. Items which were ommitted that are in the client's favour may be added, and if fraud is proved, that account will be set aside.

It does not necessarily follow that where you have converted your client's money (or indeed any other property) into something else, that the client will be unable to recover it in whatever new form it might be, so long as the new form is identifiable. Should you become bankrupt, the moneys held in the account which you administer on behalf of the client, together with any other identifiable property belonging to the client, will not form part of your general assets.

Writ of summons endorsed with statement of claim by engineer for payment of fee when plans are prepared but work is not proceeded with

In the High Court of Justice　　　　1989.C. No. 001
Queen's Bench Division
Between:　　C.A.L. Culate Partnership　　*Plaintiffs*
　　　　　　　　and
　　　　　　D.F. Ficult Limited　　　　*Defendants*

To the Defendants D.F. Ficult Limited of Llaregub, Camarthan Bay
This Writ of Summons has been issued against you by the above-named Plaintiff in respect of the claim set out on the back. Within 14 days after the service of this Writ on you, counting the day of service, you must either satisfy the claim or return to the Court Office mentioned below the accompanying Acknowledgment of Service stating therein whether you intend to contest these proceedings.

If you fail to satisfy the claim or to return the Acknowledgment within the time stated, or if you return the Acknowledgement without stating therein an intention to contest the proceedings, the Plaintiff may proceed with the action and Judgment may be entered against you forthwith without further notice.

Issued from the Central Office of the High Court this 17th day of July, 1989.

Note: This Writ may not be served later than 12 calendar months beginning with that date unless renewed by Order of the Court.

Important

Directions for Acknowledgment of Service are given with the accompanying form.

Statement of claim

1. The Plaintiffs' claim is for £750 000, being the fee calculated in accordance with the scale of fees submitted by the Plaintiffs to the Defendants and agreed to be paid by the Defendants under a contract in writing dated 1 April 1988 for the preparation by the Plaintiffs of plans, drawings and specifications for a submaritime telecommunications service tunnel, as therein specified in case the said tunnel should not be proceeded with by the Defendants.
2. The Plaintiffs have prepared the said drawings and specifications but the Defendants have not proceeded and refuse to proceed with the tunnel and in breach of the said contract have not paid to the Plaintiffs the said fee or any fee.

Particulars

Estimated cost of the said tunnel £7 500 000
Remuneration due to Plaintiffs at 10% on estimated
cost...£750 000

3. Further, the Plaintiffs are entitled to and claim interest pursuant to the contract from 1 April 1989 at the contractual rate of 10% per annum, the amount of interest due at the date of issue of the Writ being at the aforesaid rate from the date of issue of the Writ herein until judgment or sooner payment amounting to £2050 per day.

and the Plaintiffs claim:

(a) damages
(b) the aforesaid interest due under the contract and further interest at the contractual rate of 10% per annum from the issue of the Writ to judgment or sooner payment.

Served, etc.   I.V. DUNIT

5.4 GRATUITOUS AGENCY

Q. I have heard that I will not be liable if I do something for nothing. Is this true?

The belief that if you contract gratuitously for your client you will be less liable to bear the damages suffered by a third party than if you are paid a full fee is somewhat suspect. It has long been held that an agent acting gratuitously is under a duty to use reasonable care. In 1409, in the *Carpenter's Case (1409) Y.B.II Hen.IV, f.33 pl.60*, it was established that while a volunteer cannot be compelled to carry out his promise made to another, yet if he does perform it so carelessly as to injure that other person, he is liable to an action for damages.

However, you will not usually be liable for a mere mistake or an error of judgment, whereby if you had followed a different course of action, you might have averted the loss suffered, provided that it does not amount to a failure to exercise proper care and skill.

SIX

When retained by a client, how can I insert a protective clause into my employment contract limiting liability, and how effective would it be?

6.1 THE NATURE OF PROTECTIVE CLAUSES

Q. I have often heard that one can limit one's liability for negligence through protective clauses. What exactly does this term mean?

It is a very ordinary business precaution to limit liability for negligence. Though the intelligent layman is less ready than the lawyer to regard an error as likely to be negligent because he tends to regard negligence as something more heinous and unforgivable than the lawyer, who knows how easily it can on occasions occur and (if he is honest) how universally.

Under the *Unfair Contract Terms Act 1977* negligence is stated, among other things, as being the breach of any obligation arising from the express or implied terms of a contract to take reasonable care or exercise reasonable skill in the performance of the contract which may itself contain protective clauses which attempt to avoid or limit liability. Protective clauses are of three essentially distinct types. They are those which:

1. Exclude or exempt one's liability for specified aspects of one's duty;
2. Limit or reduce what would otherwise be one's duty;
3. Limit the extent to which one is bound to indemnify another person in respect of the consequences of the breach of that duty.

The word 'exclusion' may be defined as that which prevents the existence, occurrence or use of an obligation, whereas an 'exemption' is an immunity from a liability, an obligation, a penalty, the law or authority. While 'limitation' is interpreted

A cautionary tale of always thinking before you speak

Merchant bankers, Heller & Partners, were telephoned by the National Provincial Bank acting on behalf of Hedley Byrne & Co., advertising agents, and asked confidentially about the creditworthiness of Easipower Ltd, which had recently opened an account with the merchant bankers. In their reply, for which the merchant bankers undertook no responsibility, they said that the company was believed to be respectably constituted and considered good for its normal business engagements. The company was a subsidiary of Pena Industries Ltd, which was in liquidation, but the managing director was endeavouring to buy the shares of Easipower Ltd from the liquidator.

The National Provincial Bank later wrote to the merchant bankers seeking a further reference on behalf of the advertising agents, Hedley Byrne & Co., as to the respectability and standing of Easipower Ltd and whether their business was considered trustworthy to the extent of a £100 000 per annum advertising contract. The merchant bankers in their reply reiterated that while the figures were larger than they were accustomed to see, Easipower Ltd was a respectably constituted company and considered good for its ordinary business engagements.

Relying on these replies, the advertising agents placed orders on behalf of Easipower Ltd, for advertising time and space with newspaper and television companies. The agents themselves assumed personal responsibility for payment to those companies.

Easipower Ltd went into liquidation. Hedley Byrne & Co. lost over £17 000 on the advertising contracts. Hedley Byrne & Co. sued the merchant bankers for the loss alleging that the merchant bankers' replies to the National Provincial Bank were given negligently. They were misjudged, giving a false impression as to Easipower Ltd's creditworthiness.

Heller & Partners were found negligent at the initial trial. On appeal, the case was determined on the assumption that there had been negligence. The House of Lords held that but for the merchant bankers' disclaimer, the circumstances might have given rise to a duty of care on their part, yet the clear disclaimer of responsibility for their replies on the occasion of the first enquiry was adequate to exclude the assumption by them of a legal duty of care, with the consequence that they were not liable in negligence.

Pearce, L.J. concluded: 'If both parties say expressly (in a case where neither is deliberately taking advantage of the other) that there shall be no liability. I do not find it possible to say that a liability was assumed.'

Hedley Byrne & Co. Ltd v. *Heller & Partners* [1964] A.C.465.

---

as a restriction, an 'indemnity' is defined as a legal exemption from the penalties or liabilities incurred by any course of action.

Several subdivisions have been seen within the definition of the term 'exclusion clause'. Two of them relate to what have been termed primary and secondary obligations. The first type seeks relief from the primary obligations of a contract by permitting one not to do that which has been promised; the other type seeks relief from the secondary obligations of a contract, for example, the payment of damages for breach.

Breaches of primary obligations gave rise to substituted or secondary obligations on the part of the party in default, and in some cases, may entitle the other party to be relieved from further performance of his own primary obligations. Secondary obligations can be modified by agreement between the parties, although they cannot be totally excluded. Every failure to perform a primary obligation is a breach of contract. The secondary obligation on the part of the contract breach to which it gives rise by implication of the common law is to pay monetary compensation to the other party for the loss sustained by him in consequence of the breach.

Lord Denning, M.R., however, remarked in *George Mitchell* v. *Finney Lock Seeds* [1983] 1 All E.R.108, 'I do hope that we shall not often have to consider the new-found analysis of contractual obligations into "primary obligations", "secondary obligations", and "anticipatory secondary obligations". No doubt it is logical enough, but it is too esoteric altogether. It is fit only for the rarefied atmosphere of the House of Lords. Not at all for the chambers of the practitioner. Let alone for the student at the university.'

Q. What is an exclusion clause?

The term 'exclusion clause' has occasionally been used as a common term, a synonym for those types of protective clause whose general purpose is to relieve a man from his own negligence. The judicial interpretation of the purpose for which an exclusion clause is included in a contract varies depending on the circumstances of each case. An exclusion clause may be one of the following:

1. A mere warning which does not automatically give protection to the party to the contract who formulated it;
2. A defence, the contract being first construed without reference to the clause to establish the promisor's obligations after which the clause itself might be considered, to find out whether it gave an adequate defence for a breach of those obligations;
3. A simple benefit defining the promisor's obligations.

Whatever the interpretation of the purposes of an exclusion clause, clear wording is needed for it to be applied.

Q. How effective is an exclusion clause in a contract?

In commercial contracts negotiated between professional businessmen capable of looking after their own interests and of deciding how risks inherent in the performance of various kinds of contract can be most economically borne (generally by insurance), it is wrong to place a strained construction upon words in an exclusion clause which are clear and fairly susceptible to one meaning only. There is no rule of law that an exclusion clause as such will not be given effect according to its tenor in any particular circumstances, except where the performance is totally different from that which the contract contemplates. Yet a condition should not be construed so as to make it eat up the contract.

It is a fundamental consideration in the construction of most contracts, and therefore inherently improbable, that one party to the contract should not intend to absolve the other from the consequences of the latter party's own negligence. Where the words of an exclusion clause are clearly unreasonable, the courts are not bound to give effect to it. The common law would not allow a party to exempt himself from his liability at common law, when it would be quite unconscionable for him to do so.

There must always be a certain minimum, non-excludable liability for negligence. The basic principle is that you cannot be said voluntarily to be undertaking a duty of care for the purpose of the tort of negligence if, at the very moment when you say you accept it, you declare that in fact you are not.

In like manner, the problem of reconciling an exclusion clause with the existence of a contractual duty naturally arises only when one party to a contract seeks to avoid a certain responsibility which he has already accepted. Such a problem might be overcome in the following way. Should a contract contain an exclusion clause which specifically states

A cautionary tale of the dry rot contract

Lord Waleran's Kensington home was affected by dry rot early in 1958. Through his surveyor, Martin French, he employed R. Richardson and Starling Ltd, a firm who specialized in the treatment of timber decay, especially dry rot.

Having been instructed by Lord Waleran to do all that was necessary to get rid of the dry rot, the firm of specialists inspected the house and made a report to the surveyor setting out the work to be done. The whole of the dry rot growth was to be exposed, together with a 2-ft band, so as to form a clear margin around the affected area. Lord Waleran's builder would open the floors, while the specialist firm's own men would strip the plaster off the walls, and then treat the affected timbers and masonry. Timbers which were badly affected would be removed and replaced by the builder.

The specialist firm did not give a fixed-price tender for the work because the full extent of the treatment could not be determined in advance. Instead they gave a rough estimate of £130. They also enclosed a leaflet giving a ten-year guarantee in the following terms:

Adequate treatment to accessible timbers, carried out by our own trained operatives is covered by our written ten year guarantee [we] guarantee the efficacy of the treatment they apply to timber or masonry for the eradication of insect or fungal attack and, subject to the under-noted exclusions, will retreat free of charge any such timber or masonry showing signs of reinfestation during the period of ten years from the date of treatment. This guarantee holds good to any owner for the time being of the property described, during the period of the guarantee. Exclusions from the foregoing guarantee. This guarantee does not cover the cost of opening up or reinstatement.

A contract was concluded between Lord Waleran and the specialists on the basis of the report, estimate and leaflet. The treatment carried out between April and June 1958 cost £147 5s 8d, the builder's costs were £1850. Five years later in 1963 dry rot reappeared in the previously treated areas of the house and elsewhere. Considerable damage was done to the fabric of the building. The specialist firm and the builders carried out remedial work; the bill from the specialists amounted to £687 19s 3d, while the builders' was £5738 9s 2d.

Lord Waleran determined to claim against the specialists on their ten-year guarantee, but died in April 1966 before starting an action. His executors took it up and, in February 1967, brought an action for damages against the specialists on their ten-year guarantee for breach of contract, claiming the full cost of the works. The specialists, relying on Section 2 of the *Limitation Act 1939*, contended that their liability under it was limited to retreating the places which they had originally treated; it did not extend to treating new places to which the dry rot had spread, nor to any of the builder's work in opening up and reinstatement.

With Lord Denning, M.R. dissenting, it was held by Salmon and Winn, L.JJ. that the exclusion clause did limit the specialist's liability to retreatment free of charge only of timbers or masonry which became reinfested within ten years of treatment.

Lord Denning, M.R., however, remarked that the guarantee was utterly illusory:

in the one breath (the first limb) the specialists say they give a guarantee. In the next breath (the second limb) they take it away, or most of it. So much so that I think that the second limb should be regarded as repugnant to the first limb. There are scores of cases from the Year Books onwards where a party to a contract has sought all in the same document to give with one hand and take away with the other. The courts have not allowed him to get away with it. Devlin, J. put it succinctly in *Firestone Tyre and Rubber Co. Ltd* v. *Vokins & Co. Ltd.*, 'It is illusory to say; "We promise to do a thing but we are not liable if we do not do it . . ." ' In such cases it is the primary promise which holds good. The repugnant proviso is rejected.

Adams & Others v. *Richardson & Starling Ltd* [1969] 1 W.L.R.1645, C.A.

a limited number of circumstances which, if one or more arise, allow the promisor to avoid his contractual duty, then it is for the promisor to show clearly that such circumstances have arisen which justifiably permit him not to fulfil his contractual duty. By contrast, if the exclusion clause applies to the whole contract and not simply to a few events, it is for the promisee to prove that despite the exclusion clause the contract has been broken.

Q. What is the difference between an exclusion clause and an exemption clause?

It has been suggested that whereas an exclusion clause has a negative effect, an exemption clause has one which is positive. Though an exemption clause may originally have been considered as a release or absolution from an earlier obligation, an affinity gradually arose between reliance upon an exemption clause and avoiding an accrued liability. The clause was seen as a device, similar to an exclusion clause, whereby rights already conferred within a contract were taken away. Where there was no written contract, an argument of *voleni non fit injuriaie* might have been regarded as an exemption clause of sufficient weight to defeat a claim in damages for negligence.

Exemption clauses differ greatly in many respects, and the courts have found that probably the most objectionable are found in the complex standard conditions which are now so common. The principles to be applied when construing an exemption clause quite apart from considering the contract as a whole are:

1. The defendant is not exempted from liability for the negligence of his employees unless adequate words are used;

2. The liability of the defendant apart from the exempting words must be ascertained.

The particular clause in question must be considered. If the only liability of the party pleading the exemption is a liability for negligence, the clause will more rapidly operate to exempt him.

Q. How effective is an exemption clause in a contract?

The principle that a protective clause may not apply in a case of negligence if it is written in terms which are so wide that they cover a number of different liabilities, whereas it may apply if the only liability is one of negligence, applies to exemption clauses.

One test to establish what was, and what was not, the intention of the parties is if the clause contains language which expressly exempts the person in whose favour it is made (the 'proferens') from the consequences of the negligence of his own employees effect must be given to that provision. If there is no express reference to negligence, the court must consider whether the words used are wide enough in their ordinary meaning to cover negligence on the part of the employees of the proferens. If the words used are wide enough for the above purpose, the court must consider whether the head of damage may be based on some ground other than that of negligence. The 'other ground' must not be so fanciful or remote that the proferens cannot be supposed to have desired protection against it. The existence of a possible head of damage other than that of negligence is fatal to the proferens, even if the words used are prima facie wide enough to cover negligence on the part of his employees.

Such a test is, like all rules of construction, a mere guide

A cautionary tale of payment under duress

B & S Contracts and Design Ltd entered into a contract to supply and erect display stands at an exhibition of Victor Green Publications Ltd. An exemption clause was included in the contract whereby any strike which prevented B & S from completing the work was to be regarded as a *force majeure*, exempting them from any liability which might arise should they not complete the contract in time.

B & S Contracts employed workmen from one of their subsidiary companies to carry out the contract. The subsidiary company became insolvent, its employees were told that they would be made redundant on the same day on which Victor Green Publications' exhibition closed.

As soon as the workmen arrived at the exhibition centre, they went on strike claiming four weeks' severance pay. They refused the company's offer of only two weeks' pay. If the strike continued, the exhibition would have to be cancelled. Victor Green Publications therefore determined to pay to the men a further two weeks' salary. Their demand having been met, the men returned to work and completed the contract.

In settling B & S Contracts' account, Victor Green Publications deducted the additional two weeks' pay from the account as they claimed they had had to pay it under duress. B & S Contracts sought to recover the money through the courts.

In upholding Victor Green Publications' contention that the money had been paid under duress, it was noted that though B & S Contracts had not asked for the money, it was clear that unless the men were paid the contract would not have been carried out. Though B & S Contracts has sought to rely on the *force majeure* clause in the contract, contending that because of it breach of the contract had not been threatened, that clause, however, had to be read subject to the fact that B & S Contracts must take reasonable steps to prevent the strike. Here 'reasonable' means as between B & S Contracts and Victor Green Publications, not as between the defendants and the workmen.

Having regard to the calamitous effect that the failure to complete the contract would have had on the latter, and the small additional amount of money which the former had been required to pay, B & S Contracts had been unreasonable in not paying the money and could not therefore rely on the *force majeure* or exemption clause.

B & S Contracts & Designs Ltd. v. *Victor Green Publications Ltd* [1982] 1 C.R.654.

and as such should not be applied rigidly or mechanically to defeat the intentions of the parties to a contract. They have to be construed in the light of that law. Furthermore, the terms of a contract must not be so fanciful or remote that the proferens cannot be supposed to have desired protection against it. The duty of the court is to divine from the words used what the parties must have intended by their bargain.

When parties make an agreement governing their future relationship, human relationship being on balance more inclined to optimism than pessimism, the parties are more likely to be thinking in terms of non-negligent, rather than negligent, performance of the contract. The law reflects this fact of life by assuming that if there are two potential grounds of liability, both of them real and foreseeable, but one involves negligence, prima facie any words of exemption will be directed at the non-negligent ground of liability. Where another legal liability arises under an essentially technical head, so that it may act against an exemption clause being successfully applied to some negligent act, that liability should be considered, if at all, with great circumspection.

If an exemption clause excludes liability, then the courts may give effect to it. If it does not do so expressly, but its wording is clear and wide enough to do so by implication, then the question becomes whether the contracting parties so intended. If the only head of liability upon which the clause can bite in the circumstances of a given case is negligence, and the parties did or must be deemed to have applied their minds to this eventuality, then clearly it is not difficult for a court to hold that this was what the parties intended, and that this is its proper construction. Indeed, to hold otherwise would be contrary to common sense.

Q. What is the difference between an exclusion clause and a limitation clause?

There is in principle no difference between an exclusion clause and a limitation clause, between words which save you from having to pay at all and words which save you from having to pay as much as you would otherwise have to pay.

An exclusion clause may seek simply to limit or qualify rights of the innocent party upon a breach without altering the fact that the conduct of the other party amounts to a breach. Though as a general principle, the courts would not permit you to rely on a limitation clause in circumstances in which it would not be fair or reasonable to allow reliance to it.

A distinction can be drawn between clauses which exclude liability altogether and those which only limit liability to a certain sum of money. Clauses of limitation may not be related to other contractual terms, in particular, to risks to which the defending party may be exposed, the remuneration which he receives and the opportunity of the other party to insure.

Exclusion clauses may be construed strictly *contra proferentem*, whereas limitation clauses may be construed naturally. This is because a limitation clause is more likely to be reasonable than an exclusion clause. If you go by the plain, natural meaning of the words, then there is nothing to choose between them.

Q. How effective is a limitation clause in a contract?

Although a clause which seeks wholly to exclude liability may in theory be considered more severely than one which limits liability to a specific amount, the latter itself may be interpreted unfavourably, especially where liability is limited to an unrealistically low figure.

In a case which went to arbitration, furniture removers who had been hired to transport goods from London to Wales contrived to do substantial damage to an expensive double-glazed front door. It was held that the contract limiting liability to £10.00 was unreasonable and had no effect, by reason of the *Unfair Contract Terms Act 1977*. This is a point which should be considered carefully by all professionals, especially architects in the light of advice given by the RIBA.

In 1971 the RIBA Council advised chartered architects to make use of the principle contained in the Code of Professional Conduct, and incorporated into the 1982 edition of the Code under principle 1.1 the following: 'a member shall before making an engagement whether by an agreement for professional services by a contract of employment or by a contract for the supply of services and goods, have defined beyond reasonable doubt the terms of the engagement including . . . any limitation of liability.' The most suitable type of limitation clause recommended by Council was to be in a form whereby only the cost of remedial work would be

---

A cautionary tale of the limits of a limitation clause

A contract for the building and installation of a set of motor marine engines which bound the builders to replace any parts which were found to be faulty through bad materials being used or poor workmanship contained a clause which provided that all goods were to be supplied on condition that the builders would not be liable for direct or consequential damages arising from the defective materials or workmanship.

It was held that this clause, while it protected the builders, where there had been a complete breach of contract owing to a series of defects in the engines which had rendered them practically unserviceable, they would be liable for all damages justifiably claimed by their client if he should decide not to accept the goods and to treat the contract as repudiated.

Lord Dunedin said: 'Now, where there is such a congeries of defects as to destroy the workable character of the machine, I think this amounts to a total breach of contract, and that each defect cannot be taken by itself separately so as to apply the provisions of the conditions of guarantee and make it impossible to claim damages'.

Pollock & Co. v. *Macrae* [1922] S.C.192, H.L.

---

borne by an architect who was shown to be professionally negligent, liability for consequential loss being totally excluded.

Q. What is the difference between an indemnity clause and an exemption clause?

An indemnity clause may be interpreted as the obverse, or the correlative, of an exclusion or exemption clause. It concerns a claim for direct rather than for consequential damages. An indemnity clause operates where one contracting party, A, may become liable to a third party, C, and the other contracting party, B, promises to indemnify A.

These principles of interpretation do not represent rules of law, but simply the particular applications of wider general principles of construction:

1. Express language may receive due effect;
2. Omnia praesumntur contra proferentem.

While these rules apply to the construction both of a clause exempting from certain liabilities a party who has undertaken to carry out contractual work and a clause whereby such a party has agreed to indemnify the other party against liabilities which would ordinarily fall upon him, they apply *a fortiori* in the later case. It represents a less usual and more extreme situation.

However, decisions on the wording of indemnity clauses may only be applied with circumspection to the construction of exemption clauses for the following reasons:

1. Indemnity clauses are enforced by a plaintiff who claims that the defendant should indemnify him against the liability which he has incurred to the third party;
2. Exemption clauses, on the other hand, are invoked by a defendant who contends that a liability otherwise incurred by him to the plaintiff is excluded by their agreement and there is no third party;
3. In the case of exemption clauses, it is proper to enquire what kinds of liability might be incurred by the defendant

to the plaintiff apart from the exemption clause as an aid to its construction

With respect to indemnity clauses, there is no room for enquiry as to any other head of liability as between the plaintiff and the defendant.

Generally when the meaning of an indemnity clause is being considered, it is more inherently improbable than in an exemption clause that one party should agree to discharge the liability of another party to a contract for acts for which the latter is responsible. The imposition by the proferens on the other party of liability to indemnify him against the consequences of his own negligence must be imposed by very clear words. Indeed, it may be that the proferens is under a heavier duty in establishing that the other party to a contract has in fact agreed to indemnify him against his own and his employees' liability for negligence than if he were trying merely to show that he is exempted from the consequences of his own liability. Furthermore, if a person obtains an indemnity against the consequences of certain acts, then that indemnity is not to be construed so as to include the consequences of his own negligence, unless those consequences are covered either expressly or by necessary implication.

Q. When can an indemnity clause be enforced?

An indemnity clause may be enforced after liability has been established against the person seeking to rely on that clause.

In the absence of a contractual term to the contrary, time runs against a person seeking to enforce an indemnity from the date when he is called upon to pay, not from the date of the event giving rise to his inability to do so. It is settled at common law that, given a contract of indemnity, no action could be maintained until actual loss has been incurred. The common law view was first pay and then come to the court under your agreement to indemnify. In equity that was not the view taken. Equity had always recognized the existence of a larger and wider right in the person entitled to indemnity. He was entitled in a Court of Equity if he was a surety whose liability to pay had become absolute to maintain an action against the principal debtor and obtain an order that he should pay off the creditor and relieve the surety. So that in the view of the Court of Equity it was not necessary for the person entitled to the indemnity to be ruined by having to pay the full amount, in the first instance. He had full power to take proceedings under which that fate might be averted and he might substantially protect himself and secure his position by coming to court.

In cases of indemnity, such rules that while equity will safeguard the position pending the ascertainment of the fact and the extent of liability of the person to be indemnified, he has no cause of action until such ascertainment may not be merely general rules but may in fact be universal rules.

Q. Is there any particular test to decide whether or not a protective clause is reasonable?

Although a form of words may be written into a contract with the agreement of both parties, whether they be an indemnity clause, or any other type of protective clause, their effectiveness in offsetting future liability may be determined by the principle of reasonableness as set out in the *Unfair Contract Terms Act 1977*; section 4(1) and (2) of the Act states:

A cautionary tale of the dangers of electricity

In 1970 a firm of motor manufacturers with a factory at Linwood, Renfrewshire, following the practice they had had for several years, employed the electrical company, South Wales Switchgear Co. Ltd, to carry out the annual overhaul of the electrical equipment in the factory.

The maintenance work was to be carried out subject to the motor manufacturers' general conditions of contract which were available from them on request. There were three versions of the general conditions, all of which bore the same title as the original edition, namely *General Conditions of Contract 24001*. The two later editions were distinguished from the first by subtitles, 'Revised January 1969', and 'Revised March 1970'.

Though the electrical company did not request a copy of the general conditions from the motor manufacturers, in July 1970, they received the 1969 revised conditions printed on the back of a purchase-order amendment. Clause 23 of the conditions, which was similar in both revisions, provided for an indemnity by the suppliers, the electricians, as against the purchasers, the motor manufacturers, against actions in the following terms:

> In the event of the order involving the carrying out of work by the supplier and its subcontractors's on land and/or premises of the purchaser, the supplier will keep the purchaser indemnified against:
> 1. All losses and costs incurred by reason of the supplier's breach of any statute, bye-law or regulation;
> 2. Any liability, loss, claim or proceedings whatsoever under statute or common law:
>   (a) in respect of personal injury to or death of any person whomsoever;
>   (b) in respect of any injury or damage whatsoever to any property, real or personal, arising out of or in the course of or caused by the execution of this order. The supplier will insure against and cause all subcontractors to insure against their liability hereunder.

The electrical company raised no objection to incorporating the indemnity clause into the contract, nor any questions as to its terms.

A few days after receiving the purchase-order amendment, the electricians started the work. While it was being carried out, an electrical fitter employed by the South Wales Switchgear Co. Ltd was seriously injured in an accident caused by the motor manufacturers' negligence and breach of statutory duty. The manufacturers claimed that they were indemnified in respect of any liability to the fitter because of the indemnity clause in their general conditions of contract with South Wales Switchgear Co. Ltd.

It was so held by the Second Division of the Court of Session which affirmed the trial judges' decision. However, the House of Lords in allowing an appeal by the electrical company, held that on its true construction the clause did not in fact afford indemnity against the motor manufacturers' own negligence because there was no express provision for such indemnity.

Smith v. *South Wales Switchgear Co. Ltd* [1978] 1 W.L.R.165.

A person dealing as a consumer cannot by reference to any contract term be made to indemnify another person (whether a party to the contract or not) in respect of liability that may be incurred by the other for negligence or breach of contract, except in so far as the contract term satisfies the requirement of reasonableness. This section applies whether the liability in question:
(a) is directly that of the person to be indemnified or is incurred by him vicariously;
(b) is to the person dealing as consumer or to someone else.

A cautionary tale about the case of the effective indemnity clause

The main building contractors, Bovis, were employed by Price Taylors Ltd to carry out a contract. Part of the work was subcontracted by Bovis to Ellis. The latter then subcontracted a portion of that work to the plasterers, J.M. Jenner Ltd.

Mr Westcott, an employee of Jenner's, was injured when he fell into an unguarded hole on the site. At the time, Ellis was not on-site. Though Bovis and Jenner agreed that they were both jointly and equally liable either for negligence or a breach of statutory duty, Bovis sought to enforce an indemnity clause in their contract against Ellis to the effect that 'The subcontractor shall indemnify and adequately insure against all Employers' liability and third party risks arising out of the work'. It was held that despite the negligence of Bovis and the innocence of Ellis the indemnity clause was enforceable against Ellis.

Westcott v. *J.M. Jenner (Plasterers) Ltd. & Bovis Ltd.* [1962] 1 Ll.L. Rep.309.

6.2 THE *UNFAIR CONTRACT TERMS ACT 1977*

Q. What is the nature of the *Unfair Contract Terms Act 1977*?

The *Unfair Contract Terms Act 1977* came into force on 1 February 1978. Promoted as a Private Member's Bill, it was introduced to the House by Michael Ward, Labour MP for Peterborough, and was based on studies made over ten years by the Law Commission and the Scottish Law Commission.

Lord Elwyn-Jones, Lord Chancellor, speaking at the report stage of the Bill in the House of Lords, said that it had been carefully drawn up to confer benefits only on persons who were economically inferior or who had suffered as a result of negligent conduct or disregard of basic contractual rights. It went far to remove one of the worst blots in the law of contract. It was quite wrong that someone in the course of business should be able unfairly to avoid liability for negligence, especially where done in small print tucked away at the end of a contract, on the back of a ticket or in a notice on the wall. Lord Denning remarked that in future courts would be able to enquire into the reasonableness of exception clauses as people ought not to be able to exempt themselves from liability for their own negligence unless it was reasonable.

Q. What is the purpose of the *Unfair Contract Terms Act 1977*?

The stated purpose of the Act, which is applicable to England, Wales and Northern Ireland, is contained in its long title. It is to impose further limits on the extent to which civil liability for breach of contract or for negligence or other breaches of duty could be avoided by means of contract terms by subjecting them to a test of reasonableness.

It was a procedure which had begun with previous Acts such as the *Misrepresentation Act 1967* and the *Supply of*

A cautionary tale on the question of time

The partners in a firm known as Integrated Reclamation and Dredging Co. were Mr Kavanagh and Mr Taffe. In June 1970 the British Railways Board agreed that the firm could tip approved excavated material on their land, a railway cutting running east of Blackwall Way Bridge.

An indemnity clause was written into the contract whereby the firm agreed that notwithstanding any supervision given or approval expressed by the Board, they would be responsible for and release and indemnify the Board, their servants or agents, from and against all liability for personal injury (whether fatal or otherwise), loss of or damage to property and any other loss, damage, costs and expenses which might arise in consequence of the grant or existence of the agreement or of anything done as a result of its grant or existence however such injury, loss, damage, costs or expenses be caused whether by the negligence of the Board, their servants or agents or otherwise, and whether in carrying out by the third parties and the Board of the arrangements set out in the contract or otherwise. Tipping started towards the end of 1970.

In 1971 the owners of an adjoining property, R. & H. Green and Silley Weir Ltd, complained to the British Railways Board that their premises had been damaged because the tipping had been carried out without alternative support being given to them. The complaints were referred by the Board to Integrated Reclamation and Dredging Co. In February 1972 Mr Kavanagh and Mr Taffe

repudiated all claims that any damage had been caused by their work. The Board in replying drew attention to the indemnity clause which they believed afforded them a complete defence to any claim. In 1973 the Board told Kavanagh and Taffe that they would be joined in any action which would be brought against the Board by R. & H. Green and Silley Weir Ltd made so little progress in it that, in 1978, the Board applied for it to be struck out for want of prosecution. Following this, an order was made in March 1979 whereby the Board undertook that in the event of (1) the action being allowed to continue and (2) the defendants commencing third party proceedings against the present third parties and (3) the present third parties alleging that the defendants' claim against them was statute barred under the *Limitation Act 1939*, then the defendants, the Board, would seek to have determined as a preliminary issue the question whether the Board's proposed claim against the third parties was statute barred. Also they undertook that on the hearing of that issued, the plaintiffs would be at liberty to argue on behalf of the defendants, the Board, that the Board's proposed claim was not statute barred.

In March 1979, following that order, a Third Party Notice was served on Mr Kavanagh. Mr Taffe was not served. As a result of Third Party Directions which were given on 11 June 1979, a Third Party Defence was served on behalf of Mr Kavanagh in October 1979, asserting that the claim of the Board against him was in any event barred under section 2(1) of the *Limi-*

tation Act 1939, in that the third party proceedings were brought after the expiration of six years from the date on which the cause of action, if any, accrued.

On this preliminary issue it was held that as the protective clause within the contract constituted a general indemnity in favour of the defendant, time did not run against the defendants in favour of the third party until the liability, if any, of the defendants to the plaintiffs had been established.

Dillon, J. said:

> in law an action on a contract of indemnity does not normally lie until the promisee has paid the third person's claim but that the former rules of equity enable a person entitled to an indemnity to obtain relief as soon as his liability to the third person has arisen and before he has made payment, and he may, where appropriate, obtain an order compelling the person giving the indemnity to set aside a fund out of which liability may be met or to pay the amount due directly to the third person. It is, however, further pointed out that the equitable right to enforce an indemnity does not constitute a debt.

He concluded that an indemnity was not, 'against liabilities arising so much as against the payment and determination of the liabilities'.

R. & H. Green & Silley Weir Ltd. v. *British Railways Board & Kavanagh (third party)* [1980] 17 Build.L.R.94.

Goods (Implied Terms) Act 1973. In the former Act, for example, section 3 states:

> If any agreement (whether made before or after the commencement of this Act) contains a provision which would exclude or restrict:
> (a) any liability to which a party to a contract may be subject by reason of any misinterpretation made by him before the contract was made, or
> (b) any remedy available to another party to the contract by reason of such misrepresentation
> that provision shall be of no effect except to the extent (if any) that in any proceedings arising out of the contract, the court or arbitrator may allow reliance on it as being fair and reasonable in the circumstances of the case.

Such a definition of the 'reasonableness test' was further refined in the *Unfair Contract Terms Act 1977.* The question which now has to be answered is whether a protective clause was reasonably inserted into the contract. Part I, section 11(1), of the Act states:

> Of this Part of the Act, section 3 of the *Misrepresentation Act 1967* and section 3 of the *Misrepresentation Act (Northern Ireland) 1967* is that the term shall have been a fair and reasonable one to be including having regard to the circumstances which were or ought reasonably to have been known to or in the contemplation of the parties when the contract was made.

Q. In what circumstances can the test of reasonableness in the *Unfair Contract Terms Act 1977* be applied?

The test of reasonableness may be applied to a protective clause only where one of the contracting parties deals either as a consumer, such as a private client, or on the other party's written terms of business. A business not only includes the activities of any government department or local or public authority, but also a profession. It is therefore applicable, for example, to the RIBA contract of employment between client and architect.

The protective clauses are those which, first, seek to exclude or restrict liability for breach of contract; secondly, those which allow a contract performance substantially different from that which was reasonably expected; and thirdly, those protective clauses which allow the contract not to be performed either in part or as a whole.

John Fraser, while Minister of State for Prices and Consumer Protection, noted of the *Unfair Contract Terms Act 1977* that it

> does not apply across the board. It applies only to consumer contracts made on standard terms. A businessman contracting with another businessman on terms which he does not habitually use for such contracts can still exclude or limit his liability for breach of contract without fear that this may be subject to the test of reasonableness. The Act is here, in fact, tailored specially to the needs of the small businessman. It does not attempt to interfere with the freedom of those able to negotiate on equal terms to contract together on whatever basis suits them best, but it recognises that the small businessman is often in no better position than the consumer in having to accept the terms that are offered him. So far as contractual obligations are concerned, the Act gives him equal protection with the consumer in those cases where he has no choice but to accept the other party's standard terms.

Q. What do the more important sections of the *Unfair Contract Terms Act 1977* say?

Sections 3(1) and (2) of the *Unfair Contract Terms Act 1977* state:

A cautionary tale about the floor that never was

Mr and Mrs Howell-Jones bought a dilapidated house in Market Drayton, Shropshire, with existing planning permission for alterations. The plans showed that part of the house which had already been demolished was higher than it had been.

In 1978, Mr and Mrs Howell-Jones decided to sell the house through the estate agents, Barber & Son, and gave them the original plans. Mr Collins, the prospective purchaser, later received a letter from his architect stating that a previous planning application to increase the height of the former, small extension had been refused after a neighbour had complained that it would block the daylight to his property. The architects pointed out that without lifting the roof at the rear or excavating deep into the rock, which would be enormously expensive, it was only possible to build a single-storey extension. As a result, Mr Collins claimed a reduction in the contract price of the house on the grounds of the innocent misrepresentation made by the estate agents.

Mr and Mrs Howell-Jones sought to escape liability by relying on an exclusion clause which the estate agents had included in the particulars of the sale, to the effect that:

Barber and Son for themselves and for the vendors give notice that these particulars do not constitute, nor constitute any part of, an offer or a contract. All statements contained in these particulars are made without responsibility on the part of Barber and Son or the vendor. None of the statements contained in these particulars are to be relied upon as statements or representations of fact. Any intending purchaser must satisfy himself by inspection or otherwise as to the correctness of each of the statements contained in these particulars. The vendor does not make or give, and neither Barber and Son or any person in their employment has any authority to make or give, any representations or warranty whatsoever in relation to this property.

It was held by Walker, L.J. and Dame Elizabeth Lane that the exclusion clause was effective. The vendors' liability for the estate agent's innocent misrepresentation was avoided by the disclaimer which effectively excluded the agent's authority to make representations.

Collins v. *Howell-Jones & Another* [1980] 259, *Estates Gazette* 331.

1. This section applies as between contracting parties where one of them deals as consumer or on the other's written standard terms of business;
2. As against that party, the other cannot by reference to any contract term:
   (a) when himself in breach of contract, exclude or restrict any liability of his in respect of the breach, or
   (b) claim to be entitled
      (i) to render a contractual performance substantially different from that which was reasonably expected of him, or
      (ii) in respect of the whole or any part of his contractual obligation, to render no performance at all, except in

so far as (in any of the cases mentioned above in this subsection) the contract term satisifes the requirement of reasonableness.

The phrase 'standard terms of business', given in section 3(1), applies only to England, Wales and Northern Ireland. The Scottish equivalent is section 17(1), where the phrase given is 'standard form of contract'. In *McCrone* v. *Boots Farm Sales Ltd.* [1981], S.L.T.103 the judge was of the opinion that the section was to be widely applied. He remarked that it was plain that the section was designed to prevent any one party to a contract from having his contractual rights against another party who was in breach of the contract excluded or restricted by a term or condition, which might be one of a number of fixed terms or conditions invariably incorporated into some types of contract. 'If the section is to achieve its purpose', Lord Dunpark said, 'the phrase "standard form of contract" cannot be confined to written contracts in which both parties use standard forms. It is, in my opinion, wide enough to include any contract, whether wholly written or partly oral, which includes a set of fixed terms or conditions which the proposer applies.'

Though a contract may have terminated either by a breach of the contract itself or where repudiation is accepted, a protective clause may still be an effective form of defence for the party who seeks to rely on it, provided that the clause satisfies the requirement of reasonableness. Yet section 10 of the *Unfair Contract Terms Act 1977* emphasizes that liability cannot be avoided merely by looking to the terms of another, secondary, contract; it states:

> A person is not bound by any contract term prejudicing or taking away rights of his which arise under, or in connection with the performance of another contract, so far as those rights extend to the enforcement of another's liability which this Part of the Act prevents that other from excluding or restricting.

Where the protective term takes the form of a limitation clause such that liability for damages is restricted to a specified sum of money, the reasonableness of that clause may be determined when appropriate by considering both the resources which the party to the contract relying on that limitation clause could expect to be available to him and the extent to which he could be covered by insurance. In *Photo Production Ltd* v. *Securicor Transport Ltd* [1980] A.C.827, the question of insurance was considered in relation to the *Unfair Contract Terms Act 1977*. Lord Wilberforce said:

> This Act applies to consumer contracts and those based on standard terms and enables exception clauses to be applied with

regard to what is just and reasonable. It is significant that Parliament refrained from legislating over the whole field of contract. After this Act in commercial matters generally, when the parties are not of unequal bargaining power, and when risks are normally borne by insurance, not only is the case for judicial intervention undemonstrated, but there is everything to be said, and this seems to have been Parliament's intention, for leaving the parties free to apportion the risks as they think fit and for respecting their decisions.

6.3 MISREPRESENTATION

Q. How does a misrepresentation effect a protective clause?

A protective clause may be of no effect where its purpose has been misrepresented.

Section 1 of the *Misrepresentation Act 1967* states that where a contract has been entered into through misrepresentation and either that the misrepresentation has itself become a term of the contract, or the contract has been performed (or both), then the contract may be rescinded. Furthermore, under section 2(1) where loss has been suffered after a contract has been entered into as a result of a misrepresentation, then the person making the misrepresentation whether or not is was done fraudulently would be liable to damages unless he can prove that he had reasonable grounds to believe, and did believe, that the facts he put forward were true.

Any behaviour, by words or conduct, is sufficient to be a misrepresentation if it is such as to mislead the other party about the existence or extent of the exemption. If it conveys a false impression, that is enough. If the false impression is created knowlingly, it is a fraudulent misrepresentation; or if

A cautionary tale of never drawing what you do not know exists

The Dublin Corporation retained Harty & Chatterton, a firm of engineers, to draw up a scheme for a sewage outfall which involved some harbour works. Mr Hellins was appointed as job engineer under the firm's chief engineer, Spencer Harty, to prepare plans and specifications for the sewage outfall.

The backbone of the scheme was the 'North Harbour Wall', which was incorrectly shown on the drawings as a dotted line going down to a depth of 9 ft below the ordnance datum level; the foundations were in fact much shallower. The engineers had no knowledge or reason to believe that the old wall did go down to the depth indicated on the drawings. Mr Hellins himself doubted the exact depth and exact shape, and the exact character and construction, of the existing foundations. The plans, however, were designed for the purpose of saving cost. The engineers knew when preparing the plans that if a contractor had reason to believe that the wall was non-existent, his tender would be substantially increased and that he would practically have had to estimate for a coffer-dam costing £25 000.

The completed drawings and specifications, which were false and recklessly made, were forwarded by the engineers to Dublin Corporation who then went out to tender on them. The tender was won by S. Pearson & Son Ltd. The tender was for a lower price than the contractor would have offered if he had known the truth. However, he entered into contract with the corporation. The contract contained clauses to the effect that the contractors were to ascertain and judge of the facts for themselves.

The contractor sued the corporation in an action of deceit for damages for the fraudulent representations made by their engineers as to the nature of the works to be undertaken. It was held by the House of Lords that the contract and, in particular, the protective clauses truly construed did not contemplate fraud whether conscious or unconscious by either party, they provided protection only against honest mistake. Lord Atkinson said:

It would appear to me that a clause, deliberately introduced into a contract by a party to the contract, designed beforehand to save him from all liability for a false representation made recklessly and without any real belief in its truth, is as much 'conceived in fraud' and as much part of the fraud as if the representation had been false to the knowledge of the person who made it, because to use Lord Bramwell's words in *Smith* v. *Chadwick*, 'An untrue statement as to the truth or falsity of which the man who makes it has no belief is fraudulent for, in making it, he affirms he believes it', which is false.

Such protective clauses might themselves in some cases be part of a fraud and might both advance and disguise it. Those who by inserting and framing a protective clause in a contract would run a fair chance of the contractor saying, 'I assume that those with whom I deal are honest and honourable men. I scout the idea of their being guilty of fraud. An inquiry testing the plan will be expensive and difficult so I will not make it.' The protecting clause might thus be inserted fraudulently with the purpose and hope that notwithstanding its terms, no test would take place. When the fraud succeeds, those who designed the fraudulent protection cannot take advantage of it. Such a clause would be good protection against any mistake or calculation, but fraud vitiates every contract and every clause in it. As a general principle, an express term that fraud shall not vitiate a contract would be bad in law.

S. Pearson & Son Ltd. v. *Lord Mayor & Corporation of Dublin* [1907] A.C.351, H.L.

A cautionary tale of the infected potatoes

Over several years the seed potato merchants, R.W. Green Ltd, had done considerable business with Cade Brothers Farms. The latter were brothers carrying on a substantial farming business in partnership.

All dealings were carried out on the basis of the standard conditions of contract of the National Association of Seed Potato Merchants which contained the protective clause that:

Time being of the essence of the Contract notification of rejection claim or complaint must be made to the Seller giving a statement of the grounds for such rejection, claim or complaint within three days, within ten days in the case of rejection, claim or complaint specifically in respect of Skinspot, Gangrene or Dry Rot, after the arrival of the seed at its destination. It is specifi-

cally provided and agreed that compensation and damages payable under any claim or claims arising out of this Contract under whatsoever pretext shall not under any circumstances amount in aggregate to more than the Contract price of the potatoes forming the subject of the claim or claims.

Under one contract 20 tons of King Edward uncertified seed potatoes were bought by Cade Brothers in January 1974. The potatoes were infected by potato virus Y. The virus could not be detected by looking at seeds, but only by examination of the growing crop in the previous season. As a result of the infection, the crop was very poor. The farmers claimed that they had lost over £6000 in profits and therefore refused to honour their account with the merchants. The seed merchants sued

them for £2273 of debts and credit charges for seed sold in 1974. The farmers counterclaimed for loss of profit.

Griffiths, J., in remarking that the contract must like any other commercial contract be considered and construed against the background of the trade in which it operates, held that the protective clause which excluded liability if no complaint was made within a stipulated time was neither fair nor reasonable in the circumstances. In contrast, the protective clause which limited liability to the contract price was found to be worded in very wide terms and in language which was clear and easily intelligible and both fair and reasonable.

R.W. Green Ltd. v. *Cade Brothers Farms* [1979] 1 Ll. Rep. 602.

---

it is created unwittingly, it is an innocent misrepresentation. However, either is sufficient to disentitle the creator of it to the benefit of the exemption.

For example, in the case of *Southwestern General Properties* v. *Marton, The Times*, 11 May 1982, a property was misrepresented in an auction catalogue as being suitable for development if it were deemed to be in character with the existing buildings. A certain term in the documents sought to exclude liability for misrepresentation. The protective clause was held to be unreasonable and void because the buyer of the property had attended the auction at short notice and had not had time to check the information.

6.4 FAIRNESS AND REASONABLENESS

Q. A protective clause must be fair and reasonable, but what is mean by the term 'fair and reasonable'?

A protective clause will generally stand or fall depending on whether or not it is fair and reasonable. Following on the *Unfair Contract Terms Act 1977*, any requirement of reasonableness may be judged according to the circumstances at the time when any liability arose or would have arisen, whereas the test of fairness rests on whether or not the restrictions are both reasonably necessary for the protection of the legitimate interests of the promisee and commensurate with the benefits secured to the promisor under the contract. For the purposes of this test, all the provisions of the contract must be taken into consideration.

Though a protective clause be drafted in somewhat wide terms, reliance on it may be allowed where it is shown to be fair and reasonable. Nevertheless, until such a clause is shown to satisfy the requirements of reasonableness by those who rely on it, then the protective clause might be thought to be unreasonable.

6.5 CONTRA PROFERENTEM

Q. I have heard that if I write a protective clause into a contract, it will be construed against me. Is this true?

In construing or trying to reach the true meaning of a protective clause, statements made in one case may help in deciding another but cannot literally determine the answer. This is because in each case the task is one of construction to ascertain the actual or imputed intention of the parties to the contract in question. Often the test of what could be understood or intended by the ordinarily literate and sensible person will be appropriate. Where a contract is made in a specialized business such as architecture, engineering or building by two practitioners in that field, a different standard may be indicated, namely that of the reasonably informed practitioner in the field in question.

However, where a protective clause is written in language which is neither clear nor easily intelligible giving rise to ambiguity, and other rules of construction have failed to resolve it, the principle of *contra proferentem* may be applied. It has been expressed as 'verba chartarum fortins accipiuntur contra proferentem', whereby the words of the protective clause are construed against those who use them and seek their protection.

For example, in the case of *John Lee (Granthum) Ltd.* v. *Railway Executive* [1949] 2 All E.R. 581, a railway warehouse was leased by the executive to the company. The lease contained a protective clause which exempted the executive from liability for 'loss or damage (whether by act or neglect of the company or their servants or agents or not) which but for the tenancy hereby created would not have arisen'. The company's goods stored in the warehouse were damaged in a fire caused by a spark which fell from a railway engine as a result of the executive's negligence. It was held that the words of the clause were ambiguous and should be construed more strongly against the grantor, namely the Railway Executive.

The basic principle of *contra proferentem*, whereby an ambiguity in a protective clause is construed against a party who tries to shelter behind it, may be extended to cover that of 'fundamental breach' of contract. Thus a protective clause may be of no effect if it attempts to cover such a serious act which is so different from the agreed contractual obligations that it goes against the very root of the contract; it lies outside the 'four corners' of the contract.

Q. How effective is a wide-ranging protective clause?

Where a protective clause is written in such wide or general terms such that there is no clear exclusion of a particular type of liability (e.g. negligence), the clause may be interpreted against the party attempting to rely on it.

A cautionary tale of the leaking radiator pipes

F.G. Minter Ltd were the main contractors building two twelve-storey halls of residence, called Donor I and Donor II, for the University of London, Queen Mary College, in Essex. The contract was a JCT Standard Form of Building Contract, 1963 edition, dated 14 November 1966. It incorporated an FASS/NFBTE agreement for nominated subcontractors, commonly referred to as the 'green form', dated 28 April 1967. Comyn Ching were appointed nominated subcontractors to Minters for the mechanical services which included the central heating system.

In July 1966 the engineers, Kenneth Stead & Partners, whom the college had retained to advise their architects, Playne, Lacy & Vallance on the central heating system, prepared a specification for it. The radiators on each floor were to be connected to horizontal feedpipes buried in the screed. Originally the pipework was to be copper tubing. However, the feedpipes which the engineers specified were of plastic-coated steel called Gecal. Gecal was manufactured by the Oriental Tube Co. Ltd, who had recently brought it on to the market claiming that it was eminently suitable for central heating installations and for burying in screeds. It was the first such system to be installed in the UK. In November 1966 the architects issued an instruction which followed the engineers' advice in revising the system. As a result, the original quotation for the central heating system was reduced by £311.40.

As the work proceeded, Comyn Ching found that they could not make effective watertight joints with Gecal. The joints failed when hydraulically tested at a pressure of 40 lb in $^{-2}$ whereas the specification required that they should withstand a pressure of 150 lb in $^{-2}$ cold. The architects expressed their fears to the engineers about the suitability of Gecal, especially as the pipework was to be buried in the screed.

In January 1968, Comyn Ching being concerned and feeling that they could not satisfactorily continue with this part of the works sought either a variation from the engineers' specification to use different pipework or a guarantee from the Oriental Tube Co. In February, Oriental Tube gave such a guarantee to Comyn Ching in the following terms:

We the Oriental Tube Co. Ltd guarantee Gecal Tubing to be satisfactory in respect of its suitability for use in closed circuit, central heating systems both as far as the tube itself is concerned and in relation to its use with non-ferrous fittings, provided that each circuit is tested to a water pressure of 150 lbs per square inch in the presence of the Clerk of Works who is to issue the appropriate test certificate. This guarantee is extended to cover not only the cost of replacing the heating circuit but also any ancillary damage that may result from any subsequent breakdown in the heating circuit due to tube failure of the fittings in

relation to the tube.

As a result of Comyn Ching seeking further clarification that Oriental Tube would indemnify them against any claims in the event of a leak occurring after a satisfactory test, the latter replied:

We can see no point in making any additional comment or amendments to our guarantee because the points asked for by you have been fully covered and we, as manufacturers, have provided your company with a guarantee that is extremely extensive in the sense that we are prepared to accept responsibility for your own company's futures liability in every sense of the word.

On the strength of these letters, Comyn Ching completed the work using Gecal piping. The pipework passed the required pressure tests.

Donor I was completed by the autumn of 1968, and the central heating system was switched on. Almost immediately, about 166 leaks occurred. Comyn Ching repaired them under their subcontract and claimed reimbursement for £8799.85 from Oriental Tube. The latter did not accept responsibility, saying that the leaks were the result of joint failure caused by the joints being made in a fundamentally different way from that which

(continued)

the manufacturers instructed. Oriental Tube, therefore, blamed Comyn Ching.

In view of the fact that their performance was fundamentally different from that stated in the contract, the architects decided in 1969 that the entire plastic-coated steel Gecal piping should be replaced with copper, though some floors had to be ripped up where the pipework was buried in the screed.

The Court of Appeal found that the assur- ances contained in letters written by Oriental Tube to Comyn Ching operated not as a guarantee, but as an indemnity. As such, they created a legally binding contract of indemnity, consideration for the defendant's promises had been given as the plaintiffs were induced thereby to forebear from pressing for a variation order and they suffered a detriment, in that they were persuaded by the defendants for their benefit to take a risk which they did not wish to run. It was held that since the pipes passed the defendant's test the letters of indemnity were wide enough to cover the plaintiff's liability, even if it was due to their own negligence.

Comyn Ching & Co. (London) v. *Oriental Tube Co. Ltd.* (1981) 17 Build. L.R. 47, C.A.

For example, in *Price & Co.* v. *The Union Lighterage Company* [1904] 1 K.B. 412, C.A., goods were loaded on to a barge under a contract for carriage by which the barge owner was exempt from liability 'for any loss of or damage to goods which can be covered by insurance'. The barge sank and the goods were lost due to the negligence of the barge owner's employees. In an action to recover damages for the loss of the goods it was held by the Court of Appeal that the exemption being in general terms not expressly relating to negligence, the barge owner was not exempt from liability for loss or damage caused by his employees' negligence.

Likewise, a protective clause may operate against the person seeking its protection if it is construed strictly according to its written words and not extended so as to cover a different type of liability. Thus a clause excluding liability from implied terms of a contract may not give protection for liability which arises as a result of a breach of express terms. Also a clause excluding liability for latent defects may not exclude liability for an implied condition of fitness for purpose; or a protective clause which excludes liability for a breach of warranty may not cover liability for a breach of condition of the contract.

Q. Can a protective clause actually protect me?

It is a question of contractual intention whether or not a particular breach is covered by a protective clause. The courts are entitled to insist (as they do) that the more radical the breach, the clearer must the language be if it is to be covered.

The leitmotif of a protective clause must be clarity and a complete lack of ambiguity in its wording if its purpose is even to begin to bite and the principle of *contra proferentem* (against the party relying on the clause) is not to be applied in construing it.

Where no reference has been made in the contract to the particular type of liability which has arisen, certain phrases such as 'however arising', 'any cause whatsoever' or 'however caused' may be sufficient to provide some degree of protection.

For example, in *Tor Line A/B* v. *Alltrans Group of Canada Ltd*, (1983) 127 S.J. 409, clause 13 in a Baltime form charterparty imposed liability on a ship's owners for certain specified acts. The clause also provided that they were not to be responsible in any other case for damage or delay whatsoever, or howsoever caused. A clause was added to the contract which set out in detail the physical dimensions of the vessel. She did not conform to that description and, as a result, the charterers were prevented from loading as planned. This was not a default for which the owners were expressly made liable by clause 13. The question arose whether the general provisions in the clause operated to protect the owners from liability. It was held by the Court of Appeal that clear words had to be given their natural meaning. Clause 13 covered the whole of the owner's contractual obligations and clauses added to the standard form should not detract from that fact. Accordingly, clause 13 relieved the owners from liability for their description of the vessel.

6.6 ADEQUATE NOTICE OF PROTECTIVE CLAUSES

Q. Must I tell the other party to the contract that I have included a protective clause in the documents for my benefit?

The short answer is 'yes'. The principle of complete freedom of contract has within it the inherent possibility of abuse. To curtail that abuse where you, as a party to a contract, wish to rely on a certain protective clause, then it is for you to show clearly that it was included as a contract term by, for example, having taken reasonable steps to bring it to the attention of the other party.

A protective clause may be considered unreasonable because you did not draw it to the attention of the other party. The more unreasonable that a clause is, the greater the notice that must be given of it. Lord Denning, M.R. has said 'Some clauses which I have seen would need to be printed in red ink on the face of the document with a red hand pointing to it before the notice could be held to be sufficient (see *Lewison* v. *Patent Steam Carpet Cleaning Co. Ltd* [1977] 3 All E.R. 498).

Reasonable notice of a protective clause may be inferred in a new contract which is similar in its circumstances to others made earlier between yourself and the same person or company. It is the consistency of a course of conduct which gives rise to the implication that, in similar circumstances, a similar contractual result will follow. When conduct is not consistent, there is no reason why it should still produce an invariable contractual result. However, where there has been some departure from the usual course of dealing, for example, where contracts are usually in writing but the one in question is oral, this may not apply. Four contracts made during five years may not constitute such a consistent course of dealing as to include a previously written productive clause into a new contract which was merely made orally, for instance.

However, if you and the other party are of equal standing, in the same business, and both of you know which contractual terms are commonly used in that business, those terms may be considered as included in the oral contract. Where such circumstances apply, a protective clause may also be included in a contract by later varying its terms, even if the variation is contained in a letter of confirmation.

Q. Is there any way in which I can be sure that the other party to the contract knows about my protective clause?

Should a party to a contract against whom a protective clause operates have actual knowledge of it when the contract is concluded, he will inevitably be bound by it.

A signature on a contract may generally be regarded as proof that the terms of the contract were known by the signee. When a document containing contractual terms is signed, then in the absence of fraud or misrepresentation the party signing it is bound, and it may be regarded as wholly immaterial whether he had read the document or not.

A signature may be binding even when the signatory suffers from a disability which prevents him from understanding the protective clause. For example, the signee may be illiterate or a foreigner who can neither speak nor read English. However, where the signatory's disability was obvious, such additional steps which are reasonable should be taken to help him understand the meaning of a protective clause which may act against him.

Furthermore, section 2(3) of the *Unfair Contract Terms Act 1977* provides: 'where a contract term or notice purports to exclude or restrict liability for negligence a person's agreeement to or awareness of it is not of itself to be taken as indicating his voluntary acceptance of any risk.'

6.7 RELIANCE ON PROTECTIVE CLAUSES BY THIRD PARTIES

Q. Can I rely on a protective clause if a third party brings an action against me?

A fundamental principle of a contract is that only a person who is a party to it can sue upon that contract. A stranger to it cannot take advantage of its provisions. This principle is generally based on nineteenth-century cases, though in some of those cases the principle was carried to the most extrava- gant lengths. Nevertheless, they crystallized the principle that the benefit of a contract could not be conferred on a third party and similarly neither could a burden.

For example, in *Haseldine* v. *C.S. Daw & Son Ltd* [1941] 2 K.B. 343, Daw & Son were employed under a maintenance contract by the owners of a block of flats to keep a lift in good condition. The contract contained a protective clause which exempted Daw & Son from liability for any accidents caused as a result of their own negligence. Because Daw & Son had negligently repaired the lift a third party was injured and sought damages from them. It was held that Daw & Son could not shelter behind the protective clause in their maintenance contract where an action in tort was brought by a third party.

There may be a certain class of cases where third parties stand to gain indirectly by virtue of a contract, and where the deprivation of that gain can properly be regarded as no more than a consequence of the loss suffered by one of the contracting parties. In that situation there may be no question of the third parties having any claim to damages in their own right, but yet it may be proper to take into account in assessing the damages recoverable by the contracting party an element in respect of expense incurred by him in replacing by other means benefits of which the third parties have been deprived, or in mitigating the consequences of that depriva- tion.

Q. Can an employee or agent rely on a protective clause?

Where there is a contract which contains a protective clause, the employees or agents of the principal who acted under that contract could have the benefits of that clause and be able to shelter behind it. However, a number of conditions have to be satisfied before a person acting as an agent, hence as a third party, to a contract can rely on a clause excluding or limiting third party liability; these conditions are:

1. The contract between the principal parties must not only make it clear that a third party is intended to be protected by the protective clauses limiting or excluding liability, but also establish that one of the principals in addition to contracting as the agent for that third party;
2. It must be shown that that principal has authority from the third party so to contract, though later ratification may suffice;
3. The third party must give consideration to the other principal to the contract.

The word 'agents' in this context includes those people employed as subcontractors to do the work. However, whether or not in any given contract performance can properly be carried out by the employment of a subcontractor must depend on the proper inference to be drawn from the contract itself, the subject-matter of it and other material surrounding circumstances. Vicarious performance of a contract which has been made by one party specifically with another because of the latter's particular skill, judgement, competency, taste or other personal qualification, may not be considered a true performance of the contract, but rather a breach of contract, even where it had been completed by a third party in accordance with the general terms of that contract. An action for that breach may be continued against the representatives of the party at fault in the event of his death, though the liability of those representatives may only extend to the value of the assets in their hands.

A protective clause whose purpose was to exclude or limit the liability of a third party to a contract could not be construed as a promise not to sue him. Nevertheless, a clause may be written into the contract whereby an undertaking is given by one party to the other that no legal proceedings will be instituted by him against a third party. However, such an undertaking may not be used by way of defence should an action arise.

SEVEN

What must I do to limit

effectively my liability

by insurance?

Q. What is a contract of insurance?

Risks, especially commercial contracts within the building industry, are generally covered by insurance in the form of a contract of insurance.

Statutes are of little assistance when it comes to defining the nature of a contract of insurance; and there has been no all-embracing definition. Probably it is undesirable that there should be because definitions sometimes tend to obscure and occasionally to exclude that which ought to be included.

A partial definition was given by sections 96(1) and 95 of the *Insurance Companies Act 1982*. Section 96(1) states that a contract of insurance includes any contract, the effecting of which includes the carrying on of insurance business by virtue of section 95. Section 95 states:

> For the purposes of this Act 'insurance business' includes (a) the effecting and carrying out, by a person not carrying on a banking business, of contracts for fidelity bonds, performance bonds, administration bonds, bail bonds, or custom bonds or similar contracts of guarantee being contracts effected by way of business (and not merely incidentally to some other business carried on by the person effecting them) in return for the payment of one or more premiums.

One type of 'contract of guarantee or indemnity' is professional indemnity insurance.

A contract of insurance is a concept which is easier to describe rather than to attempt to define. Essentially it possesses three characteristics:

1. It provides for the insured to be contractually entitled to money or money's worth or the provision of services to be paid by the insurer when a certain event occurs;
2. There must be some uncertainty as to whether or not that particular event will ever arise and the time at which it would occur;

3. The insured must have an 'insurable interest' in the subject-matter of the contract.

Q. What is the purpose and what effect can a professional indemnity insurance policy have on my liability?

The purpose of a professional indemnity policy is to cover you as the insured against a claim for damages, which may arise as a result of injury or loss caused by your, or your employees', negligent act, error or omission. In other words, it provides cover for a liability which arises because of a breach of a certain professional duty to be expected of you when carrying out your profession, but not liability which arises because of your own, or your employees', dishonesty or fraud; nor does it cover claims for breach of warranty or guarantee or punitive or exemplary damages. It may include cover for costs incurred in taking legal action for the recovery of outstanding fees, replacing lost or damaged documents and the dishonesty of employees.

Unless an additional premium is paid, most policies do not cover libel or slander or infringement of copyright. There is also no cover for claims made involving the dishonest misappropriation of clients' moneys by the practice's employees or for claims involving loss of documents.

Q. How does a professional indemnity policy operate?

A professional indemnity policy, which may be renewed annually, is based on the principle of only providing cover for those claims made during the period for which the policy runs rather than providing an indemnity for those acts, errors and omissions actually made during the time of that particular policy but which might only give rise to liability at some future date when the current policy has expired.

Though the negligent act may have occurred several years previously, and the claim be made after the policy has lapsed and take a considerable time to settle, once notice has been given by you to your insurers that you are aware of a particular occurrence that might give rise to a claim being made against you, the insurers to whom that notice has been given will continue to deal with it under the current policy.

Unless otherwise agreed, the amount of the indemnity provides protection in the aggregate during any one year and is not an amount of coverage provided for each and every claim. The insurers' total limit of liability during any one year is the amount of the indemnity quoted.

7.1 UBERRIMAE FIDEI

Q. I have heard that the basis of contract of insurance is 'uberrimae fidei', what does this mean?

A contract of insurance of whatever type is based on the principle of *uberrimae fidei*; on disclosures being given in the utmost good faith and in the fullest confidence of their truth.

Section 17 of the *Marine Insurance Act 1906* clearly states, 'A contract of marine insurance is a contract based upon the utmost good faith, and if the utmost good faith be not observed by either party, the contract may be avoided by the other party'. There is no obvious reason why there should be

A cautionary tale about the bugbear called 'professional indemnity insurance'

A firm of architects practised in Exeter. In 1973 they were engaged by the Devon & Cornwall Housing Association in connection with the construction of a housing development known as the Rose Duryard Development. The architects designed the scheme and supervised its construction. The building works were completed and taken into possession by the Association between November 1976 and November 1977.

Problems arose with the brickwork. The association notified the architects in July 1979. The Association set out in detail the remedial works which they required to be undertaken at no cost to them. The architects were insured in respect of professional liabilities with the New Hampshire Insurance Co. Their insurance policy contained the following conditions:

4. The insured should, as a condition precedent to their right to be indemnified under the policy, give New Hampshire immediate notice in writing of any claim made against them or of the receipt of notice from any person of an intention to make a claim against them;

7. In the event of New Hampshire being entitled to void the policy by reason of inaccurate or misleading information given by the insured in the proposed form, New Hampshire could treat the policy as being in full force and effect, apart from the exclusion from the indemnity of any claim which was related to circumstances which ought to have been disclosed in the proposal form which were not disclosed;

8. Where events occurred which made it likely that there would be a claim under the policy, and written notice was given to the company of such occurrence, then any actual claim subsequently made arising out of that occurrence would be deemed to be a claim arising during the period of cover where the occurrence took place whenever such claim was actually made;

12. New Hampshire would have no liability to indemnify under the policy to the extent that the insured was entitled to an indemnity under any other policy.

When Home Insurance took over the scheme from 1 October 1983 it retained the policy wording used by New Hampshire subject to two relevant qualifications. First, Home Insurance included a term in the contract that it would not exercise its right to avoid the policy in respect of non-disclosure or misrepresentation of material facts contained in the proposal form, provided that the insured established that such non-disclosure, etc. was innocent and free from any fraudulent conduct or intention to deceive.

Secondly, one of the exceptions to the cover concerned any circumstances disclosed in the proposal form likely to result in a claim against the insured.

The claim, which was notified by the Association to the architects in July 1979, related to defective brickwork, and it was in connection with this that notification was subsequently given by the architects to New Hampshire.

Liability was contested by the architects. The problem related to cracks in the brickwork from differential movements in the elements of the structure. It may have been that expansion joints should have been included at the points where the brickwork cracked. In September 1979 the architects agreed with the consulting engineers for the development to share the cost of some of the remedial works to the brickwork. The architects did not seek reimbursement from New Hampshire. They did, however, inform them of the contribution which they had made.

In May 1982 the Association's solicitors notified the architects of its intention to issue a writ arising out of problems on the Rose Duryard Development. This notification was passed on by the architects to New Hampshire. The Association's solicitors were asked for details of any allegations of negligence and of any apparent problems which were alleged to have arisen.

In June 1982 the writ was issued. It stated that the claim was for negligence in advising

(continued)

upon, designing and supervising the construction of the development and/or in carrying out the functions and duties of an architect in connection with the development and for breach of statutory duty in carrying out these functions. However, the writ was not immediately served although the Association's solicitors did inform the architects of its issue. In August 1982 the Association's solicitors wrote, stating that they had at that stage obtained only a preliminary report from their expert consulting engineers.

Eventually, in May 1983, the Association's solicitors informed the architects' solicitors that they had evidence suggesting that an action would go ahead against both the architects and the consulting engineers for the development. They requested an extension of time for service of the statement of claim (which normally has to be served within 28 days of service of the writ) until the end of October 1983.

Their request was granted by the architects but not all other potential defendants were prepared to agree to the extension of time and, in June 1983, the Association was successful in applying to the court for an extension to the validity of the writ (a writ must normally be served within 12 months of its issue unless extended by order of the court).

Shortly after this, on 30 September 1983, the last New Hampshire policy expired, and from 1 October 1983 the Home Insurance policy took effect. At this point, the architects had been notified of a claim in respect of brickwork and they had contributed towards the remedial works. They had subsequently received notice of a claim relating to the development of which no precise details had been given, but they had notified the existence of this claim to New Hampshire at the time when it arose.

In December 1983 the writ, without a statement of claim, was served, and the Association's solicitors sent to the architects' solicitors a number of technical reports which broadened the Association's allegations beyond mere problems with the brickwork. On 10 January 1984 the statement of claim was served; this document made clear the Association's case, it was far more broadly based than the claim which had originally been notified in respect of the brickwork in July 1979.

Upon learning of these broadened allegations extending beyond brickwork, New Hampshire informed the architects that it did not regard its policy as covering any heads of damage other than in relation to brickwork. Accordingly, Home Insurance was notified of the position. Its response was that the claim was notified in 1979 to New Hampshire and the fact that parts of the claim – that other than the brickwork claim – had not been fully detailed or investigated, were not relevant. It maintained that there was no fresh claim, but only parts of an original claim which had not been investigated. The company concluded by saying that none of the matters set out in the statement of claim were first made during the currency of the Home Insurance policy.

As a result of this dispute, the architects sought a declaration from the High Court that they were covered for any potential liability to the Association under one policy or the other. Home Insurance not only argued that the claim was covered by the New Hampshire policy, but also advanced a defence of non-disclosure at the time when the scheme changed hands. The Home Insurance proposal form, in question, related to existing claims against the architects. The architects admitted to two claims, one of which was the Rose Duryard Development claim. The architects' answer in the proposal form stated that the claim was in the policy year 1978/79 and had been settled at nil. Further, in answer to question 8 on the Home Insurance proposal form which asked the architects if they were aware, after enquiry, of any pending claim or circumstances likely to give rise to a claim, they answered 'no'.

It will be recalled that by the summer of 1983 the architects were aware of the issue of the writ although it had not been served, and they still did not have details of the alleged claims. The architects had, however, kept New Hampshire informed of such information as they had.

On the basis of the architects' responses to the questions raised in the Home Insurance proposal form, Home Insurance alleged that there had been a misrepresentation of the position amounting to a non-disclosure of a material fact. Home Insurance alleged that it was not told of the outstanding claim being

(continued)

dealt with by New Hampshire at the time of the changeover in insurers. As far as Home Insurance was aware, there had been a claim in 1979 which had been settled.

The judge had first to decide what was meant by the word 'claim' in the context of the insurance policies. The judge said that 'claim' must relate to the object that was claimed and was not the same thing as a cause or right of action by which a claim might be supported or as a group upon which it might be based. In other words, the claim was a claim for damages rather than a claim for bad design or supervision.

In the Home Insurance proposal form in the light of the claim made in 1979 and subsequent events, the important question was how a reasonable man placed in the position of the architects would have regarded matters. He held that the architects had answered the questions based upon a reasonable understanding of what the questions meant.

Home Insurance had argued that a careful analysis of correspondence regarding the development which came into existence before the architects had completed the 1983 proposal form should have made them aware that the problems extended to more than just brickwork. However, it was held that a reasonable architect would not have understood these as referring to anything other than those alleged defects in the brickwork which had already been detailed in 1979. The architects had not become aware of those allegations contained in items 4–8 of the Scotts Schedule until at least October 1983, i.e. after the new insurance cover took effect.

The judge next turned to an alternative argument that there had been a material non-disclosure on the part of the architects, namely that despite the fact that they were aware that a writ had been issued but not served they did not specifically refer to this in the proposal form, but instead referred to the 1979 claim which had been settled at nil.

However, looking at the answer itself, the architects had made reference to the Rose Duryard Development and to its reference claim number with New Hampshire Insurance. This was a disclosure of the claim of 1979 and the subsequent issue of the writ which had been notified to New Hampshire and been dealt with by them. Home Insurance could have investigated this further with New Hampshire but failed to do so.

Home Insurance brought into the arguement the existence of claims, experience of which accompanied the proposal. However, it had been prepared by the brokers and not the architects themselves. In effect, this form had intimated to Home Insurance that the Rose Duryard claim was not settled.

The judge accepted the weight of the Home Insurance argument in this respect and that the details given in the claims experience form, which the brokers submitted to Home Insurance, contained a material inaccuracy. Had the form been accurately completed, it would have affected Home Insurance in its decision to take on the insurance risks.

It had been agreed between Home Insurance and the brokers ABS that they would prepare a claims experience record of each insured. The architects had no knowledge of this document. It had not been expressly incorporated within the proposal form and was not in fact mentioned anywhere in it. It was held that it did not form part of the broker's presentation on behalf of the architects and was never intended to be regarded as such. Furthermore, the brokers had no actual or apparent authority to deliver what was in truth their own particular internal record of claims experience to Home Insurance on behalf of the insured architects.

Accordingly, New Hampshire was liable to indemnify the architects in respect of any claims for which the architects may be found liable relating to brickwork, and Home Insurance was liable in respect of the other items on the claim.

Thorman & Others v. *New Hampshire Insurance Company & Another, (1987) Times, 12 October.*

a rule of disclosure in marine insurance which is different from the rules in other forms of insurance.

For centuries it has been the law in connection with insurance of all sorts – marine, fire, guarantee, and every kind of policy – that as the underwriter knows nothing and the person who comes to him to insure knows everything, it is the duty of the assured to make a full disclosure to the underwriters without being asked about all the material circumstances.

No proposition of insurance law is better established than that the party proposing the insurance is bound to communicate to the insurer all matters which will enable him to determine the extent of the risk against which he undertakes to guarantee the assured.

Q. How much must I disclose to my insurers?

It is a somewhat dangerous exercise for you, as the proposer, to speculate upon the maximum amount of information you must disclose. Nevertheless, it is possible to distinguish between four possible standards of the duty of disclosure:

1. It may be sufficient to satisfy that duty if such facts as you believe to be material only are disclosed;
2. To disclose such facts as a reasonable man would believe to be material;
3. To disclose such facts as the particular insurer would regard as material;
4. To disclose such facts and circumstances as a reasonable or prudent insurer might have treated as material.

Section 18 of the *Marine Insurance Act 1906* states that every circumstance is material which would influence the judgement of a prudent insurer in fixing the premium or determining whether he will take the risk. Whether any particular circumstance which is not disclosed is material or not is, in each case, a question of fact, the term 'circumstance' including any communication made to, or information received by, the insured.

Q. On what grounds can my insurers refuse to pay out on my insurance contract?

The general principle for disclosure is to disclose material facts which would influence the mind of a prudent insurer.

The practical effect of this principle is that your insurers are entitled to repudiate liability wherever they can show that a fact within your knowledge was not disclosed which, according to current insurance practice, would have affected their judgement of the risk. A fact may be material to insurers in the light of the great volume of experience of claims available to them, which would not necessarily appear to you as a proposer for insurance, however honest and careful you are to be one which you ought to disclose.

For insurers to succeed in repudiating liability, it must clearly be shown that they *would have been influenced*, and not merely *might have been*, by the particular fact which when seeking insurance you withheld from them. The balance is tipped in favour of the insurers against the insured, not least because the *Unfair Contract Terms Act 1977* does not apply to contracts of insurance.

Q. Are there any circumstances in which the principle of 'uberrimae fidei' ('utmost good faith') does not apply?

The principle of *uberrimae fidei* may not be relied on by an

A cautionary tale about the meaning of simple words

By birth, Sapsy Glicksman was a Polish Jew. He could neither read nor write, but only sign his name. His native tongue was Yiddish and his grasp of English was poor. Sapsy Glicksman was a ladies tailor in a small way. He and his then partner insured their stock in trade against burglary with the Lancashire and General Assurance Co.

The proposal form which had been accepted by the insurance company asked whether any company had 'declined to accept or refuse to renew *your* burglary insurance'. The partners replied, 'Yorkshire accepted, but proposers refused'. However, another insurance company, the Sun Insurance, had refused a proposal for burglary insurance made sometime previously by Sapsy Glicksman alone. Nevertheless, the partners signed a declaration at the foot of the form pledging that the answers to the questions were true and that they had withheld no information that might tend to increase the company's risk. They agreed that the declaration and answers should be the basis of the contract between them and the company and to accept a policy, subject to the *usual* conditions prescribed by the company.

The policy which the insurance company issued contained the proviso that the statements made by the assured in the proposal and declaration were true in *all* respects, and that if the policy were obtained through any misrepresentation, suppression, concealment or untrue averment whatsoever by the assured, then the policy should be void.

During the currency of the policy, Sapsy Glicksman, who was again carrying on the tailors' business alone and in whom the benefit of the policy had been vested, made a claim. His premises had been burgled and £1656 6s 3d worth of stock was either stolen or damaged. The insurance company resisted the claim and the dispute was referred to arbitration under the terms of the policy.

When the proposal form was looked at in detail, it was clear that confusion had arisen because of Sapsy Glicksman's poor grasp of English over the wording of the question whether or not 'you' had had a previous proposal for an insurance policy refused or accepted by another company. At the time the proposal was made, Sapsy Glicksman was in partnership; and the word 'you' in English is both singular and plural, and there is an inextricable confusion between them. If the word 'you' is used in the plural, as naturally it should have been because two people were applying, then it was quite true that there had not been any refusal of an insurance; but it was not true if it were taken in the singular.

The arbitrator by an award stated in the form of a special case found that a false answer had been given to the question and that the policy had been obtained by suppression or conceal-ment of a material fact. An appeal was taken to Roche, J. who came to an opposite conclusion in favour of Sapsy Glicksman.

The Court of Appeal reversed the judgment of Roche, J. and their decision was affirmed by the House of Lords where it was held that there was sufficient ground for supporting the finding of the arbitrator that the refusal by the insurance company of the proposal made by Sapsy Glicksman on the former occasion was a material fact and that that fact had been concealed.

However, Lord Atkinson said, 'I think it is a lamentable thing that insurance companies will abstain from shaping the questions they put to intending insurers on these occasions in clear and unambiguous language'; while Lord Wrenbury remarked: 'I think it a mean and contemptible policy on the part of an insurance company that it should take the premiums and then refuse to pay upon a ground which no one says was really material. Here, upon purely technical grounds, they, having in point of fact not been deceived in any material particular, avail themselves of what seems to me the contemptible defence that, although they have taken the premiums, they are protected from paying.'

Glicksman (Pauper) v. *Lancashire & General Assurance Co. Ltd.* [1927] A.C. 139, H.L.

insurer as a defence in avoiding liability under a policy if it is shown that an inaccurate answer came about because the wording of a particular question was ambiguous, especially if the interpretation which the person seeking insurance cover put upon it was both fair and reasonable and the answer when related to that interpretation was truthful.

However, an insurer might be able to avoid a policy if the answers contained within the proposal form were not merely untruthful but incomplete and thus misleading, though the statement itself was truthful. Also, in certain circumstances, an insurer might shelter behind the principle of *uberrimae fidei* because of an untruthful reply to an ambiguously worded question.

7.2 WARRANTIES AND BASIS OF CONTRACT CLAUSES

Q. What does a 'warranty' or 'basis of contract clause' mean?

Words in a policy stating that the proposal shall be the basis of the contract and be held as incorporated therein are words apt to convert answers to questions into conditions of the policy; and similarly, where the policy expressly provides that 'if anything averred in the declaration shall be untrue, this policy shall be void and all moneys received by the said company in respect thereof shall belong to the said company for their own "benefit"'. The same effect results from the word 'basis'.

A warranty or condition (these words are used as equivalent in insurance law), though it must be strictly complied with, must be strictly, though reasonably, construed. A statutory definition of the nature of warranties was given in clause 33 of the *Marine Insurance Act 1906*. A warranty is a promissory warranty whereby the assured undertakes that the existence of a particular state of facts is affirmed or denied.

A warranty, whether it be expressed or implied, is a condition which must be complied with whether it be material to the risk or not. If it is not complied with, then subject to any express provision in the policy the insurer is discharged from liability as from the date of the breach of warranty, but without prejudice to any liability incurred by him before that date. The term 'basis of contract' means that an insurer may avoid a contract of insurance for the non-disclosure of a material fact.

Insurers may pre-empt the issue of whether a fact is, or is not, material by including in their proposal form a declaration, which the proposer is obliged to sign, that he warrants the accuracy of all the answers to the questions asked. That declaration is commonly termed the 'basis of contract clause'; the effect of such a clause is that all answers in the proposal form are incorporated into the contract as warranties. Should any one answer be inaccurate, the insurer may repudiate the whole of the contract on the ground of a breach of warranty. This may be done regardless of whether a particular answer is material to the risk, or that the person seeking the insurance cover answered the questions in good faith and to the best of his knowledge and belief. Where the answer relates to past and present facts, the breach of warranty is committed at the moment when the contract is made, therefore, the insurer may refuse to pay any claim under the policy.

Q. What is the practical result of a 'warranty' or 'basis of contract clause' in an insurance form?

Insurers, by changing the questions asked in a proposal form, by means of a basis of contract clause, from simple representations to a guarantee, prepare nothing less than a trap for the person seeking insurance cover because it allows a major mischief in the present law, on three main grounds:

1. They allow insurers to repudiate a policy for inaccurate statements, even though they are wholly immaterial to the risk;
2. They entitle insurers to repudiate policies because of a statement of fact which is objectively inaccurate, even though the insured could not reasonably be expected either to know or to have the means of knowing the true facts;
3. The elevation *en bloc* of all such statements into warranties binding on the insured means that if the insurers can establish any inaccuracy, however trivial, in any of the statements, they can exercise their right to repudiate the policy.

A representation as to a matter of fact is true if it is substantially correct, that is if the difference between what is represented and what is actually correct would not be considered material by a prudent insurer, while a representation as to a matter of belief or expectation may be considered true if it be made in good faith. In either case, a representation may be withdrawn before the contract is concluded.

Injustice could best be avoided if the person seeking insurance was treated as having discharged his duty of disclosure and truthful representation if questions contained within the proposal form had been answered to the best of his knowledge and belief, though the answer itself might be inaccurate, provided enquiries had been made which were reasonable having regard to both the topics covered by the question and the nature and extent of the cover which was sought. Any 'basis of contract' clause should be ineffective if

it sought to convert a statement representing past or present facts into a warranty, for example, a policy clause which declared that the insured's answers to specific questions in the proposal form are true would not constitute a warranty.

Q. How do I know whether my answers will form the basis of the insurance contract?

If an insurance company means to stipulate that the truth of answers to questions put to you when seeking insurance should be a condition precedent to the validity of the contract, that is they will form the basis of the contract, the insurance company must do so in such unambiguous terms as a layman can, without difficulty, understand.

The insurers must establish clearly that you consented to the accuracy, and not the truthfulness of your statements being made a condition of the validity of the policy. No ambiguous language suffices for this purpose. You, as the applicant, can be called on to answer all questions relevant to the matter in hand. But this is merely the fulfilment of a duty – it is not contractual. To make the accuracy of these answers a condition of the contract is a contractual act. If there is the slightest doubt that the insurers have failed to make clear to you that they have exercised their right of requiring full information that you consent and to this contract, the courts may refuse to regard the correctness of the answers given as being a condition of the validity of the policy. In other words, the insurers must prove by clear and express language the *animus comprahendi* on your part as the applicant; it will not be inferred from the fact that questions were answered and that you declared that your answers were true.

Furthermore, the matters to be disclosed should be those which you had knowledge of. The duty is a duty to disclose, and you cannot disclose what you do not know. Therefore, the obligation to disclose necessarily depends on the knowledge you possess. Your opinion of the materiality of that knowledge is of no moment. Insurers are in a highly favourable position because:

1. They are entitled to expect you to use bona fides, that is, the utmost good faith in your dealings with them.
2. Your answers to the various questions asked by the insurers or their agents must be given in the utmost good faith.
3. The validity of the insurance policy is conditional upon you acting (and answering the insurers' questions) with the utmost good faith.

This might be reasonable in some matters, such as your age and parentage or information as to your family history, which you must know as facts. Or it might be justifiable to stipulate that these conditions should obtain for a reasonable time, say, during two years, during which period the insurers might verify the accuracy of the statements which have been made bona fide by yourself.

But insurance companies have pushed the practice far beyond these limits, and have made the correctness of statements of matters wholly beyond your knowledge, and which can at best be only statements of opinion or belief, conditions of the validity of the policy. The policies issued by many are framed so as to be invalid unless this and many other like questions are correctly – not merely truthfully – answered, though the insurers are well aware that it is impossible for anyone to arrive at anything more certain than an opinion about them. Few of those who insure have any idea how completely they leave themselves in the hands of the insurers, should the latter wish to dispute the policy when it falls in.

Q. How much or how little background research should I do before answering the insurers' questions?

The duty of disclosure placed upon you is not such as for it to be necessary to carry out a detailed investigation of all facts related to the thing being insured, but rather to make such reasonable enquiries which you may discover during the ordinary course of your profession or business.

To impose an obligation for detailed investigation upon you as the proposer would be tantamount to saying that insurers only insure those who conduct their business prudently, whereas it is commonplace that one of the purposes of insurance is to cover oneself against one's own negligence or the negligence of one's employees.

Q. Does an insurance agent owe me a duty?

A duty of disclosure and truthful representation rests equally upon the person seeking insurance as it does upon an insurance agent who may be involved in the transaction.

Where an insurance is effected for the assured by an agent, the agent must disclose to the insurer every material circumstance which is known to himself and which the assured is bound to disclose, unless it came to his knowledge too late to be communicated to the agent. The agent himself is deemed to know every circumstance which in the ordinary course of business ought to be known by or to have been communicated to him.

During the course of an insurance transaction it is often inevitable that the agent will complete, or help, in filling in

A cautionary tale about the exploding mill

Mr Beauchamp was a builder who took out an insurance policy dated 31 October 1935 with the National Mutual Indemnity Insurance Co. to insure, among other things, against accident and negligence on one of his jobs. The job was the demolition of Alexandra Mill at Oldham; it was the first job of this nature that he had undertaken.

The mill was to be demolished by a controlled explosion carried out by a gentleman whom the builder had employed for this purpose. The builder himself would not handle any explosives. Because of this, the builder answered 'no' to one of the questions on the insurance company's proposal form – namely, are any acids, gases, chemicals, explosives or any other dangerous preparations used in your business'. The builder agreed his answers would form the basis of contract between himself and the insurers.

In July 1936 explosives were used to demolish the mill. During the course of the work three people accidentally lost their lives. They were killed by falling masonry. It was found that, negligently, insufficient precautions had been taken by the builder to prevent an accident. This stemmed from the fact that one of his employees, a Mr McCormick, had been made responsible for the task of demolishing the mill. Though a very good and intelligent labourer and though he would not have been using the explosives, he was not a qualified foreman and did not have the training necessary for him to carry the heavy responsibility for that type of job. The builder made a claim under the policy but the insurance company repudiated liability on the grounds of non-disclosure.

Finley, J., in giving judgment for the insurance company, held that the denial of the use of explosives amounted to a warranty that they would not be used:

The Plaintiff as I mentioned was a builder. He was a person who was not doing any other demolition work. This insurance was solely in respect of the one isolated demolition job, so to speak, at this Alexandra Mill at Oldham, and it seems to me, therefore, that the proposal form must inevitably have reference to the future because though, in fact, the Plaintiff was in business he was not insuring anything with regard to his general business, but was insuring in respect only of this special job in the future. Accordingly, it seems to me that the whole of the proposal must be regarded as having reference to a future event, and when in these circumstances, he is asked, 'Are any acids, gases, chemicals, explosives, or any other dangerous preparations used in your business', that does not, of course, mean his present business of a builder: it means the business on which he is going to embark, the business of demolition. Accordingly, it seems to me that it does have the nature of a warranty or a condition. I think that the true view to take is that he was insuring what I may conveniently call (the phrase is not elegant, but intelligible) a non-explosive demolition. I think the risk, where the demolition is an explosive one is greater than where it is a non-explosive one and what he was insuring was, I think, a non-explosive demolition. I cannot doubt that the view taken by an insurance company of a case where explosives were to be used would be widely different from that taken of a case where explosives were not to be used.

Beauchamp v. *National Mutual Indemnity Insurance Co. Ltd* [1937] 3 All E.R. 19.

A cautionary tale of the problems of having only one eye

Mr Bawden was illiterate. Apart from being able to sign his name, he could neither read nor write. He had only one eye.

Quin was the local agent of the London, Edinburgh and Glasgow Assurance Co., and though he had no authority to make an insurance contract from the company, he could negotiate and settle the form of the assured's proposal for insurance and was supplied with proposal forms for that purpose.

The answers to the questions on the form were dictated by Mr Bawden to Quin, who wrote them down. Those answers were all correct. However, no details of Mr Bawden's having one eye were given by him or Quin in reply to the declaration on the form, 'I have no physical infirmity, nor are there any circumstances that render me peculiarly liable to accidents. I agree that the statements contained in this proposal shall form the basis of the contract between me and the company. (If not strictly applicable particulars of any deviation must be given at back).' Mr Bawden signed his name to the proposal and Quin forwarded it to the insurance company who accepted it. The policy was renewed from time to time.

During the currency of the policy, Mr Bawden was involved in a accident and lost the sight of his remaining eye. He made a claim under the policy which the insurance company refuted on the grounds of non-disclosure. It was held that the insurance company's knowledge was that of their insurance agent. They must therefore be taken to have contracted with a man whom they knew had only one eye.

Bawden v. *London, Edinburgh and Glasgow Assurance* [1892] 2 Q.B. 534.

---

the answers to an insurance company's proposal form. The form itself may then be signed by the proposer to the effect that the truth of the answers shall form the basis of the contract. If they are inaccurate, the proposer though he has signed the promise that those answers are true, may successfully allege that the fault is that of the agent of the insurance company who completed the form and therefore he should be able to rely on the policy without being prejudiced by the inaccuracy of the answers he had certified as being true.

For example, in *Holdsworth* v. *Lancashire and Yorkshire Insurance Co.* (1907) 23 T.L.R. 521, a business was not described correctly on a proposal form, though the insurance agent knew the true nature of the work carried out by the person seeking insurance. It was found that the insurance company being assumed to have the same knowledge as the agent, gave insurance for the actual business and not simply the one incorrectly described in the policy.

7.3 WITHHOLDING INFORMATION

Q. Are there any circumstances when I can withhold information from insurers?

In general terms, a duty of disclosure exists only while there is no contract binding upon both the insurer and yourself when seeking insurance. When such a contract does arise, your duty of disclosure ceases. Thus the insurance company must be informed of any material alteration to the facts which have been disclosed in the proposal form by yourself before completion of the contract.

The point at which a contract of insurance is deemed to be concluded occurs when the proposal of the assured is accepted by the insurer, whether the policy be then issued or not; and for the purpose of showing the proposal was accepted, reference may be made to the covering note or other customary memorandum of the contract, although it is unstamped.

This duty of disclosure placed upon a person seeking insurance may be qualified; there are a number of circumstances in which the material facts need not be disclosed:

1. Any circumstances which diminishes the risk;
2. Any circumstance which is known, or presumed to be known, to the insurer; the insurer is presumed to know matters of common notoriety or knowledge, and matters which an insurer in the ordinary course of his business as such ought to know;
3. Any circumstances as to which information is waived by the insurer need not be disclosed;
4. Any circumstances which it is superfluous to disclose by reason of any express or implied warranty.

Q. Do I have to tell my insurers everything about my past even if, for example, I had a conviction many years ago?

It was thought that if any convictions of whatever nature had been borne by a person seeking insurance, then they had to be disclosed, even though they belonged to a dim and remote past, otherwise the insurers might refuse to indemnify the insured.

For example, in *Rose-Lodge Ltd. v. Castle* [1966] 2 Ll.Rep. 113, diamond merchants took out an all-risks insurance policy for their business. When they brought a claim against their policy, the insurance company refused to honour it on the basis that the previous convictions of one of the company's directors in 1946 for bribery of a policeman, and their sales manager's conviction for smuggling diamonds in 1956, had not been disclosed. McNair, J. partially upheld the insurers' contention. He determined that while the 1946 bribery conviction of a company director was immaterial as it bore no direct relationship to his trading as a diamond merchant, the 1956 smuggling conviction, on the other hand, was material because of the its direct relationship to the diamond business.

Following on the *Rehabilitation of Offenders Act 1974*, an insurance company may not under certain circumstances reject a claim or repudiate a policy where the person seeking insurance has not disclosed certain information which, but for the Act, may have been considered a material fact. The purpose of the Act, which is contained in its long title, is to rehabilitate offenders by allowing them not to disclose a previous conviction where the offender has not been reconvicted of any serious offence for a number of years. At the same time, the Act penalizes the unauthorized disclosure of any of their previous convictions. The effect of the rehabilitation scheme is given in section 4(1) of the Act:

a person who has become a rehabilitated person for the purpose of this Act in respect of a conviction shall be treated for all purposes in law as a person who has not committed or been charged with or prosecuted for or convicted of or sentenced for the offence or offences which were the subject of the conviction . . . (2) . . . where a question seeking information with respect to a person's previous convictions, offences, conduct or circumstances is put to him or to any other person otherwise than in proceedings before a judicial authority:

(a) the question shall be treated as not relating to spent convictions or to any circumstances ancillary to spent convictions, and the answer there to maybe framed accordingly, and
(b) the person questioned shall not be subject to any liability or otherwise prejudiced in law by reason of any failure to

A cautionary tale of always making sure that what you have said is written correctly

One of the partners in a firm signed an insurance proposal form. The proposal form contained a warranty that the answers to questions contained in the form were true, that no information had been withheld and that they should form the basis of the contract between the firm and the insurance company. The answers to the questions were filled in by one of the insurance company's agents.

Although the partner had told the true facts to the insurance agent, unknown to the insurance company, their agent had answered three of the fourteen questions wrongly, either because he had unintentionally written untruths as he did not understand his partner's replies or he forgot what he was told or he did not understand the questions asked or he intentionally wrote down untrue facts to earn his commission.

A policy was issued by the insurance company to the firm. During the currency of the policy the firm made a claim under it. The insurance company repudiated liability because of untrue statements in the proposal form.

The insurance company successfully contended that their agent in filling in the proposal form was merely acting as an amanuensis, or copying secretary, who wrote to the dictation of the proposer. Furthermore, the knowledge of the true facts by the agent could not be imputed to the insurance company.

Scrutton, L.J., in the Court of Appeal, said of cases where the insurance agent at the request of the proposer fills up the answers in purported conformity with the information supplied by the proposer, that:

If the answers are untrue, and he knows it, he is committing a fraud which prevents his knowledge being the knowledge of the insurance company. If the answers are untrue but he does not know it, he has no knowledge which can be imputed to the insurance company. In any case a man who has signed without reading a document which he knows to be a proposal for insurance, and which contains statements that in fact are untrue and a promise that they are true and are to be the basis of the contract, cannot escape from the consequences of his negligence by saying that the person he asked to fill it up for him was the agent of the insurance company.

Newsholme Brothers v. *Road Transport & General Insurance Co.* [1929] 2 K.B. 356.

acknowledge or disclose a spent conviction or any circumstances ancillary to a spent conviction in his answer to the question.

Rehabilitation periods vary for differing sentences. However, there are a number which are excluded from rehabilitation. Apart from life imprisonment, perhaps one of the more important exceptions is that where a sentence of imprisonment for a term exceeding 30 months has been imposed, the person convicted may derive no benefit from the Act in completing an insurance proposal form.

Q. Do I have to answer every insurance question which asks for personal information?

The *Sex Discrimination Act 1975* and the *Race Relations Act 1976* makes certain kinds of sexual and racial discrimination unlawful. One field which both Acts specifically refer to is insurance.

Both Acts make it unlawful for anyone concerned with the provision of insurance, among other things, to discriminate against a person because of their race or because they are a woman who wishes to take out insurance cover by refusing or deliberately omitting to provide them with that particular cover or one of like quality, in the like manner and on the like terms which would normally be given to a man or to a person not of that race.

An insurance company cannot claim that where a person seeking insurance is a woman or is of a particular race, colour, nationality or ethnic group it is a material fact. Any questions put by the insurers, seeking such information may not be answered by the insured.

Nevertheless, the *Sex Discrimination Act 1975* makes a proviso that a person may be discriminated against by the insurers where an annuity, a life assurance policy, accident insurance policy or a similar policy involving the assessment of risk is being considered, and the information was acquired by reference to actuarial or other data from a source on which it was not only reasonable to rely, but also reasonable having regard to the data and any other relevant factors.

Q. To what extent does an insurance company require me not to answer its questions?

Though a proposal form may contain a considerable number of questions which must be answered, other facts known to you when seeking insurance but which fall outside the general scope of the questions should not be withheld. But the extent of the duty of disclosure may be limited by the application of the doctrine of waiver whereby the insurer renounces or disclaims the need to be given that information. An insurer's decision to waive certain information could be inferred from the payment of a large premium, or if the insurers seem to be indifferent or uninterested in whether or not particular matters should be disclosed.

Where an insurance company makes no attempt to obtain further information concerning a question they have asked in their proposal form which has clearly been answered in an incomplete manner, then waiver of such information by the company may be assumed.

If the insurance company is in a position to avoid liability on a particular contract because of information being withheld, the fact that the company has undertaken or continues to act in the defence of a claim may be construed as a sufficient indication that they have waived their right to refuse payment because of the insured's breach of duty.

7.4 INSURANCE CLAIMS

Q. What is the position if an insurers' consent has to be obtained before legal proceedings can be started?

The insurers' consent must not be unreasonably withheld if it is a condition of the insurance policy that that consent must be obtained by the insured before he undertakes any action to fight a claim made against him. Where the insurers have not informed the insured of their decision within a reasonable time, it may be assumed that they have agreed to such a course of action.

The insurers' decision may be guided by the advice given by counsel on whether or not the insured's action is likely to be successful. For example, a clause, commonly known as a Queen's Counsel clause, may be inserted into a professional indemnity policy to the effect that the insurers will cover any

A cautionary tale of never having a 'good guess' at something you do not know

Mr Hyde, an architect, had lived in Hitchin, Hertfordshire, since the age of 7. He designed an industrial building with a pre-cast concrete frame and brick wall panels in Hitchin for his father-in-law's firm. The firm later sold the building to Eames London Estates Ltd.

The site was on made-up ground. Through the centre ran a 100-year-old railway embankment. On one side was a recent chalk fill and on the other a rubbish tip topped with fill.

The architect thought the site was an old railway embankment. He satisifed himself about the land's bearing capacity by agreeing a figure with the local authority. No other soil survey was carried out. The building later cracked badly because of the unsuitable foundations.

Of the four defendants, the developers, the specialist building contractors, the by-law authority and the architect, it was held that the architect was primarily liable for the defective building. In other words, an architect cannot shed his responsibility for foundations by ascertaining what will get by the local authority.

Eames London Estates Ltd. & Others v. *North Hertfordshire District Council & Others* (1980) Build.L.R. 50.

---

claim, or claims, which might be made against the insured, in respect of

> any act of neglect, default or error on the part of the assured . . . or their partners or their servants in the conduct of their business . . . without requiring the assured to dispute any claim unless a Queen's Counsel . . . advise that the same could be successfully contested by the assured and the assured consents to such a claim being contended, but such consent not to be unreasonably withheld.

Apart from being used as an indication of the possible outcome of a claim, one purpose of the Queen's Counsel clause is to prevent underwriters insisting that the assured should dispute his liability to a third party and thus face the publicity of legal proceedings which, whether the case is successful or not, the publicity might be damaging to the insured's reputation.

The right of an insurance company to determine what is, and what is not, the most suitable way to deal with an actionable claim may be limited by the proviso that they

consider not merely their own interests, but also pay due regard in all honesty and good faith to those of the assured; the same principle applies to any solicitors appointed by the insurers. Though an insurance policy may enable insurers to conduct a claim as they wish, even to the extent of retaining the services of solicitors, it does not entitle them to force the insured to accept those solicitors in preference to another firm. The solicitors, though they may be appointed by the insurance company, are the insured's solicitors.

Q. In what circumstances can an insurance company pay all litigation costs?

An insurance policy may expressly state that the insurers will pay all costs arising from litigation. Quite apart from such a clause, insurers may be liable for all the costs which stem from taking a claim to court, even though the insurance

A cautionary tale of the cat-cracker

Lindsey Oil Refinery Ltd owned the freehold land at Killingholme, South Humberside, on which stood an oil refinery. The refinery was operated by Lindsey for Petrofina (UK) Ltd and Total Oil (Great Britain) Ltd, who between them owned all the shares in the Lindsey Oil Refinery Ltd Co.

Lindsey proposed to extend the oil refinery and build a substantial catalytic cracking unit. The unit, commonly called a 'cat-cracker', was made up of eight large cylindrical vessels each weighing up to 380 tons. To raise money for the project, Lindsey entered into a contract with a consortium of companies called the Omnium Leasing Co. The contract provided that Omnium would put up the money for the new buildings which they would then own. Lindsey would lease their freehold land to Omnium. On completion of the works, Omnium would lease the buildings back to Lindsey.

Foster Wheeler Ltd were appointed as main contractors for the Works under a contract which was post-dated 31 January 1979. Foster Wheeler subcontracted the heavy lifting operations including the installation of the cat-cracker unit to Greenham (Plant Hire) Ltd.

Two of the heaviest vessels which formed part of the cat-cracker unit needed specialist lifting equipment. Greenham therefore subcontracted that part of their contract to another firm for £185 000. That firm was the Dutch company, Mammoet Stoof BV, who owned 50% of the English company Magna-load Ltd. For administrative reasons, the sub-subcontract was in the name of Magnaload rather than Mammoet, though it was Mammoet who would reimburse Magnaload for their services, remain responsible for the lifting operations and provide the heavy lifting system called a Hydrajack. The Hydrajack was made up of a gantry which rested on two vertical masts each 67 m high and 30 m apart.

The cat-cracker vessels were successfully lifted into position. While the Hydrajack was being dismantled on 2 September 1978, the gantry was displaced and fell to the ground due to the negligence of both Mammoet and Magnaload. The accident not only caused considerable damage to the oil refinery, but also killed two men.

The main contractors, Foster Wheeler, had taken out a contractors' all-risks insurance policy for £50 000 000 to cover the construction, erection and testing of the new extension with the New Hampshire Insurance Co. This insurance cover was later increased to £92 000 000. Under the policy the insured was defined as the main contractors, subcontractors, Omnium Leasing Co. and Lindsey Oil Refinery Ltd. The insured were indemnified against third party liability by the insurance company under the terms of the policy:

Against all sums for which the insured shall become legally liable to pay as damages consequent upon:
(a) Accidental bodily injury to or illness or disease of any/person;
(b) Accidental loss or damage to property occurring as a result of and solely due to the performance of the insured contract happening on or in the immediate vicinity of the contract site.

The insurance policy was extended on 23 April 1978 by an endorsement which specifically included: 'The erection operation and subsequent dismantlement of the following items of equipment being used on the Greenham (Plant Hire) Ltd subcontract for the erection of eight large vessels . . . Hydrajack system £2 150 000.'

As a result of the accident with the Hydrajack gantry, Lindsey Oil Refinery Co. made a claim against the insurers under the policy which was settled for about £1 250 000. Having paid the claim, the insurers sought to exercise their right of subrogation by bringing an action in the names of Petrofina, Total Oil, Omnium and Lindsey Oil Refinery (the plaintiffs) for the recovery of damages against Magnaload Ltd and Mammoet Stoof BV who had caused the accident through negligence.

Magnaload and Mammoet in defence claimed that the insurance company was not entitled to exercise any right of subrogation against them as they were insured under the same policy as the plaintiffs in respect of the

(continued)

same property. They were subcontractors under the main contractor's all-risks insurance policy. The term 'subcontractor' was defined in the main building contract as: 'Any person to whom the preparation of any design the supply of any plant or the execution of any part of the works is subcontracted, irrespective of whether the contractor is in direct contract with such person.'

It was held that a contractor's all-risk insurance policy was not a liability insurance, but an insurance on property comprising the works and temporary works on the site and all the insured, including subcontractors, were on the true construction of the policy, insured for loss and damage in respect of the whole of that property. It was commercially convenient for all parties concerned in building and engineering contracts that a single policy should be taken out to cover all the contractors and subcontractors working on the site for any loss or damage to the works, and that there was nothing in law to prevent the main contractors taking out such a policy. But since a subcontractor was entitled to insure the whole of the contract works and not merely that part for which he was responsible, and as the defendants had so insured, the insurers had no right of subrogation against the defendants in the name of the plaintiffs.

Lloyd, J. remarked, 'It frequently happens that businessmen do not tie up their contracts in ways which seem satisfactory to lawyers; particularly where the parties are companies which, though not members of the same group in the strict sense, are nevertheless closely associated as these were'. Lloyd J., in considering subrogation, applied the basic principle of subrogation, that it cannot be obtained against the insured himself. In the case of true joint insurance, there is no problem: the interests of the joint insured are so inseparably connected that the several insureds are to be considered as one with the obvious result that subrogation is impossible. In the case of several insureds, if the different interests are pervasive and if each relates to the entire property albeit from different angles, again there is no question that the several insureds must be the reason why an insurer cannot sue one co-insured in the name of the another, it must apply in the case of contractors and subcontractors engaged on a common enterprise'.

Petrofina (UK) Ltd. & Others v. *Magnaload Ltd. & Another* [1984] Q.B. 127.

policy might limit their liability to a certain sum, if they do so without consulting the insured first. Nevertheless, an insurer may be entitled to recover from the insured the excess under the policy, together with other sums which the latter was required to bear under the terms of the insurance policy.

A proposal form may expressly ask whether the insured wishes to be covered for the costs of defending an action, and the policy then makes specific provision as to the proportion of the costs which will be paid by the insurers. Such a provision would be sufficient to cover the costs of a successful third party claim if the action was originally entered into by the insured with the agreement of the insurers.

Should the insured become insolvent, the benefit of an insurance contract may be conferred on to a third party, even though they are not a party to the contract itself under the *Third Parties (Rights Against Insurers) Act 1930*. The Act allows a bankrupt person or company who has been insured against third party liability to transfer his rights against the insurer to the third party against whom liability has been incurred by the insured, either before or after his insolvency.

The insurer will then be under the same liability to the third party as he would have been under to the insured. But if the liability of the insurer to the insured exceeds the liability of the insured to the third party, nothing in the Act will affect the rights of the insured against the insurer in respect of the excess; while if the liability of the insurer to the insured is less

A cautionary tale about insurance companies

A company by the name of Soole & Son Ltd entered into a contract, in May 1964, to buy a plot of land at 196 Kew Road, Richmond, from the vendor, Mr Betsford, for £20 000.

The controlling shareholder in Soole & Son Ltd was Mr Soole, a builder. Mr Soole's intention was to demolish the existing house at Kew Road and build six houses on the land. Planning permission was granted for the development, despite objections made by adjoining owners.

In September 1964, before the sale of the property had been completed, Waterhouse & Co., solicitors of Lincoln's Inn, wrote to the vendor on behalf of Mr and Mrs Hayman, owners of the adjoining property, 194 Kew Road, that they having the benefit of a restrictive covenant which limited the number of houses which could be built at 196 Kew Road to one, would bring such action as they were advised to ensure that the covenant was not broken. The vendor forwarded the letter to Soole & Son Ltd.

In November 1964 the opinion of junior counsel was sought by Mr Soole and later, in March 1965, that of leading counsel on whether or not the restrictive convenant was enforceable, and whether or not there was in existence a building scheme to which a covenant could be annexed. Following both counsels' cautious advice that it was doubtful whether the restrictive covenant could be enforced and whether it was annexed to the particular plots now occupied by the adjoining

owners, a policy was taken out by Soole & Son Ltd, with the Royal Insurance Co. Ltd, to cover the possibility that the restrictive covenant might prove enforceable and make it either impossible or impracticable to develop the land.

A single premium of £525 was paid on 7 May 1965. Three days later, on 10 May 1965, the insurance cover commenced, though the actual policy was not issued until 1 June 1966 because the Royal Insurance Co. was making arrangements for the re-insurance of part of the risk. The policy provided that in the event of any person or persons at any time within a period of 30 years (from 10 May 1965) claiming to be entitled to enforce the restrictive covenant, the insurance company would indemnify Soole & Son Ltd against certain specified losses; it continued, 'In the event of any claim being made against the Insured which is covered by this Policy the Company shall be entitled at its own expense and in the name of the Insured to take or defend legal proceedings'.

Though the insurance company had not been told that neighbours had already indicated their intention to enforce the restrictive covenant before the premium was paid on 7 May 1965, they were nevertheless aware that such proceedings were taking place by the time they issued the backdated policy in June 1966, for on 28 May 1965, Mr and Mrs Hayman, together with Mr Matthias and Mr Protheroe, who both owned adjoining houses

which formed part of the same estate, issued a summons against Soole & Son Ltd that they were entitled to the benefit of the restrictive covenant.

At the beginning of 1966 the Royal Insurance Co. Ltd took over the conduct of their insureds' defence. In May 1966 the insurers through their solicitors decided to consult an eminent leading counsel who gave an opinion which was less confident than previous counsels that the restrictive covenant did not ensure for the benefit of adjoining owners and was not annexed to adjoining plots of land. Nevertheless, the insurers continued to control the conduct of the defence.

On 16 November 1966 judgment was given that the covenants were not void for uncertainty and were validly annexed to each of the respective properties of the plaintiffs so as to entitle them severally to the benefit of the covenants, but that was without prejudice as to whether or not the covenants were still enforceable.

Mr Soole then took the only course which appeared to be open to him and which he believed, should things go amiss, would be covered by insurance. In the spring of 1967 he told the owners of the three neighbouring properties that he intended to carry out a development of six houses at 196 Kew Road, as originally proposed. The three neighbours applied for an injunction which would prevent

(continued)

more than one house being built. It was granted on 6 December 1967.

On 11 April 1967, Soole & Son Ltd assigned the benefit of their insurance policy to Mr Soole. The following month Mr Soole claimed an indemnity under the policy from the Royal Insurance Co. Ltd. However, the insurance company denied liability claiming that the loss fell outside the terms of the policy, for Mr and Mrs Hayman had indicated that they would take legal action against the plaintiff before the date on which the policy started. The risk insured against was confined to loss, damage or expense from claims to enforce the restrictive covenant only when those claims arose between the policy's commencement date 30 years later. However, the plaintiff maintained that the defendants were estopped from setting up this plea because of their conduct after January 1966, when having become aware of all the circumstances, they continued to control the defence of the proceedings originally brought by Mr and Mrs Hayman.

In giving judgment for the plaintiff, it was held that though the plaintiff's claim had been intimated before the commencement of the policy, the consequences of that claim were not excluded from the scope of the indemnity given by the policy. Yet, Shaw, J. remarked obiter that the assumption of the control of the defence of the proceedings was equivocal and did not necessarily imply a representation by the insurance company that they regarded the claim as one which must give rise to a liability to indemnify the plaintiff.

Soole v. *Royal Insurance Co. Ltd.*, unreported.

than the liability of the insured to the third party, nothing in the Act will affect the rights of the third party against the insured in respect of the balance. Moreover, the Act imposes a duty on the insured, his representative or the insurers to give such information as may be reasonably requested by the third party to establish whether or not any rights may have been transferred to him from the insured. Any clause within a contract of insurance will be of no effect if it prevents or prohibits the giving of such information.

Q. I have heard the word 'subrogation' used in connection with insurance policies, what does it mean?

Upon the insurer paying to the assured the amount which had been lost, subject to the various terms of the insurance policy there may arise a right of subrogation in favour of the insurer.

Subrogation may be defined as the substitution of one person or thing for another, so that the same rights and duties which attached to the original person or thing attach to the substituted one. If one person is subrogated to another, he is said to 'stand in that other's shoes'.

One of the rights of the insurer upon payment of a claim is the right of subrogation. In other words, where the insurer pays for a total loss, either of the whole or in the case of goods of any apportionable part, of the subject-matter insured, he thereupon becomes entitled to take over the interest of the assured in whatever may remain of the subject-matter so paid for and he is thereby subrogated to all the rights and remedies of the assured in and in respect of that subject-matter as from the time of the casualty causing the loss.

Q. What does estoppel mean in insurance terms?

In an insurance claim the question of estoppel may occasionally arise. Estoppel may be defined as the rule of evidence or doctrine of law which precludes a person from denying the truth of some statement formerly made by him, or the existence of facts which he has by words or conduct led others to believe in. If a person by a representation induces another to change his position on the faith of it, he cannot afterwards deny the truth of his representation.

EIGHT

What is my pre-contract

liability?

8.1 LIABILITY FOR SURVEYING

Q. What is my liability in surveying a new site for a client?

An architect, engineer, surveyor or other professional should, as a matter of course, thoroughly survey a new site to avoid designing a structure which would infringe or interfere with the rights of others. If this occurs, he may be liable in damages.

Although an architect is to visit the site and carry out an initial appraisal, it is to be inferred from the RIBA Architects' Appointment that the preliminary or basic services which an architect will normally provide places no greater personal obligation upon him to search and find background information concerned with the site than specifically to ask the client to provide such information on the ownership of land, lessees, easements, encroachments, underground services,

rights of way and support, boundary fences and other enclosures and restrictions affecting the land. To accept without checking information about the site given by a client or some person unauthorized by a client is unwise.

For example, in *Columbus Co.* v. *Clowes* [1903] 1 K.B. 244, Mr Clowes was an architect who was commissioned by Columbus Co. Ltd to prepare plans and specifications for a factory and offices to be built on land in the City of London. Mr Clowes was informed by a former employee of the company, who had no authority from them to give any such information, that the site in question was of certain dimensions which were in fact considerably less than the real dimensions of the site. The architect assumed that this information was correct and without taking any steps to measure and survey the site drew his plans on the assumption that the site was smaller than it actually was. Wright, J. remarked that it was the architect's duty 'to have surveyed the site and measured it and taken out the proper dimensions before proceeding with his plans'.

Q. Must I physically survey a site, or can I rely on any documents?

To determine the boundaries of a site by relying on information contained within the title deeds or on Ordnance Survey maps, which may be drawn to such a small scale that simple enlargement leads to error or which may be out of date, is as ineffectual in discharging one's duty of skill and care as, in some cases, relying on information about the encumbrances of land deposited with the Office of Local Land Charges.

For example, in *Mower* v. *Hurr* [1983], a dispute arose over the ownership of an area of land which lay between a roadway at the front of a lodge and the well-established hedge which enclosed it. The plan showing ownership of each part of the land was unclear for several reasons. It was drawn to so small a scale (1 : 2500) that it did not show the disputed area; the road ran alongside or very close to the wall of the lodge; and the precise boundary did not tally with the position on the ground whereby, in 1978, the parties to the conveyancing of the hedge intended the disputed land should be included in the sale. Furthermore, although a surveyor did take detailed measurements of the site which were inserted on the plan, they only related to the rear of the property, no one felt the need to record the dimensions in the front of the lodge. So acrimonious was the dispute that the Court of Appeal remarked unfavourably upon the use of small-scale plans which are seldom satisfactory in indicating precise boundaries. Such acrimonious disputes could easily be avoided if a degree of care had been take in the preparation of plans.

The failure of an architect, engineer, surveyor or other professional to exercise reasonable skill and care in producing an inaccurate survey renders him liable to a client for any reasonable cost in making good the plans. Nevertheless, the client is under an equal obligation to act reasonably, not to incur unnecessary expense.

It would be reasonable for you first to be given the opportunity to correct the drawings and make good the plans without charge; indeed, you would be bound to do so. If, however, the clients had called in another architect or other professional, he would in all probability insist on beginning afresh and refuse to make any use of your existing plans. That, then, would be a reasonable course for the client to pursue.

Q. If I get a survey wrong, for how much will I be liable?

The assessment of what are reasonable damages fluctuates by as much as what is considered reasonable skill and care, where you are commissioned to carry out a structural or measured survey on behalf of a client who then buys the property on the strength of the report which turns out to be inaccurate.

There is no universal rule for damages. Generally the proper measure of damages is the cost of repair of the defects, which a proper inspection by a competent surveyor would have brought to light, rather than the difference between the purchase price and the value of the property as it should have been described.

Q. When and in what detail should I do a soil survey to discharge my duty of skill and care?

Of all the unknown quantities in building, the substructure is the most variable, often the result of limited or no preparatory investigations. Careful and detailed soil surveys are, as a general rule, vital to avoid liability in this area.

A number of criteria have been foward as suitable for determining the detail in which a soil survey should be done to find out the load-bearing capacity of the soil, including the nature of the substrata, the watertable, etc., the weight of the proposed building and its estimated cost relative to the cost of trial holes, bores or percussion tests, the acceptable levels of settlement and the extent of existing knowledge on ground conditions in the area. All these have inherent weaknesses. A low-cost, light-weight building in a place with which you are familiar may suggest that a detailed survey is unnecessary, especially if ground conditions in the area are normally good and reliable. Such a presumption may be foolhardy.

You must take the consequences if you accept the results of soil tests taken by a previous employee of your client which turn out to be false or insufficient and you have not examined the ground to determine the correct design of the foundations. This may be considered your bounden duty, especially when the cost estimates for substructure work may be wildly inaccurate. Even carrying out what may be considered, in some circumstances, a full and detailed survey with the correct type of soil investigation may be insufficient to discharge the duty of skill and care in others.

For example, engineers were held liable in damages when on being commissioned to design a pumping station they carried out boreholes on a grid pattern over the entire site apart from the centre where there was a mature oak which marked the position of the pumping station. From the boreholes it was found that the substrate was clay. A figure for excavating this was agreed with the contractors and entered into the bills of quantity. On felling the oak, it was found that a stratum of rock rose up directly under its roots. The foundations, contrary to the information gained from the boreholes, had to be blasted through rock which

significantly increased the substructure costs to the extent that the client's budget was exceeded. In another case, an architect was brought into an action on the grounds of contributory negligence, against an engineer employed under a separate contract to the architect for failing to carry out the correct type of soil tests. Pits were dug, not boreholes, though the site was known to be particularly bad. It was argued that the architect, being in total control of the contract, should have insisted on boreholes being drilled by the engineer. They were not, and the architect did not forcibly bring it to the attention of the client.

A question of negligence will arise where there has been a failure to use 'reasonable' skill and care in making sufficiently exhaustive enquiries as to soil conditions and, as a result, failing to give proper advice to a client, the advice being neither accurate nor correct. Thus you may be found negligent in not making the proper enquiries which a competent practitioner would do as to whether or not there had been trees on a site whose subsoil was clay, and on finding that there had been, causing moisture content and plastic limit tests to be carried out.

8.2 THE EFFECT OF PRIVATE RIGHTS, EASEMENTS, RESTRICTIVE COVENANTS AND PROFITS *À PRENDRE*

Q. What is the difference between an easement and a natural right?

A major difference between an easement and a natural right is that an easement has to be acquired, while a natural right automatically exists and is protected by a right to damages or an injunction for nuisance if it is infringed. An example of a natural right is the right of a landowner to have his land supported by that of his neighbour. The support must not be removed by the latter.

However, there is no natural right of support for a building by other buildings. Thus when a building is demolished, no support need be provided for adjacent buildings. Nevertheless, care is needed in this respect as a right to have a building supported by other buildings can be acquired as an easement.

Q. What is the difference between an easement and a restrictive covenant?

An easement and a restrictive covenant are, in some respects, similar:

1. Both allow the owner of land to restrict the use a neighbour makes of his own land;
2. Both require a dominant and servient tenement to exist;
3. Some types of negative rights may exist under either an easement or a restrictive covenant – e.g. rights to light, air, water or support.

However, in other respects, they differ; in contrast to a restrictive covenant, an easement:

1. Exists at law as well as in equity;
2. It may be acquired by long enjoyment, that is by prescription.

Essentially a restrictive covenant is negative in nature, for example, it may be used to preserve an amenity of a particular area. It should be noted that usually the original covenantor will continue to be liable on the restrictive covenant as his liability is contractual, even if he has parted with the servient tenement. The person to whom it is assigned will be bound by the restrictive covenant only in the following:

1. The restrictive covenant is by nature negative, even if the words used in connection with it are positive; one test is to ask whether or not the restrictive covenant requires money to be spent; if the covenantor has to put his hand into his pocket it will not be negative;
2. The restrictive covenant is made for the protection of land retained by the covenantee; thus where he parts with all such land (with some exceptions), he will not be able to enforce the covenant;
3. There must be an intention that the burden of the restrictive covenant will run with the covenantor's land; clearly, if only the covenantor is bound by the words of the restrictive covenant, then the assignees of his land will not be bound;
4. Only equitable remedies, such as an injunction, are available to enforce a restrictive covenant, for example, for the demolition of a building which has been put up in breach of a restrictive covenant designed to protect a view; damages may be awarded where an injunction or specific performance could have been granted, though you are not entitled to insist upon damages if you make out your case, nor if you cannot be awarded an injunction; and furthermore, an injunction may be refused where the character of an area has been so completely changed that the restrictive covenant is valueless.

Q. What is my liability in respect of nuisance or trespass?

In the design of a new building, and its location within the site, care must be taken not to infringe any existing covenants and so cause trespass or nuisance. Similarly, care should be taken to stop or prevent any which already exist and have been adopted by the client, through his very ownership of the land. A nuisance will also be adopted if the client makes use of that which causes it, or does nothing to bring it to an end through having knowledge, or presumed knowledge, about it and ample time to stop it.

Failure by an architect or other professional who is in a position to take effective steps to prevent the nuisance by advising the client in an appropriate manner is a breach of the duty of care which is owed not merely to the client, but also to neighbours as well. However, ignorance may be a defence as no one is liable for nuisance unless he either created it or continued it after it coming to his knowledge, provided that the lack of knowledge was not due to failing to use reasonable care to discover the facts.

For example, a person may be considered free from liability after having had built on their land a wall which, due to its pressure, fractures a sewer running some 3 m beneath it if they were ignorant of the sewer's existence and could not reasonably be expected to know of it.

Q. To what extent must I advise my client on restrictive covenants?

It is your duty, particularly if you are an architect, to advise your client on the discharge or modification of restrictive covenants as they affect freehold land.

It would be almost impossible to obtain a declaration that a restrictive covenant after 1925 is not enforceable. Nevertheless, under the *Law of Property Act 1969*, the Land Tribunal can order the modification or discharge of a covenant, subject to the payment of compensation to those who would suffer trivial injury, because it impedes some reasonable use of the land or is contrary to the public interest by impeding the user.

Furthermore, a covenant can be deemed obsolete where its original purpose can no longer be achieved because, for example, the character of the property has changed or the neighbourhood has altered.

Q. I am an architect, to what extent must I advise my client on easements such as a right of support?

An architect is under an obligation not merely to consult the client about easements, that is any limitations which may exist as to the use of the land because of the rights of adjoining owners or the public, such as the right of support, but more important, to advise on their discharge and the ways in which their infringement can be avoided. Failure to so advise may be indicative of the negligent performance of your personal contractual duty to your client to exercise reasonable skill and care.

In the case of the right of support, an easement is unnecessary to support land as it is a natural right which follows upon the ownership of property. However, the mere withdrawal of support is not of itself a nuisance, it only becomes wrongful if and when subsidence occurs.

For example, a landowner whose land has subsided and the buildings standing on it subsequently crack because support from the adjacent land has been withdrawn may be entitled to recover not merely damages for the injury to his land, but also for his buildings, although in the case of the latter there is no natural right of support. Nevertheless, an easement may be acquired, either expressly by grant or deed or impliedly by prescription, which is similar in character to a natural right.

You should ensure that there have been no previous excavations which are likely to cause subsidence as a result of present excavations, although the latter by themselves pose no danger. This is because liability for damages rests with the person who made the excavation and not on the lessee or owner in possession at the date of subsidence. If an excavation if made under the same land by another person and subsidence is caused, the person making the second excavation will be liable for all damage caused by the subsidence, even though there would have been no subsidence but for the first excavation.

Q. What is the effect of interfering with a right of light?

If you carelessly design a building which interferes with the light reaching a window, not merely a doorway or a piece of open ground, not specifically designed to admit light to a building, you will be liable as the originator of the nuisance for all damages which naturally flow from it. As with the right of support, so too with the right of light, that the person liable for the nuisance is the one who actually created it, even though he cannot prevent its continuance because he does not own the building.

Light, like air, is the common property of all, or more accurately, it is the common right of all to enjoy it, but it is the exclusive property of none. There is no natural right to light as there is a right of support for land, but a legal right, a negative easement which may prevent the owner or occupier of adjoining property from building anything which obstructs or obscures the ancient light of the dominant tenement.

Difficulties arise where attempts to create an easement of light are made by a simple deed. Although the deed is sufficient where the title is unregistered to bind all future owners of the burdened land, whether or not they know about the easement, it is insufficient where the title is registered. Under section 19 of the *Land Registration Act 1925*, as amended in 1936, any disposition of property such as the creation of an easement is merely equitable and only a minor interest which will not bind a purchaser – i.e. the easement is not protected by an entry on the Land Register.

Q. What are my liabilities if I interfere with private rights?

It is your duty, if you are an architect, to discover any private rights which would affect a new building. If the building does interfere with a neighbour's right, the client may be left open to a mandatory injunction requiring him to demolish the offending part of the structure, or an action for damages which he may recover from you. Damages can be assessed so as to include the loss in value of the entire site, though it is not yet suitable for development, and not just the value of the part which is affected.

Whether or not a new building does affect another's rights can be established by expert evidence. Only where it cannot be so established by the balance of probabilities will you avoid liability. For example, in respect to a right of light in order to give a right of action and sustain the issue, there must be a substantial privation of light, sufficient to render the occupation of a building uncomfortable and to prevent the occupier from carrying on his accustomed business on the premises as beneficially as he had formally done.

Some slight inconvenience caused to a neighbour, such as the result of your advising the client as a matter of course to use the building site to its best advantage, should be distinguished from real injury which severely affects a neighbour's enjoyment of his property. In the former, the case itself may not be actionable because the damage is so minimal or the adjoining owner is being purely vexatious in his objections. Where it is actionable, a value may be placed upon the damage as adequate compensation for any loss. The owner of a dominant tenement cannot claim the right to more light merely by altering his building, thereby placing an additional burden on the servient tenement, for example, by putting new windows into a room which has been so built as to be poorly lit. Equally, an easement giving a right of light is not diminished by the use to which a room is put. If an owner chooses in future to use a well-lighted room for a storeroom for which little light is required, he does not lose his right to use the same room or building for some other purpose for which more light is required.

When a room in a building receives light through windows or different sides which are ancient lights, the owners of land on either side can generally only build to the same height as a building on the opposite side, so that together they would not cause a nuisance by obstructing too much light and so making the room unpleasant because it was dimly lit. Though in deciding the extent of damages, the effect of both external and internal reflected light should be considered, together with the amount of clearly visible sky, and the actual distance of the new building to the existing: the closer it is, the more unpleasant it may be for the occupiers of an existing building.

Q. Are there any guidelines to indicate whether or not a right to light has been substantially interfered with?

The calculation that no one is or ever will be entitled to more light than amounts to not less than 1 lumen over 50% of a room at table level is questionable.

Its universal application is unsuitable to decide whether the design of a new building is such that it substantially infringes an easement because what is a socially acceptable standard of lighting has increased since the calculation was originally devised.

The truth may well be that the standards of light required by normal inhabitants are increasing, and it is hardly to be doubted that they will increase because modern offices are built on the whole with more light than old offices. Moreover, the general nature of the locality should be considered, that is whether the building is in an industrial or residential area, or indeed an area of some other nature.

Q. What is my liability for designing a building which interrupts a view?

The erection of a building may not be considered a nuisance merely because it was built in such a way as to interrupt a view or to invade a neighbour's privacy, but it may be unlawful because it might be a breach of the Building Regulations. It demands that more attention be given in the initial survey to an examination of the site's surroundings.

For example, in *Re Trafford's Application*, owners of a farm objected to a covenant being modified by their neighbours so as to allow two dormer windows to be built into their bungalow roof on the grounds that the windows would detract from the view seen from the farm. They would result in a loss of harmony with the other bungalows. The Land Tribunal held that the restriction impeded a reasonable use of the land without securing any practical benefit of substantial value for which £500 would be adequate compensation. Yet is has been found that there would be a serious loss of privacy if a restrictive covenant which secured a practical benefit of substantial advantage by preventing any further building to take place on a property was altered to permit the building of a four-bedroomed house in part of the garden of an existing house, although planning permission had been granted for it.

Q. What is an easement?

An easement is a right which an owner of land may acquire over another's land. For example, a right of way or a right of light.

An easement must satisfy a number of criteria in order to exist:

1. There must be a dominant and a servient tenement; that is, if Mr Selwyn owns Sospan Fach and grants a right to use a path across Sospan Fach to Mr Davies, the owner of Dolmanol, on a neighbouring piece of land, then Sospan Fach is the servient tenement and Dolmanol the dominant tenement. If Mr Selwyn had granted the right to Mr Owen, who owned no land, the latter would have acquired a licence to walk over Sospan Fach, but his right could not exist as an easement as there is no dominant tenement;
2. The easement must accommodate the dominant tenement; in other words, there must be a benefit to the land or dominant tenement, otherwise the right cannot exist as an easement. Furthermore, the servient tenement must be sufficiently near to the dominant tenement to give to it a practical benefit;
3. The dominant and servient tenements must be owned and occupied by different people: one cannot have an easement over one's own land or rights against oneself;

4. The easement must be able to form the subject of a grant by being created by a deed; this principle applies even where an easement is established by its long use, it merely gives rise to a presumption to this effect.

Q. If I have planning permission for a scheme, will I be liable if I breach a restrictive covenant?

Planning permission, whether it is granted by the local planning authority to an individual or to itself, does not authorize the breach of a restrictive covenant.

There are certain exceptions to this general principle. Where a local authority has either acquired land or appropriated land which it already owns for development, then the erection, construction, carrying out or maintenance of any building or work on that land in accordance with planning permission is authorized by statute, even if a restrictive covenant is breached. When a restrictive covenant is breached in this way, the owner may claim compensation.

Q. My client believes he has a profit *à prendre*, what does this mean and how does it differ from an easement?

A profit à prendre is essentially a right to take something from another person's land which is part of that land, such as minerals, crops, timber or wild animals existing on it, and is capable of being owned at the time it is taken. A profit *à prendre* differs from an easement, in that it need not be appurtenant to the land.

Q. How does an easement come into existence?

A legal easement exists only when it is held for an interest equivalent to a fee simple absolute in possession or terms of years absolute and is created by the following:

(1) *Statute* – for example, a public utility may be given certain rights by an act in connection with the laying of gas and water pipes, sewers or electricity cables;

(2) *Deed* – no particular form of words need be used if an easement is created by deed. However, an easement cannot be created so as to take effect at some time in the future; thus a developer who is selling plots of land cannot create easements in advance of each sale. An implied easement may also arise from an express grant of land, for example, in *Wong* v. *Beaumont Property Trust Ltd.* [1965] 1 Q.B. 173, a landlord let cellars to a tenant who covenanted to:

(a) use them as a restaurant;
(b) eliminate smells;
(c) comply with health regulations.

Neither the landlord nor the tenant knew that this could not lawfully be done without installing a ventilation system; it was held that the tenant had an easement of necessity to construct such a system, partly on the landlord's part of the property, and use it.

(3) *Prescription* – an easement may be created by its long enjoyment or continuous use as of right. In other words, it must be enjoyed without the use of force, without secrecy and without permission. The user must be with certain limited exceptions by or on behalf of a fee simple owner against a fee simple owner. There must be a continuity of enjoyment which is without excessive intervals. There are three methods by which an easement can arise by prescriptions:

(a) Common law, where there has been a continuous user as of right from time immemorial, which is fixed at 1189 as the limit of legal memory. For practical purposes, if 20 years' use can be established, the court will presume that it has continued since 1189;

(b) Lost modern grant, overcame the possibility that if use was established as beginning after 1189 prescription at common law would be lost. It presumes from long use that an easement had been granted after 1189 but prior to the user supporting the claim and that the deed of grant has been lost;

(c) The *Prescription Act 1832* provides that:
   (i) an easement enjoyed for 20 years as of right and without interruption cannot be defeated by proof that use began after 1189;
   (ii) an easement enjoyed for 40 years as of right and without interruption is deemed absolute and indefeasible unless enjoyed by written consent.

NINE

What is my design

liability?

9.1 EFFECT OF POOR DESIGN

Q. What is my liability for design?

The law does not usually imply a warranty from the architect or the engineer when employed to design a structure that where the work is carried out to his design the desired result will be achieved, but rather that he will use reasonable skill and care. Yet a reasonable standard of skill and care changes and is extended; as building products develop new skills are required.

The positive duty placed upon the architect and engineer to use reasonable skill and care may lead to 'defensive design', the oversizing of structural members (whether or not new or traditional materials are selected) with the attendant increase in construction costs. It is justifiable only because of a fear that a structure will fail early in its life, though considerable care may have been taken in its design, and a professional fear of increased liability, a desire to escape the principle of 1% to blame 100% liable for damages.

The failure of a building of ordinary design and well-used construction could in itself be evidence of a lack of competent skill on the part of an architect. But simply to state that there has been a negligent lack of care and skill, except in the simplest and most obvious cases, is insufficient; and indeed quite unjust without calling the 'best evidence', which need not necessarily be the evidence of experts. The 'best evidence' is actual documentary evidence, which in money cases unhappily cannot be produced.

Should the design result in a constructional or technical defect which can be proved to stem from the architect's or engineer's breach of duty, all the costs which result from it may be recovered by the client though he has given the plans, specification and other contract documents his approval; while approval by a client of an aesthetic detail in the design may be an adequate discharge of personal liability, provided it does not affect the property's commercial value.

A cautionary tale of always making sure your design works

A warehouse and some office accommodation were constructed as part of a group of four similar buildings in Brewery Road, London. The architects carried out the detailed design for the speculative development.

There was trouble with the four warehouses due to ingress of water and flooding. In January 1977 after the architects recommended additional rainwater drainage, the developers sought a quotation for modifications to the drainage system and these were carried out during that year.

The original design as built provided a roof and gutters made of asbestos. The gutters were valley gutters situated between the roofs, and it was necessary for the gutter outlets to be run through the inside of the building. These gutter outlets led to a downpipe which after it reached a point where the gutter pipes converged on the downpipe went diagonally from right to left and then led into a manhole in the basement. Thus there was only one outlet from each of the two gutters and one downpipe into which these two outlets led. This downpipe led into one manhole. All the pipes were 150 mm in diameter.

The modifications which were carried out were of two types. First, in all four buildings two extra gutter outlets were introduced into each gutter making three in all per gutter, together with upstands to prevent overflows. Secondly, in the case of three of the buildings (but not no. 12), an additional outlet was provided which led to an extra manhole, so that gutters could be led out of the building in two different ways by means of two exit pipes.

At no. 12, this was not done, with the result that the water from the gutter could still outflow through only one pipe, with all six pipes leading to this one outlet. Apparently it had been considered impracticable to employ the same extent of modification to no. 12 as to the other three buildings because the area leading out of the building had a reverse fall. Thus instead of the water running away from the building as it did in the other three, it would run back into the building if the second manhole had been built.

The guttering system employed had obvious dangers in the event of overflow. An eaves gutter would have caused an overflow to be thrown outside the building, whereas the drainage system designed and used posed a threat to the inside of the building. It was therefore a less safe system with greater risk of damage if anything went wrong.

The architects designed the building such that the drainage could cope with 75 mm of water per hour, which was a generally accepted standard. Two floods occurred on 2 June and 9 July 1981 which damaged the lessee's stocks of materials stored in no. 12. The first flood was not discovered until about 9 a.m., the storm had occurred during the early hours of the morning. The loss adjuster's report had stated that it was quite evident that the rainwater pipes serving the gully around the pitched roof were unable to cope with the excessive rain and that the water rose above the flashings and penetrated into the building. The water first of all collected on the ground floor, but eventually reached the basement.

The second storm on 9 July was even worse. Significantly more damage was caused to the plaintiff's stored materials. This storm and flooding occurred in the afternoon. The pipes seemed to be bursting in different places with joints blowing, and water was pouring down the walls. There was a rushing noise at the manhole (this suggested that it was not blocked).

None of the other three buildings suffered such flood damage. The lessees subsequently had remedial works carried out including a second outlet pipe leading to a second manhole.

It was held that whatever the position when the original design was constructed, it had become apparent that modifications were required to the stormwater drainage system at the time when three of the four buildings were modified. However, in the case of no. 12 these modifications did not include the provision of a second outlet pipe descending into a second manhole. It ought to have become

(continued)

apparent to the architects that, for whatever reason, something additonal was required.

The cause of the flooding was that no. 12 lacked a second outlet and manhole. The architects when they designed the remedial works should have appreciated that there was a risk of internal flooding and damage to no. 12. The lessees had not had the building surveyed professionally before they took on their lease.

It was normal practice in cases of commercial leases to have buildings surveyed even when new. Had there been a survey, it may well have revealed to an expert surveyor that the stormwater drainage system was not adequate.

It was held that the lessees' failure to employ surveyors was not such as to absolve the architects of all liability. However, there was some degree of contributory negligence on their part in failing to have a professional survey, and this contributed to the floods and the damage caused.

D. Landau & Sons Ltd. v. *The Hind Woodhouse Partnership,* (1987) unreported.

Q. To what extent will I be liable for another professional's designs?

A professional such as an architect or an engineer may remain liable where he has delegated design work to a specialist subcontractor, particularly where he has had no authority from his client to delegate the design of any part of that structure. However, under the RIBA Conditions of Engagement, an architect may nominate a suitable specialist to carry out work which he is not equipped to do himself. Thus where the conditions are part of the architect's contract, he will normally carry no legal responsibility for the work to be done by the expert.

For example, in *Investors in Industry Commercial Properties* v. *South Bedfordshire District Council* [1986] Q.B. 1034, a firm of architects designed four warehouses on an infill site in Leighton Buzzard. The foundations were designed by structural engineers. Their design was totally inadequate. Within a few months of practical completion two of the warehouses broke up and had to be demolished. The owners claimed approximately £600 000 from the local authority which had approved the foundation plans. The local authority brought in as third parties the architects and the structural engineers; the structural engineers were uninsured and therefore the case against them was dropped. However, the case against the architects was continued as they were insured. It was found that the local authority had not come near to establishing that the architects were in breach of their professional duty in failing to reject the foundation plans.

Q. Do I have a duty to warn of defects caused by poor design?

A term may be implied into a JCT contract which imposes upon the contractor a duty to warn the client and architect if he has reason to believe that the design is or has become defective. Likewise, an architect may owe a duty to the contractor, by implying a term within a JCT contract to warn him if the contractor is making a serious and potentially expensive error in defective design.

Two cautionary tales of being on your guard for design defects, from the contractor's and architect's points of view

A development company retained a firm of architects and a main contractor for the construction of a new office block in Ashford, Kent, under a JCT 63 building contract.

The curtain walling for the office was designed, supplied and fixed by nominated subcontractors. The design was defective, the building, which was particularly exposed on its south face, let in rainwater. The subcontractors' attempts to remedy the problem failed.

The architects had sent the main contractors copies of the nominated subcontractors' drawings. The main contractors were aware of difficulties which occurred in applying sealants in accordance with the drawings, they lacked 'buildability'. The nominated subcontractors went into liquidation. The development company sued the architects and the main contractors.

It was held that there was to be implied into the contract between the development company and the main contractors a term requiring the latter to warn of design defects as soon as they came to believe that they existed.

The main contractors also owed to the development company and the architects a common law duty to inform the architects of design defects known to them. However, the main contractors would up to the time when they discovered the lack of 'buildability' probably have been entitled to an indemnity from the architects, and as the architects were the development company's agent, from the latter as well. Once the main contractors had discovered the defect, they should have given notice of it. They did not do so and were therefore liable.

Equitable Debenture Assets Corporation Limited v. *William Moss Group Limited & Others* [1985] 2 Constr.L.J. 131.

In 1963, Manchester University entered into a JCT 63 contract with main contractors for erecting student accommodation and an ancillary complex. The university's architects had designed a reinforced concrete structure, partly clad in ceramic tiles and partly in brickwork.

The waterproofing of concrete buildings with ceramic tiles was at the time a novel application. In many respects, the design was defective. It failed to protect the ceramic tiles from rain and insufficient attention had been given to the building problems of fixing the tiles. The architects specified that the tiles should be fixed using a grout which was not waterproof. In time many of the tiles fell off.

The university sued the architects for breach of contract and negligence. It was found that there was an implied term in JCT 63 requiring the contractors to warn the university of design defects of which they became aware. They had complied with this duty in notifying the architects of their concern that in the light of their general knowledge and practical experience, they had come to believe that an aspect of the design was wrong. Belief that there were defects required more than mere doubt as to the correctness of the design, but less than actual knowledge of errors.

Furthermore, because of proximity architects may sometimes owe a duty of care to contractors, even in relation to how they carry out their work. For example, if an architect knew that on a site with which they were concerned contractors or subcontractors were making a major mistake which would involve the contractors in expense, then the architects would probably owe a duty to the contractors to warn them.

Victoria University of Manchester v. *Hugh Wilson & Lewis Womersley & Pochin (Contractors) Ltd.* (1984) CILL.126.

Q. How is my liability affected if I use new design concepts or materials?

You may not be negligent if the state of knowledge at the time when the building was designed indicated that the design was satisfactory. Subsequently acquired knowledge cannot convert a design accepted by competent members of the profession at the time into a faulty design.

Where the design is at the frontiers of technical knowledge and only later knowledge can prove how defective the design was, you nevertheless have a contractual duty to ensure that the design will not be negligently erected. The law requires even pioneers to be prudent. The graver the foreseeable consequences of failure to take care, the greater is the necessity for circumspection. Those who engage in operations which are inherently dangerous must take precautions which are not required of persons engaged in the ordinary routine of daily life.

Q. How may I best discharge my design duties and liabilities?

Where a constructional technique is involved, your duty of reasonable skill and care may be discharged not merely by warning the client of the risks, but also of taking the best advice available on the matter. You can either advise your client to employ consultants himself or you can do so, with the client's clear knowledge and consent, to undertake some part of the design work with which you are unfamiliar.

You are effectively obliged continually to update your knowledge to ensure that new developments within the profession are incorporated into your practice. However, this does not imply that every new technique or material proposed in professional literature should be adopted immediately. It is only when a new technique has been proved and accepted as good and used as an invariable practice in the profession that you are at fault in failing to adopt it. Equally, you would be lacking in your duty of skill and care if you continued to use techniques and materials which, though having the reputation of being traditional, tended to lead to defects rather than discard them.

To suggest that while you are not required to read every article appearing in the technical press, you should nevertheless have a thorough knowledge of all technical information, even on a single product, ranging as it does from manufacturers' literature, Agreement Certificates and British Standard Code of Practice (BSCP), is an ideal which bends to practical commerical necessity. This is not merely because the quantity of the information is so great and the quality of the information given so variable, but also because of continuous innovations in techniques and new materials being introduced.

There is a tendency for those who specialize in a particular aspect of architecture, engineering or construction to be more aware of and have a greater knowledge of developments within that field than one who is in a general practice. Arguably, a greater responsiblity and a higher degree of the duty of skill and care should be attached to those who hold themselves out as being especially skilled in a particular field.

Q. How is my liability affected when I specify certain materials to be included in my design?

Despite the large number of new products available to designers, a conservative attitude prevails when specifying materials. This is often the result of lack of time available for:

1. making decisions;
2. checking thoroughly each product and component on every job.

A cautious attitude can itself be a great weakness. Materials may be preferred which have been used for some time before by others and those which are considered a 'failed product' avoided. This attitude to materials is often adopted regardless of the underlying reasons:

1. Lack of quality in design and workmanship due to cost restrictions;
2. Lack of testing small models or prototypes to aid selection;
3. An unwillingness to admit to a lack of experience and knowledge, thus strongly relying on the 'office memory' which could be suspect;
4. The acceptance of manufacturers' advice and recommendations as being reliable though further enquiries may indicate that it is questionable.

In the case of (4), it is a contractual duty either specifically stated or implied that materials specified will be fit for their purpose. If they are not, you may be held liable, especially where the materials are relatively new and it is found that thorough enquiries as to their suitability have not been made.

For example, in the British Columbian case of *Sealand of the Pacific* v. *Robert C. McHafie Ltd.* (1974) 2 Build L.R. 74, it was found that a contractual duty was owed by naval architects to their clients to make further enquiries as to the suitability of concrete products to be used for alterations to an underwater aquarium which would have revealed their unsuitability and not have relied on the supplier's faulty recommendations.

Again, in *Pirelli General Cable Works Ltd* v. *Oscar Faber & Partners (a Firm)*, [1983] 2 W.L.R. 6, a breach in duty of skill and care resulted from the consultant engineers specifying a relatively new material for the refractory inner lining of a chimney which was so unsuitable for the purpose that cracks developed and the chimney had to be partly demolished and replaced.

The question which immediately arises is: where does one stop seeking information after having one's own design model tested if not to rely on the one body who presumably knows most about it, namely the manufacturer who developed the material. It is a sad reflection that a manufacturer may be under an obligation to give honest, factual, provable performance specification information yet that information can be presented in such a way that it implies the product is more acceptable than it actually is in order to encourage its commercial success.

For example, due to the rapid growth in the market for insulation brought about among other things, by tighter Building Regulations requiring higher thermal resistance in buildings, manufacturers of urea formaldehyde foam strongly marketed the product. No mention was made that toxic gases and irritant dust particles would be given off after it had been injected into a cavity whose internal face was not totally sealed. Although the foam was accepted in the UK, it was banned both in Canada and the USA.

Where such materials are being considered, the client should be advised of their advantages and disadvantages in order to reach a valid decision as to their use. If the materials are used by reason of your own personal decision rather than on the client's express instructions, you may leave yourself more open to an action for failing in your duty of skill and care to the client if the materials prove to be inadequate.

9.2 DESIGN COPYRIGHT

Q. In what circumstances am I liable for breach of copyright if I use someone else's design?

An architect who is a member of the RIBA is under a professional obligation to make 'reasonable' enquiries and to notify any other architect who has been working or is commissioned to carry out work on the same scheme by the same client of his own engagement. Such a matter of courtesy sidesteps the issue of copyright, as it does not automatically mean that the architect can use another's design.

The pitfalls are well illustrated in *Meikle* v. *Maufe* [1941] 3 All E.R. 144. Meikle, an architect, had a beneficial interest in the copyright of work of a former practice which he carried on under the names of its original partners, Smith Brewer. The latter was a member of the Heal family who had, in 1912, designed their showrooms in Tottenham Court Road. In 1935, Maufe was engaged to extend the original building. Both he and his clients informed Meikle of this. However, despite a most courteous reply from Meikle, it was held that there could be no implied term that this gave either the client or the architect the right to reproduce the original design, which they had done (though the new design was slightly different) for sound aesthetic and commercial reasons.

Through the *Copyright Act 1956*, if you own the copyright in a design, you may dispose of the right to exploit it in two ways:

1. Assigning the whole copyright and retaining no further interest in the design;
2. Granting a licence to use it.

In the case of the latter you remain the owner of the copyright and if what is granted is a restricted licence, say, to one person to use it on one occasion, then you can subsequently grant further licences to use it again. However, if the copyright is not assigned or an explicit licence granted, then use of your design or 'artistic work' is illegal.

A breach of copyright may amount to a criminal offence, even though the owner may have given some form of acknowledgement to you that your design was going to be used.

Q. What does design copyright mean?

Section 2 of the *Design Copyright Act 1968* defines 'artistic work' as works of architecture being either buildings or models for buildings, irrespective of their artistic quality, paintings, drawings and photographs.

In terms of 'authorship' of the building, copyright is not vested either in the client, unless otherwise agreed, or in the contractor, who is merely part of the machinery employed in the production of the structure which embodies the design and the ideas of the architect. For copyright purposes, the author of the architectural work of art is the author of the original plans, namely the architect.

As for the quality of the design embodied within the plans, this is immaterial to the legal mind, 'I think it unlikely that any legislative would be so addle-pated as to appoint the judiciary to decide whether Frank Lloyd Wright, Palladio, Pheidias, or Corbusier had produced buildings of artistic

A cautionary tale on knowing too little about law

The principles underlaying a statute or embodied within a by-law may be open to a wide variety of interpretation. The multiplicity of the regulations, sometimes written in a confusing style, themselves lead to misunderstanding. On occasion, legal defects are unwittingly designed into a building. *B. L. Holdings Ltd.* v. *Robert J. Wood & Partners* is a case in point, especially when the conclusions of the High Court are compared with those of the Court of Appeal.

In the High Court it was held that the architects, Robert J. Wood & Partners, were negligent and in breach of their duty of skill and care, as professional men who ought to have had sufficient knowledge of legal principles to protect their client's interests; and having gone ahead with a scheme after planning permission was received without warning their client that the policy of the local council to exclude car parking and residential accommodation from an application when considering granting an Office Development Permit was surprising as the policy was incorrect and unlawful and that, therefore, the planning permission was invalid. To have such a breadth and depth of knowledge in such a specialized field as planning law would for many architects be unusual, and would exceed that of one whose daily work it is to interpret the law. The trial judge yet conceded that, 'not a few architects engaged in this work would have been misled in exactly the same way as this architect was', and 'he might well have been followed in error by some lawyers'.

In contrast, the Court of Appeal in overturning the lower court's decision held that the architect was not negligent. In other words, an architect was not required to know more law than an expert in his own field, it could not be expected to be minutely accurate. Conversely, if an architect holds himself out as being an expert, particularly if his personal contract with a client revolves around a speciality, then his duty of skill and care in knowing the law may be greater.

B.L. Holdings Ltd. v. *Robert J. Wood & Partners*, [1979] 123 S.J. 570.

---

character or design in the sense that they are artistically' Stewart, J. in *Haig* v. *Sloan* [1957] 16 Fox Pat.C. 189. For example, in Camden Town, the owner of a fish and chip shop had the front of the shop rebuilt as a copy of a design drawing he had seen. As the drawing was held to be an original literary work, the designer successfully sued the fish and chip shop owner for breach of copyright.

Copyright will not be infringed if a client instructs another architect to use the original design for a building on the site for which it was intended, provided that the first architect's fees have been paid in full. Here the operative word is 'full', for where a purely nominal fee has been agreed and paid by the client for certain drawings, a licence to build is not then automatically assumed to exist particularly if those drawings were intended purely for planning permission.

With the withdrawal of the mandatory fee scale and its replacement by one which is purely a recommendation entirely open to negotiation, it may be more difficult to determine what is a full and appropriate standard fee for similar work when it is carried out by a specialist as against a general practitioner. What is suitable for one may not be so for the other.

Q. Can anyone other than my client use my design drawings?

The implied licence given by you to erect a building on a

particular piece of land from your set of drawings may be extended from your client to another person, for example, the purchaser of that land for which planning permission may have been granted. This may occur, for instance, when it has become uneconomic for the client to proceed any further with the scheme itself. Such a licence takes effect upon payment. The principle is that you impliedly promise that in return for your fee you will give a licence to the owner client to use the plans for the building on that site.

However, in the RIBA Conditions of Appointment which state that unless a minimum of work has been completed up to and including work stage D, an implied licence will not exist. In other words, where the RIBA contract is used, copyright may be infringed where the original architect has not only carried out preliminary services up to D, inception of the scheme feasibility studies and outline proposals, but also where the work involved in illustrating the design in sufficient detail for the client to agree to spatial arrangements, materials, appearance, cost estimates and work programme is incomplete.

Q. How can I stop a breach of my design copyright?

You may apply to the court for an injunction to restrain the breach of copyright. An injunction may not be obtained if building work has already started, though punitive damages for the flagrant infringement of a design could be awarded.

In setting the value of the damages, though all the surrounding circumstances of the case may be taken into account, they would not normally be considered; rather it is the amount of profit which would accrue if you had been commissioned to carry out the infringing building, not the fee which might be charged to reproduce the design.

9.3 EFFECT OF PLANNING AND BUILDING LEGISLATION

Q. To what extent must I know the law as it relates to planning and Building Regulations?

The extent and detail in which you should not only know the law but apply it fluctuates. Differing judgments may serve but to declare that truth lies somewhere if we knew but where. As a matter of principle, you owe a duty of skill and care to discover and then comply with all relevant legislation, check the legality of the work and advise the client on the subject. The 'general' degree of skill and care which you are bound to bring to the performance of any service which you undertake is one of competent knowledge in the general rules of law applicable to the subject.

As a matter of principle, you are liable to the client for any loss he has suffered from your lack of knowledge. Ignorance or disregard of the legal requirements in relation to Building Regulations may result in a fine being levied against the client, together with an enforcement notice being served for the whole or part of the building to be rebuilt in accordance with the regulations. Yet you will not be liable for making a mistake about the law, provided that it is not made carelessly. Though where a building is designed which contravenes the relevant legislation, an opportunity does exist to rectify it by seeking a relaxation or dispensation under section 6 of the *Public Health Act 1961* on the ground that the specified requirements in relation to the particular circumstances of the case are unreasonable.

Though a contract may provide that the builders are to comply with all local authority regulations, by-laws and statutes, the responsibility of the architect remains to ensure that the building actually does. In the circumstances surrounding *Eames London Estates* v. *North Hertfordshire District Council & Others*, (1980) B18. L.R. 50, Judge Fay QC, the official referee, held that liability for breach of statutory duty, as contained within the Building Regulations for example, existed irrespective of negligence. The duty to comply with by-laws is absolute, there is strict liability with no need to prove any negligence. In comparison, it was held in *Worlock* v. *Savis & Rushmoor Borough Council* (1983) 22 B.L.R. 66, C.A. that contractors were not liable for breach of statutory duty imposed by the Building Regulations on the basis that it would be wrong to regard those regulations as giving rise to a statutory duty creating an absolute liability.

A careless mistake made when the law on a subject is relatively common knowledge within the profession as a whole will lead to liability for damages. For example, *Hatchway Properties Ltd* v. *C. Henry Bond & Co.*, [1983] 266 E.G. 316, was a successful action for damages for breach of duty against surveyors acting as property managers for not submitting a full planning application before the lapse of outline approval for part of a site for a projected housing development in Norfolk. Outline planning consent was obtained for the erection of 86 dwellings. This was conditional on an application being made for approval of certain reserved matters, namely design, siting, external appearance and means of access within the normal three years. Detailed consent was given for part of the land, most of which had been sold, but no application was made within the three years for approval of the reserved matters regarding the rest of the land. As a result, outline consent lapsed. A new application was made but rejected because changes in the structure plan were made after the original permission had been given. The surveyors admitted liability for such damages as flowed directly from it which were assessed as being the difference in the price of the land if it had been sold with full planning permission and without.

Q. Is there any particular time by which I must know the effect of a legal decision?

The question of 'reasonableness' arises when the problem is considered of the time within which you should not merely know of a legal decision or a statute which affects the profession, but also when it should be applied.

Positive steps must be taken to keep one's legal knowledge up to date; it may fairly by held to be part of the duty of one who holds himself skilled in that branch of professional knowledge to become acquainted with a decision which had such an important bearing upon his practice.

Knowledge to be gained in reasonable time could mean as soon as the decision or act is published, depending on its effect and what it implies with regard to the duties and consequent actions of the architect. They could occur in the very midst of negotiations and be of such a nature as to alter totally their course, yet not to give them immediate effect would in itself be an act of negligence.

Q. Inadvertently I may have failed to notify all owners and occupiers of land which my clients propose to develop. What is the position?

Every planning application requires the applicant or you, as his agent, to certify:

1. Who owns and occupies the land;

A cautionary tale of how easy it is to fall foul of planning legislation

A travel agent who built a spiral staircase connecting his ground-floor shop premises with the residential premises above was obliged to remove the staircase under an enforcement notice issued to remedy the unauthorized development involved in converting the residential premises into office space, notwithstanding that the construction of stairs was permitted without planning permission under section 22(2)(a) of the *Town and Country Planning Act 1971* and the travel agent would be entitled to rebuild the stairs the day after complying with the enforcement notice.

It was held that the test to be applied when considering such situations is to ask whether the apparently permitted activity was an integral part of the unauthorized material change of use. In this case, it was clear that the only possible reason for building the staircase was to enable the staff in the travel agency to communicate quickly with the office staff above. The staircase was therefore clearly integral to the development and would have to be removed under the enforcement notice.

Somak Travel Ltd. v. *Secretary of State for the Environment & Another, The Times,* 2 June 1987; [1987] J.P.L. 630.

---

2. That they have all been notified that the application is being made to the local authority;
3. Brief particulars of it.

The certification procedure allows those directly affected by the proposals to submit representations before any decision is taken. It reassures the authority that the notifications have taken place, releasing it from the administrative burden of doing its own investigations.

If there is a parcel of land within the site that is not in the applicant's ownership or there are tenants with a legitimate long-term interest who were not notified problems may arise. If the oversight is found prior to a decision being made on the application, it can be corrected by delaying consideration of the application while notices are again served and objection periods elapse. However, it may not become apparent that someone has been missed out until the planning permission has been granted. If it is discovered that there was an error in the certificate, the planning permission is potentially void-able. It remains valid until it is challenged and the court strikes it out.

In other words, your clients may have contracted to purchase the land subject to planning approval being granted. In due course it is granted; however, there is an error on the certificate, an occupier of the land has not been informed of your planning application. In such circumstances your clients may have paid the purchase moneys on receipt of the planning approval which they later find is voidable at the court's discretion, in which case the clients may look to you for damages.

Determination of ownerships within a site can only be ascertained from examination of title. It is important that you adequately research the certificate.

Provision is made in the certification procedure for circumstances where part or all of the land cannot be attributed to any particular owner, or where ownership is uncertain, by using certificate B or C as appropriate. This does mean publication of the application in the local press. It is important that the significance of this point is drawn to the clients' attention when seeking instructions on which certificate to serve.

Q. I am confused about the local authority's liability to my client for approving plans for Building Regulations. Can you help?

The duty of care owed by a local authority to an owner will arise only in exceptional circumstances. It is unlikely to arise where the developer has obtained professional advice. It would not be reasonable or just to do so. The purpose of health and welfare by-laws is to protect occupiers and members of the public from risks to health and safety. A non-resident owner is not at risk in this way.

In other words, a local authority's liability may arise in two ways:

1. Is there any risk to health and safety of the person claiming? If not, no duty may be owed;
2. Even if there is a risk to health and safety, is the owner himself in breach of the Building Regulations? If he has been personally negligent, there will be no duty. If he has not been personally negligent but is still in default, then it may depend upon the degree of expertise available to him as the owner occupier.

The duties of the local authority may be summarized as follows:

1. The purpose of local authorities' powers is to protect occupiers and the public against dangers to health and safety;
2. The duty will be owed not only to original occupiers, but also to subsequent occupiers;

3. Where the duty is broken, the damage is the reasonable cost of eliminating the danger to health and safety;
4. There is no duty to an original building owner occupier who has himself failed to comply with the Building Regulations even if his failure to comply is not negligent – i.e. where he has relied upon professional advice; exceptionally in the absence of such professional advice a duty may still be owed;
5. If the defaulting building owner has had the benefit of advice of architects or engineers or contractors, it will be neither reasonable nor just to impose a liability on the local authority to then indemnify the building owner.

Q. What is the liability of an approved inspector vis-à-vis the Building Regulations?

An approved inspector undertakes functions in relation to the inspection of plans, the supervision of work and the giving of certificates and other notices. A failure on his part to discharge these functions, or any one of them, properly may render him liable for breach of contract if he undertakes work on payment of a fee and/or liable for breach of statutory duty and/or liable in negligence.

The inspectors must be diligent, visiting the work as occasion requires and carrying out their inspection with reasonable care. An approved inspector may delegate work to another person, except the power to issue a plans certificate or final certificate. Legal responsibility for the acts of the delegatee remains with the approved inspector.

It is an offence:

1. to give a notice or certificate which the person giving it knows to contain a false or misleading statement;

A cautionary tale of letting everyone know about your planning application

In October 1976 an application was made for a residential development. The certificate on the application stated that the requisite notice had been given to all other owners of the land. It transpired that a small parcel of the land (2%) was owned by someone whose identity remained unknown. In January 1977 outline planning permission was granted, with the approval of reserved matters in April 1980.

In June 1980, Mr Main challenged the planning permission granted in 1977 by way of judicial review, claiming the 1977 consent was invalid because the certificate accompanying the application was incorrect and therefore the subsequent approval of reserved matters in 1980 was also invalid. Since the unidentified 2% of the land was not considered 'demini-

mus', the court determined that the error in the certificate was sufficient for it to strike down the planning consent at its discretion.

In exercising its discretion the court considered:

1. The period of time between 1977 when outline consent was granted and 1980 when the reserved matters were approved, between which time Mr Main made no objection to the original consent;
2. The scheme did not involve development on that 2% of the land;
3. The Secretary of State had known about the position for some time and had taken no action;
4. That it was too late, at least for Mr Main

who was not the relevant owner, to have the consent quashed.

However it was suggested that even after a substantial lapse of time between the grant of consent and appeal, the court might be sympathetic to an owner who challenges the validity of the consent as soon as he is aware of it. This could even be after development has taken place, if he has no reason to have had the matter drawn to his attention prior to that time.

Main v. *Swansea City Council & Others* [1985] J.P.L. 558.

---

2. to give a notice or certificate recklessly where it contains a false or misleading statement.

A written statement may be false not only because of what is stated, but also because of what it withheld, omitted or implied.

Q. What is the effect of a breach of the Building Regulations?

Any person, for example, a developer, who is in breach of a duty imposed by Building Regulations and which results in

damage under section 38 of the *Building Act 1984* may be the subject of civil proceedings. The term 'damage' includes the death of, or injury to, any person. It also covers any disease and any impairment of a person's physical or mental condition. However, this civil liability is subject to the regulations themselves providing for prescribed defences to such an action.

Furthermore, if any work to which Building Regulations are applicable contravenes any of the regulations, the owner may be required by a local authority notice to pull the work down or alter it. However, no such notice may be served after the expiration of 12 months from the date of completion of the work.

A cautionary tale of who is liable for defective buildings

Investors' claim in Industry Commercial Properties Ltd arose out of the rapid disintegration and subsequent demolition of two of four warehouses built on the Spinney Pool Estate at Leighton Buzzard, a site that was once an exceptionally large pool and had then been filled in by tipping. The demolition was a result of inadequate design of the foundations.

Despite their denying negligence or breach of statutory duty, it was found that the local authority had, in connection with their approval of plans and inspections carried out by their inspectors of the foundations during laying, woefully failed to discharge the responsibilities imposed upon them by the *Public Health Acts* of *1936* and *1961*. The relevant statutory provisions were contained in section 4(1) of the *Public Health Act 1961* and sections 61 and 62 of the 1936 Act: they concerned the making and enforcement of building regulations.

During 1973 the local authority had carried out site and trial pit inspections and had seen and approved the plans and calculations relating to the proposed functions. They had raised no objections to them and their inspector approved all the foundation bases on the site before concrete was poured in. Within weeks of the buildings being completed cracks appeared and, in 1979, two of the warehouses were demolished and rebuilt on proper foundations.

The local authority were in breach of the relevant building regulations. The all-important question of law was whether the local authority, in exercising their functions under the 1936 Act, owed a duty of care to the building owners. The five propositions of law were:

1. The purpose for which the legislature had conferred supervisory powers over building operations on local authorities was to protect the occupiers of buildings and members of the public against dangers to health or personal safety; it was not to safeguard the building developer, or anyone else, against purely economic loss;
2. It could well be that a local authority in exercising its statutory powers would be held to owe a duty to a subsequent occupier other than the original building owner to take reasonable care to ensure that a building was erected in accordance with the building regulations so as not to cause danger to health or personal safety of the occupier;
3. Where that duty of care had been broken and, as a result, the condition of the property gave rise to danger to health or safety, then an occupier to whom the duty was owed might be at liberty to restore the property to a condition in which such danger was eliminated and recover the amount of any such necessary expenditure from the local authority; whether he had such right of recovery had to depend on the particular facts;
4. A local authority in exercising its supervisory powers would normally owe no duty to an original building owner because it was normally incumbent on the owner himself to ensure that the building was erected in accordance with the building regulations and it could not have been the intention of the legislature that, save perhaps in exceptional circumstances, a local authority could owe a duty to a person who was in such breach;
5. A local authority in exercising its supervisory powers would normally owe no duty to an original building owner who had had the benefit of the advice of architects, engineers and contractors and had relied on it; it would not be reasonable nor just to impose on local authorities a liability to indemnify builders against liability resulting from such reliance.

The legislature in imposing on local authorities for the general protection of the public the obligations under section 64 of the 1936 Act could not have intended to protect building developers such as investors in Industry Ltd against damage which they might suffer through their failure to comply with building regulations — or to entitle them to an indemnity from their fellow ratepayers against the consequences of any such failure.

The facts of the case were not exceptional. Propositions 4 and 5 fairly and squarely applied to it. The local authority, in considering whether or not to approve plans and in the site inspections, owed no duty of care to them whatever duty they might have owed to other persons.

Investors in Industry Commercial Properties Ltd. v. *South Bedfordshire District Council*, [1986] Q.B. 1034.

A cautionary tale of the moving floor slab

Mr and Mrs Kimbell were the owners of 12 Tavistock Road, Fleet, Hampshire. The plans were approved in 1962 and the house built in or shortly before 1964. They had purchased the house in December 1975, and sometime in 1978 they noticed that gaps had appeared between the skirting-boards and the flooring at ground level. They discovered that the ground floor slab was laid on top of hardcore which had been placed on 'gravelly organic silt'. The slab supported only non-loadbearing walls. The loadbearing walls were taken down to a strata of green sand known as the Bracklesham Beds. There was no problem with the loadbearing walls which had been founded in this strata.

Mr and Mrs Kimbell began legal proceedings against Hart District Council, alleging negligence in the inspection and approval of building plans and in site inspections of foundations. The writ was issued on February 1984. It was held that this was within 6 years (the appropriate limitation period) from when damage to the property was first suffered as a result of settlement of the floor slab. The limitation defence raised by the local authority therefore failed.

However, to succeed there were two other hurdles which Mr and Mrs Kimbell had to clear:

1. They had to show that the damage suffered was of the type for which they were entitled to protection under local authority Building Regulations;
2. Was the local authority in breach of a duty to act with the care and skill of a competent local authority in relation to its Building Regulations functions?

The damage to the property did not affect its stability. It consisted of gaps appearing between skirting-board and floor slab, together with hollow areas beneath the floor slab. The settlement of the floor slab had now ceased. As any cause of action against a local authority could only arise when damage to property put at risk the health or safety of persons present on the premises, the defendants could not be liable for mere physical damage to the property. This finding was sufficient to dispose of a claim against the local authority.

It was found that settlement had occurred 14 years after the ground floor slab had been laid because of the exceptional drought conditions in the summer of 1976 followed by unprecedented wet weather in autumn, winter and spring of 1976–7. It was this exceptional climatic condition which had caused the unusual lowering of the water table followed by its subsequent rise which had caused the settlement.

It was held that at the time (1962–4), the 'state of the art' was such that a competent local authority would not foresee that the construction of a floor slab on such a subsoil would be likely to give rise to settlement problems in the floor slab. At that time, the method used for construction was very common. Accordingly, the local authority had not acted in breach of its duty of care either in relation to the approval of plans or in inspecting the construction of the floor slab.

Though there was a breach of by-law, in that the foundations did not sustain the appropriate loads, that in itself did not render the local authority liable, nor was it liable for negligence in failing to reject plans.

Graham Frances Kimbell & Daphne Anne Kimbell v. *Hart District Council*. (1986), unreported.

9.4 PROFESSIONAL ADVICE

Q. If I do not know enough, what would be my liability in giving professional advice to a client or accepting advice from others?

Inexperience is a reason for seeking more experienced advice, it is not a shield against liability.

You are under a professional obligation to advise your client to seek further advice on matters of which you have little knowledge, that is to appoint a consultant. It is a moot-point whether you should then advise your client that the consultant's advice is correct or incorrect. Arguably, you owe a duty of care to advise your client whether or not the consultant's recommendations should be accepted, and whether or not they are in the client's best interests. It is an obligation which may be implied if it is not stated as an actual term within your personal contract with the client, that you will act consistently in the latter's interests and protect them from loss and harm so far as possible.

The duty of care which arises in giving advice, be it written or verbal, and the consequences which stem from it are similar for both yourself and the consultant. You are both responsible to the client and to each other that your own information is correct and accurate. The duty of care would only arise if the person making the statement or giving advice held himself out as possessing the necessary skill and competence to give the advice and being prepared to exercise the necessary diligence to give reliable advice.

In other words, whenever a person gives information to another, whether it is actively sought or merely accepted, on a serious matter and particular on a matter of business, and the relationship is such that the speaker ought to realize that he is being trusted, and particularly if he realizes that the other believes him to have special knowledge or information if it is reasonable for the other party to seek and act upon the advice, then a duty arises to use reasonable care in his selection of information in the exercise of his judgment.

Q. To what extent does a client's expertise affect my liability in advising him?

Occasionally a low level of care in giving a client advice may be justified, particularly where the client is knowledgeable in the matter, though there is a certain level, either stated or implied within your contract, below which you should not fall even if the client is experienced.

Conversely, where the client is inexperienced or the scheme by its very nature is dangerous or where new techniques and materials are being used, the duty of care and skill may be increased. A professional person should not adopt a policy of providing the same level of service for all those with whom he deals as particular individuals pose particular risks.

Q. What is my liability in respect of consultants?

If you as an architect or engineer advise a client, whether or not you have been asked for the advice, to employ a consultant, you must act with no small degree of circumspection. You have a prima-facie responsibility for a consultant's performance. The essence of the proposition that liability arises is reliance. The professional man must be aware that the other is relying on his skill to guide him, and that other must in fact rely on it and act on it.

Wherever possible, the consultant should be employed by the client and selected by him from a shortlist. They should be chosen because:

1. they have worked with you or the client before;
2. they are fully qualified in their field;
3. they have worked on similar contracts;
4. their indemnity insurance policy is adequate, preferably the cover being on an each and every claim basis.

Nevertheless, in determining the architect's or engineer's liability for the negligence of others whom he had selected, it would be of little avail to show that he had selected reputable and sufficiently qualified people to do the work and thus was not guilty of personal negligence.

However prudently the selection is made, you remain responsible to the client as the overall success of the design rests with you. That responsibility cannot be delegated unless your commission quite clearly and specifically provides otherwise and the term itself does not fall within the ambit of the *Unfair Contract Terms Act 1977*.

When advice is accepted even on minor matters and the payment of the consultant by you is quite minimal, liability immediately arises for damages against you if you use it. For example, an engineer is 'appointed' by an architect to carry out structural calculations, which prove wrong, and they were carried out on the back of a beer mat and the price paid for them was a pint of beer; the architect will be liable.

A similar principle applies with regard to the appointment of a clerk of works. Where an architect advises the employer to appoint a clerk of works and it is later found that he is incompetent, the fact that the clerk of works was not employed by the architect may not be used as a defence in an attempt to limit the architect's liability. For example, in *Leicester Board of Guardians* v. *Trollope* [1911] 75 J.A. 197, it was held that the architect was liable for a defective floor which had dry rot in it, though it was the result of the clerk of works fraudulently deviating from the design while he had specific responsibility for ensuring that there was constant quality control of the work.

If someone possessed of a special skill undertakes quite irrespective of contract to apply that skill, a duty of care will arise. The fact that the service is given by means of words can make no difference. Furthermore, if in a sphere in which a person is so placed others could reasonably rely upon his judgement or skill, and the person takes it upon himself to give information or advice to be passed on to another person who as he knows, or should know, will place reliance upon it, then a duty of care will arise. In other words, there is a duty of care by a person such as an architect or engineer who takes it upon himself to give advice to a person whom he is aware, or should be aware, will depend on the truth and accuracy of that advice, no matter how many removes from him he may be from the original communication so long as the communication remains accurate as to what the original information was.

Q. What is my liabililty if I do not accept a consultant's advice and do the work myself?

An architect, engineer or other professional will be held liable, if damages result, where he does not accept the advice of the consultant who has warned of possible danger and recommended a certain course of action.

Needless to say, where an architect decides to undertake a particular aspect of the work himself, which is not part of the basic services offered by the architect and for which he is entitled to charge additional fees rather than give the work to a consultant, for example, taking out quantities for inclusion in a bill of quantities, then he is solely liable for loss caused by any errors resulting from lack of skill, rather than jointly liable, possibly, where a consultant is employed. Normally, however, an architect or employer would not warrant that the bills of quantity were an accurate or indeed a complete description of the works.

Nevertheless, where the architect gives an estimate of the likely cost of the building or a figure is given to him by the client, he is under an obligation to design the scheme in such a way that the cost will be reasonably near to it. One should not estimate a work at a price at which no one would contract for it, for if he does, he deceives his client.

If a surveyor or indeed an architect gives an estimate greatly below the sum at which certain work can be done and thereby induces a client to undertake what he would not otherwise do, then the client may be entitled to recover. But no liability will arise if the client can achieve a similar desired object, despite a reduction being made elsewhere, which he must give the surveyor or architect the opportunity to do, acting reasonably to mitigate his loss. By implication, it is a good practice that all expenditure, or likely expenditure, should be approved by the client beforehand.

TEN

What are the basic principles

for choosing a standard

form of building contract?

10.1 MEANING OF A STANDARD FORM AND CONTRACT

Q. What does the term 'a standard form of contract' mean?

There has been much argument by the advocates of one form of contract that that particular form is the standard form, all others are the client's own and will be interpreted *contra proferentem*.

The *Shorter Oxford English Dictionary* gives the meaning of 'standard' as an authoritative or recognized exemplar of correctness, perfection or some definite degree of any quality. Standard forms of contract are generally of two kinds, building contracts tend to fall between the two.

The first, of very ancient origins, are those which set out the terms on which mercantile transactions of common occurrence are to be carried out. The standard clauses in these contracts have been settled over the years by negotiation by representatives of the commercial interests involved and have been widely adopted because experience has shown that they facilitate the conduct of trade. Contracts of these kinds affect not only the actual parties to them, but also others who may have a commercial interest in the transactions to which they relate. If fairness or reasonableness were relevant to their enforceability, the fact that they are widely used by parties whose bargaining power is fairly matched would raise a strong presumption that their terms are fair and reasonable.

The same presumption, however, does not apply to the second kind of standard form of contract; this is of comparatively modern origin. It is the result of the concentration of particular kinds of business in relatively few hands. The terms of this kind of standard form of contract have not been the subject of negotiation between the parties to it, or approved by any organization representing the interests of the weaker party. They have been dictated by that party whose bargaining power either exercised alone or in conjunction with others providing similar goods or services enables him to say, 'If you want these goods or services at all, these are the only terms on which they are obtainable. Take it or leave it.'

Where the contract is of the latter kind, the court has to consider all its provisions to see whether the bargain made was fair – i.e. whether the restrictions were both reasonably necessary for the protection of the legitimate interests of the promisee and commensurate with the benefits secured to the promisor under the contract.

Q. What type of clauses can be included in a standard form of contract?

Common forms of clauses may be included within a standard contract which has been evolved by negotiation between bodies concerned to protect the rights of their members and which are regarded as representing what the consensus of opinion in the trade or profession regards as fair and reasonable. Though those clauses may be of long standing, that fact alone does not entitle them to the automatic accolade of fairness and reasonableness.

Furthermore, it is virtually impossible for there to be an equal base between a number of parties to a contract, though some degree of balance may be sought by limiting the number of representatives from each body involved in the negotiations, as happens, for example, at JCT. Rather the result is a contract to which the parties agree equally, but the obligations of each which are created by the contract are not all equal.

Q. To what extent are clauses in a standard form of contract binding?

The parties who enter into a contract, whether or not it is a standard form of whatever kind, will be bound by its terms unless it falls under the provisions of the *Unfair Contract Terms Act 1977*.

The basic principle is that the court does not make a contract for the parties. The court will not even improve the contract which the parties have made for themselves, however desirable the improvement might be. The court's function is to interpret and apply the contract which the parties have made for themselves. If the express terms are perfectly clear and free from ambiguity, there is no choice to be made between different possible meanings. The clear terms must be applied, even if the courts think some other term would have been more suitable.

An unexpressed term can be implied if, and only if, the court finds that the parties must have intended that term to form part of their contract.

Q. Do valid standard forms of building contracts have a policy or philosophy?

The philosophy which lies behind the terms of some building contracts is that the established contractor should bear the risks of building operations rather than the client who may be building for the first time, because the former has more experience than the latter, and is therefore better able to foresee any risks and allow for them. That philosophy or policy of the contract is to be discerned from the terms of the contract alone.

The building contracts produced by the JCT, PSA, ACA,

FAS, ICE and FIDIC are all in one respect or another standard forms. The question of whether or not a contract is validly a standard form may be of less importance than the question of whether or not the clauses it contains are valid. Invalidity may be dependent on whether or not unfair advantage has been taken of one party by another.

In other words, the public interest requires, in the interest both of the public and of the individual, that everyone should be free so far as practicable to earn a livelihood and to give to the public the fruits of his particular abilities. The main question to be considered is whether and how far the operation of the terms of an agreement is likely to conflict with this objective. In refusing to enforce provisions of a contract whereby one party agrees for the benefit of the other party to exploit or refrain from exploiting his own earning power, the public policy which the courts implement is not a nineteenth-century economic theory about the benefit to the general public of freedom of trade, but the protection of those whose bargaining power is weak against being forced by those whose bargaining power is stronger to enter into bargains that are unconscionable.

Q. To what extent are clauses in the standard form of contract influenced by judgments of the court?

The JCT contracts have been amended many times to take account of courts' decisions. Occasionally the tribunal has not changed a clause. An illustration of the former is clause 2.2.1 of JCT 80 (Private with Approximate Quantities), as amended, which states, 'Nothing contained in the Contract Bills shall override or modify the application or interpretation of that which is contained in the Articles of Agreement, the Conditions or the Appendix'. That clause was substituted for the former clause 12 in JCT 63 which stated, 'Nothing contained in the Contract Bills must override, modify or affect in any way whatsoever the application or interpretation of these Conditions'. Clause 2.2.1 was modified from clause 12 as a result of the findings in *English Industrial Estates Corporation* v. *George Wimpey & Co. Ltd* [1973] 1 Lloyds Rep. 118. The courts felt that they had the right to look at any special terms written into the bills 'to follow exactly what was going on', even though they were prohibited from allowing the *ad hoc* terms found in the bills from effectively governing the Conditions.

By way of contrast, the JCT in considering clause 16.1 of JCT 80 decided not to introduce terms which would override difficulties where suppliers retain their title in materials until payment by the client under clause 30. The reasons which the JCT gave for not changing clause 16.1 were that the administration involved would be considerable and costly. Tenders might be increased to cover the risk that some materials may fail to qualify for payment before incorporation into the works, the period of risk running mainly from the date of payment by the client to the date of their incorporation into the works by the contractor. Furthermore, the risks of repossession or claims by sellers generally arise only if the contractor becomes insolvent. Also contracts of sale frequently permit the contractor to pass on his title in the goods to the client, so defeating any alleged right to repossess.

Q. How do you construe a standard form of contract?

A contract, even though it be in a standard form, should be

construed in the context of the scheme for which it is used. The facts and circumstances which surround any contract are many and varied, together they are unique to it.

This is in spite of the fact that other contracts may be used to help in understanding a particular point which is not especially clear. To some extent, decisions on one contract may help by way of analogy and illustration in the decision of another contract; but, however similar the contracts may appear, the decision as to each must depend on the consideration of the language of the particular contract, read in the light of material circumstances of the parties in view of which the contract is made.

It must be remembered that the court, while it seeks to give effect to the intention of the parties, must give effect to that intention as expressed, that is it must ascertain the meaning of the words actually used; and the words actually used must be construed with reference to the facts known to the parties and in contemplation of which the parties must be deemed to have used them. Such facts may be proved by extrinsic evidence or appear in recitals. Again, the meaning of the words used must be ascertained by considering the whole context of the document and so as to harmonize as far as possible all the parts: particular words may appear to have been used in a special sense, or in a special meaning adapted by the parties themselves as shown by the whole document. Terms may be implied by custom and on similar grounds.

Q. How are clauses in a standard form of contract interpreted?

To arrive at the meaning of the clauses within standard forms of contract, regard must be paid to precedent, particularly where a previous decision on a similar point has the weight of long standing, and indeed other contracts may be used by way of illustration to help construe a particular term.

As a general principle, a court in construing a document may not break away from previous decisions, even if in the first instance it would have taken a different view, because all the documents made after the meaning of one has been judicially determined are taken to have been made on the faith of the rule laid down.

10.2 WHEN A CONTRACT IS A CONTRACT

Q. When is a contract a contract?

An usual feature of any building contract is that an offer from a builder, in the form of a tender, to do certain work set out within a bill of quantities, specification, drawings or other documents has been accepted by the client in return for 'valuable consideration'. That is, the contract sum which the ICE contract defines as 'the sum to be paid in accordance with the provisions hereinafter contained for the construction, completion and maintenance of the Works in accordance with the Contract'.

A contract need not be invalid merely because the contract sum has been omitted from it. A mere promise by a constructor to perform work without any mention of price needs to be supported by some consideration in order to become binding on him. Consideration may be implied where the contractor has been retained to do the work, there being an implied obligation from the client that he will pay the contractor a reasonable sum for the work done and the materials supplied. Indeed, where work is carried out before a fully complete and formal contract is drawn up, the contractor may recover his outlay on the basis of *quantum meruit*, literally as much as he deserved. In other words, quantum meruit is a fair reward for services rendered where there is no agreed rate of payment.

A tender which is unconditionally accepted results in a contract being formed when its acceptance is notified to the tenderer.

Q. Are there any general principles for construing words?

As a general principle, words or terms used within a contract should be construed according to the plain, ordinary and popular sense in which they are understood, unless they have acquired a peculiar meaning because of their use within a trade or profession which is distinct from the popular sense of the same words. Where the terms of the contract are perfectly clear and unambiguous though onerous (but not punitive), they will be upheld.

For example, in *Jackson* v. *Eastbourne Local Board*, (1866) H.B.C. (4th edn 194) vol. 2, p. 88, H.L., Jackson, a local builder, undertook to build a sea-wall at Eastbourne expressly agreeing within the contract to 'take upon himself the risk of, and be answerable for, all accidents and damages from or by seas, winds, drift of craft, fire or any other cause, whatsoever, which may occur during the construction of the works under this contract, and in case of such accidents or damages arising, shall make good and repair the same as soon as possible at his own cost and charges'. There was no qualification to these obligations in the contract. A severe storm occurred on 22 October 1881 and a large part of the completed wall was washed down. The House of Lords found the case so plain that it was impossible not to find the builder liable for damage.

If a contract contains words which in their context are fairly capable of bearing more than one meaning, and it is alleged that the parties have negotiated on an agreed basis that the words bore only one of the two possible meanings, then the extrinsic evidence, such as pre-contract negotiations, relied upon by the parties may be examined to see whether they have in fact used the words in question in only one sense. The effect is that they have given their own 'dictionary meaning' to the words as a result of their common intention.

While you may look to pre-contract negotiations to construe a word or term, you may not look to post-contract actions, the principle being that it is not legitimate to use as an aid in the construction of the contract anything which the parties said or did after it was made. Otherwise you might have the result that a contract meant one thing the day it was signed but, by reason of subsequent events, meant something different a month or a year later.

Although subsequent conduct cannot be used for the purpose of interpreting a contract retrospectively, it is often convincing evidence of a course of dealing which may give rise to legal obligations. It may be used to complete a contract which would otherwise be incomplete. It may be used so as to introduce terms and conditions into a contract which would not otherwise be there. If it can be used to introduce terms which are not already there, it must also be available to add to, or vary, terms which are there already, or to interpret them. If parties to a contract by their course of dealing put a particular interpretation on the terms of it, on the faith of which each of them, to the knowledge of the other, acts and conducts their mutual affairs, they are bound by that interpretation just as much as if they had written it down as being a variation of the contract. There is no need to enquire whether their particular interpretation is correct or not, or whether they were mistaken or not, or whether they had in mind the original terms or not. Suffice it that they have, by the

A cautionary tale on the delicate question of money

In February 1972 building contractors Bernard Sunley & Sons Ltd entered into a contract valued at over £1 million with Mottram Consultants Ltd to build a supermarket at Kinshasa in the Republic of Zaïre, formerly the Congo. The contract was on a 'cost plus' basis. Mottram were to pay Sunley the prime cost of all the materials and labour used in the erection of the supermarket plus a fee of 10% of such cost.

On account of exchange control restrictions, it was arranged that SGA, an agency of the government of Zaïre by whom the supermarket would eventually be owned, should make local currency available to Mottram Consultants for such local expenditure as paying for local labour and materials used in the erection of the supermarket.

The contract provided for the architect to issue weekly interim certificates for the amount due in respect of total prime cost for local expenditure and monthly certificates for other expenditure, that is money spent in purchasing materials outside Zaïre. It was agreed to vary the main contract terms to the effect that the weekly certificates be subject to any necessary adjustments in the monthly certificates.

Sunley's representative in Zaïre was inexperienced in managing contracts in African countries. Owing to his negligence, large overpayments were made to fraudulent subcontractors. In some cases, there were payments for goods which were never delivered, in others there were payments for more goods than were delivered. Mottram Consultants discovered in August 1972 that they had been defrauded by the subcontractors and credited Sunley's with sums which Sunley's had paid to them. Sunley's contended that £33 526.33 was still owing to them and did not pay the imprest accounts for five weeks as they had an arguable case for being allowed to set off the money.

When information came to SGA that large sums of money supplied by them for building operations had been squandered by being misapplied and lost, they stopped feeding Mottram's bank account in Zaire. Mottram, as a result, did not have zaïres with which to pay the interim certificates. The contract was terminated.

It was held that the variation to the main contract expressly providing that any necessary adjustments should be made by the architects in the monthly certificates showed clearly that Mottram's were not entitled to withhold payment of any part of the sum appearing in the weekly interim certificates because they thought that some of the expenditure included in a former account, or that account itself, had not been properly incurred and accordingly it was for the architect to put that right if need be in the monthly certificates.

Mottram Consultants Ltd v. *Bernard Sunley & Sons Ltd* [1975] 2 Lloyd's Rep. 197.

course of dealing, put their own interpretation on their contract and cannot be allowed to go back on it.

When the parties to a contract are both under a common mistake as to the meaning or effect of it and then embark on a course of dealing on the footing of that mistake, replacing the original terms of the contract with a conventional basis on which they both conduct their affairs, then the original contract is replaced by the conventional basis. The parties are bound by the conventional basis; each party can sue or be sued upon it just as if it had been expressly agreed between them.

Q. How precise or detailed should a contract be?

The greatest difference between standard forms of building contract is often the degree of precision and detail adopted for a particular provision, the principle behind the clause being essentially similar in a number of contracts. For example, clause 6 of JCT 80 covers within nine subclauses and sub-subclauses the contractor's obligations to comply with statutory requirements; the FAS contract in clause 1.3 contains three subclauses covering the same principle.

Because the parties to a contract are more often than not businessmen, they ought to be left to decide what degree of precision is essential to express in their contracts where no legal principle is violated. The duty of the courts is to construe such contracts fairly and broadly without being too astute or subtle in finding defects. Though the grammatical construction of a sentence or group of words used in a document may be difficult to understand, it is not a sufficient reason for finding them to be too ambiguous or uncertain to be enforced if the fair meaning of the parties can be extracted.

Meaningless words can be ignored so as to preserve an agreement which might otherwise fail for lack of certainty. Indeed, if the parties' common intention is clear from other evidence, the court can correct a mistake by ordering that the contract should be rectified, so that it accords with the parties' intentions. An ambiguous clause should be construed in a manner which would avoid an unreasonable result, while retaining the validity of that clause. This does not mean that the court will make a contract for the parties or go outside the words they have used except in so far as there are appropriate implications of law; for example, the implication of what is just and reasonable is to be ascertained by the court as a matter of machinery where the contractual intention is clear but the contract is silent on some detail.

Q. How do I know what is the correct meaning and construction of a contract clause?

A contract which is connected with building has to be construed not only according to its own terms and provisions, but also according to rules and principles which are of general application. It is made more difficult by the forms of building contract in common use not being as clearly worded as they might be. It is a truism that businessmen often record the most important agreements in crude and summary fashion; modes of expression, sufficient and clear to them in the course of their business, may appear to those unfamiliar with the business far from complete or precise. Indeed, the JCT form has been described as made up of a farrago of obscurities.

The true construction of a provision within a contract is often made more difficult when some of the printed conditions are struck out or altered without sufficient regard being paid to their effect on the contract as a whole. The principle of construing such a clause is that when your client and the contractor use a printed form and delete parts of it, you can pay regard to what has been deleted as part of the surrounding circumstances in the light of which you must construe what they have chosen to leave in.

Q. What happens if the priority of contract document is unclear?

Where the clause covering the priority of contract documents is less clear than that of JCT 80 or GC/Works/1, the question of construction arises. Though a standard form is the same for every scheme the circumstances of that scheme are unique to it. It is impossible for a standard form to cover every contingency unless it be by giving the architect or engineer some degree of discretion in interpreting the terms of the contract, that is in deciding whether the printed or the written clauses should have priority over the other.

Clause 1.3 of the ACA Form allows for exceptions to the general rule that the form of agreement has priority over all other written contract documents to be identified and set down under that clause.

Contract documents are taken as mutually explanatory in both ICE clause 5 and FIDIC clause 5.2. They contain essentially the same clause, to the effect that:

> The several documents forming the Contract are to be taken as mutually explanatory of one another and in case of ambiguities or discrepancies the same shall be explained and adjusted by the Engineer who shall thereupon issue to the Contractor appropriate instructions in writing.

By way of contrast, the FAS contract is silent as to the priority to be given between the standard form and the other contract documents, apart from clause 1.54, which states that the architect is to be notified of any discrepancies between the specification, the bills of quantity and drawings and shall determine which course is to be followed.

Q. If the wording of a clause in a number of contract documents which should be similar but in fact differ, which wording has priority?

Because the printed language of a standard form of contract is by its very nature uniform and invariable, it may have acquired from its use a known and definite meaning.

A bill of quantities may be used in conjunction with a standard form as one of a number of documents which together form the contract; however, the terms it contains may not have acquired such a definite meaning as those within the standard form. The terms of the bills of quantities are written specifically to cover the detailed construction of a building which is not and cannot be wholly covered by the terms within a standard form. Those terms are drafted in such a general way that they apply equally to all schemes on which that standard form is used. Should there be any reasonable doubt upon the sense and meaning of the contract as a whole, generally the written words of the bill of quantities should have a greater weight placed upon them than the printed words of the standard form. This is because the written words are the immediate language and terms selected by the parties themselves for the expression of their meaning, and the printed words are a general formula adapted equally to their case and that of all other contracting parties upon similar occasions and subjects.

In a number of standard forms, however, there is a clause which specifically states that priority is to be given to the printed terms of the standard form where they conflict with the written words. JCT 80, clause 2.2.1, is an example:

> Nothing contained in the Contract Bills shall override or modify the application or interpretation of that which is contained in the Articles of Agreement, the Conditions or the Appendix.

Again, clause 4(1) of GC/Works/1 states:

> In cases of discrepancy between these conditions and the Specification and/or the Bills of Quantitites and/or the Drawings the provisions of these Conditions shall prevail.

Where such clearly worded clauses are used, the printed form would prevail. For example, bills of quantities provide for a scheme to be completed in five sections. The first four are finished earlier than the completion date for the whole of the works, but the last section is not. The conditions and appendix of the contract are not amended. The bills are ineffective to make the contractor liable in liquidated damages for failure to complete in sections. In other words, the provisions of the standard form of contract may be applied to nullify contrary provisions in the bills of quantities.

WHICH CONTRACT TO USE

A cautionary tale of a contract in all but name

On 14 February 1959, Nuclear Civil Contractors submitted to Atomic Power Constructions Ltd a tender for carrying out civil engineering subcontract work on a new nuclear power station at Trawsfynydd, Merionethshire, being built for the Central Electricity Generating Board.

The tender, which was for a lump-sum price, incorporated conditions authorizing Atomic Power Constructions to make variations in the form, quality or quantity of the work and adjustments to the contract price according to costs of labour and materials. Some changes in the work were made by the Board before the tender was submitted, and further substantial changes were made after the submission of the tender which necessitated the amendment of some of the tender drawings, specifications and bills of quantities.

Both Nuclear Civil Constructors and Atomic Power Constructions intended from the outset that a legally binding contract should be made between them and, in June 1959, Nuclear Civil Constructors began work on the station at the request of Atomic Power Constructions. However, it was not until April 1960 that the form of the general conditions of contract was agreed.

The question arose of whether or not there was a contract between the two which governed their rights as to the work done since June 1959, and their payment for it.

It was held that as both had acted in the course of negotiations on the understanding that when the contract was made it would govern what work had been done before it came into existence, the contract of April 1960 therefore governed the rights of the main contractor and the subcontractor. It was necessary to imply a stipulation for the business efficacy of the contract that the variation clauses should apply retrospectively.

Trollope & Colls Ltd. & Holland & Hannet Cubitts Ltd. trading as Nuclear Civil Constructors v. *Atomic Power Constructions* [1963] 1 W.L.R. 333.

10.3 WHICH CONTRACT TO USE

Q. What points should I bear in mind when advising a client which contract to use?

The basic premiss on which any building is founded is that a contractor will do and complete a defined piece of work in a given time for a given sum of money. In other words, reasonable workmanship in a reasonable time for a reasonable price are the minimum clauses which are needed to make a contract viable in commercial terms. Though, if the terms are somewhat wide and imprecise or if the contract is silent on a particular point, this of itself will not prevent a contract from being formed.

The object of the law of contract is to facilitate the transactions of commercial men, not to create obstacles in the way of solving practical problems.

Familiarity with the standard form of contract used for a scheme should be a prerequisite to its recommendation. It is a positive duty in advising a client on which standard form to adopt for you to be aware of the strengths and weaknesses of each contract in relation to the particular scheme being considered, so that the client may make a well-informed decision. For example, a department store in Swansea pioneering the 'Eurostore' system was built in 1974 under an ICE contract normally used for works of civil engineering construction.

The breadth and depth of advice to be given to a client in selecting a contract centres on the extent to which the client

---

A cautionary tale of accepting tenders

Willcocks & Barnes were building contractors who claimed damages from the Co-op for breach of contract to employ them to carry out building work in Paignton.

The Co-op had invited tenders for the work by advertising that applications for bills of quantities should reach their office not later than 4 December 1928. Willcocks and Barnes applied for, and received, the bills of quantities. They were told by letter that their priced bills of quantities were to be sent to the architects Bridgman & Bridgman in a separate, sealed envelope with their name on the outside. The bills would be returned to them unopened after the contract had been signed if their tender was not accepted.

On 18 December the builders delivered their tender to the Co-op and their priced bills of quantities to the architects. On the same day, the Co-op's managing committee met and asked the architects to verify and report on Willcocks & Barnes' bills through quantity surveyors. The quantity surveyors recommended the acceptance of the tender. At a special meeting of the committee ten days later, it was resolved to accept the tender of another firm.

Willcocks & Barnes contended that the opening of their bills of quantities constituted an acceptance by the defendants of their tender, and that the return of these opened indicated a completed contract between themselves and the Paignton Co-operative Society.

It was held that the returning of the builders' open bills of quantities could not be regarded as the communication of an acceptance because, before they were returned, the architects informed Willcocks & Barnes that the Co-op had decided to accept another builder's tender. An intention to accept an offer was not an acceptance, unless and until the intention was communicated to the person by whom the offer was made. But an offeree cannot accept a withdrawal offer after he has learnt by whatever means that it has been withdrawn.

Willcocks & Barnes v. *The Paignton Co-operative Society Ltd.* (1930) 74 Sol.J. 247.

---

places reasonable reliance on your skill and experience in guiding him. It is of course your duty to advise your client about any abnormal or unusual term in a contract, though it is perfectly normal and proper for you to use standard forms. Depending on the circumstances, you need not go through the small print of those somewhat lengthy conditions with a tooth-comb every time you are advising a client or to draw the client's attention to every problem which on a careful reading of the conditions might in some instance or other conceivably arise.

Whatever is the advice, it should be given clearly and concisely in a manner which, above all, avoids confusion or misunderstanding, otherwise you may be liable for any financial loss suffered by the client should he act on that advice.

Q. Are there any special rules about accepting a tender by post?

If it is reasonable to accept a tender by post, such acceptance is effective when posted.

In other words, where the circumstances are such that it must have been within the contemplation of the parties that the post might be used as a means of communicating the acceptance of an offer, the acceptance is complete as soon as it is posted. It will constitute a contract, even if the letter goes astray and is lost. However, this postal rule may not apply in all cases, such as in the majority of building contracts where a contractor submits a tender which both he and the client must have expected to be accepted by post, when the express terms of the offer specify that the acceptance must reach the offeror.

Unless a letter of intent is specifically written in such a way as to ensure that a binding agreement does not come into existence until a formal contract document has been prepared, such a letter of intent within a building contract is usually indicative of a firm intention by the client to enter into a contract with the builder. It may be a binding acceptance of a tenderer's offer. Yet a contract binding all parties may not be prevented by a statement in the letter of intent that a formal contract was being prepared. It is a question of construction to establish whether or not a condition precedent existed which would stop a concluded contract from arising if the letter of intent made the acceptance of an offer subject to a formal document being executed.

The explanatory notes on the ICE Conditions of Contract regard the written acceptance of the tender as part of the contract, any clarification or other matter in the letter of intent becoming part of that contract. However, a letter of intent has been found to be no more than the expression in writing of a party's present intention to enter into a contract at a future date, save in exceptional circumstances it could have no binding effect. Thus a letter of intent will ordinarily have two characteristics:

1. It will express an intention to enter into a contract in the future;
2. It will itself create no liability in regard to that future contract.

ELEVEN

How do I choose the best standard

form of building contract to

limit my liability?

11.1 THE *SUPPLY OF GOODS AND SERVICES ACT 1982*

Q. How can a building or engineering contract be evaluated?

There are three basic principles within building and engineering contracts:

1. reasonable workmanship;
2. in a reasonable time;
3. for a reasonable price.

They establish a common starting-point and are codified in the *Supply of Goods and Services Act 1982*, which itself forms a neutral basis for evaluating standard forms of contract. Part II of the Act states:

13. Implied term about care and skill.
    In a contract for the supply of a service where the supplier is acting in the course of a business, there is an implied term that the supplier will carry out the service with reasonable care and skill.
14. Implied term about time for performance.
    (1) Where under a contract for the supply of a service by a supplier acting in the course of a business, the time for the service to be carried out is not fixed by the contract, left to be fixed in a manner agreed by the contract or determined by the course of dealing between the parties, there is an implied term that the supplier will carry out the service within a reasonable time.
    (2) What is reasonable time is a question of fact.
15. Implied term about consideration.
    (1) Where, under a contract for the supply of a service the consideration for the service is not determined by the contract, left to be determined in a manner agreed by

the contract or determined by the course of dealing between the parties, there is an implied term that the party contracting with the supplier will pay a reasonable charge.

(2) What is a reasonable charge is a question of fact.

Q. What does 'reasonable skill' or workmanship mean?

The term within the *Supply of Goods and Services Act 1982* that 'the supplier will carry out the service with reasonable skill' itself implies that the supplier has the ability to do the job skilfully. There is an implied warranty that he is reasonably competent to undertake that task which he is to do. Where the design of a building of traditional construction fails, it is evidence of a want of competent skill on the part of the architect, especially where considerable experience has been gained of the type of structure involved.

The principle was illustrated in the case of *Greaves & Co. Ltd* v. *Alexander Duckham & Co. Ltd* [1975] 1 W.L.R 1095, 1095, where an oil company wanted a new factory, office and warehouse to be built at Aldridge, Staffordshire. The warehouse was to be used for the storage of barrels of oil which were intended to be moved about with fork-lift trucks. They entered into a package-deal contract with a single firm of building contractors, Greaves & Co. (Contractors) Ltd. They were to do everything for them, and not only providing the usual labour and materials, but also employing the architects and engineers as subcontractors. The contractors employed Baynham Meikle & Partners, structural engineers, to design the structure of the building including the floors. The building owners made known to the contractors the purpose for which the building was required. Shortly after the warehouse was brought into use, the floors began to crack because of the vibrations produced by the fork-lift trucks. The contractors, accepting that they were liable to the owners for the cost of remedial work, claimed an indemnity from the engineers who were held liable for a breach of the implied contract term that the warehouse would be fit for its intended purpose and for the breach of their duty to use reasonable skill and care in and about the design.

Q. What does 'reasonable time' mean?

At the turn of the century the general rule of law as it then stood was that any act necessary to be done by either party in order to carry out a contract must be done within reasonable time. The principle was interpreted that except where time was of the essence of the stipulation, a breach of contract was only committed in the case of unreasonable delay in the performance of any act agreed to be done. For example, where time was not essential, a party failing to complete a sale of land on the day fixed by the agreement did not commit a breach of contract either in equity or at law; it was only on failure to complete within a reasonable time after that day that the contract was broken.

However, by the middle of the century it was found that whether or not time was of the essence, anyone who was actually injured by the breach of a time stipulation could recover damages. In other words, a breach of a contractual stipulation as to time which is not of the essence of a contract would not be treated as a breach of a condition precedent to the contract, that is as a breach which would entitle the innocent party to treat the contract as terminated or which would prevent the defaulting party from suing for specific performance. Nevertheless, it was a breach of the contract and entitled the injured party to damages if he had suffered damage.

The current view of the law with regard to time within all contracts may be summarized as follows. Time will not be considered to be of the essence unless:

1. The parties expressly stipulate that conditions as to time must be strictly complied with;
2. The nature of the subject matter of the contract or the surrounding circumstances show that time should be considered to be of the essence;
3. A party that has been subjected to unreasonable delay gives notice to the party in default making time of the essence.

In mercantile contracts, that is contracts which deal with commercial matters, building contracts being analogous to them, time will be considered of the essence out of practical necessity. Time is of the essence in building contracts because, for example, the landowner has some use for the building on a specific date.

Q. What does a reasonable price mean?

The general rule governing all building and engineering contracts is that the main contractor is bound to complete the works by the date stated in the contract or be liable for liquidated damages to the client. This is subject to the exception that the client is not entitled to liquidated damages if by his acts or omissions he has prevented the contractor from completing the works by the completion date.

The *Supply of Goods and Services Act 1982* codifies the existing common law as it relates to a reasonable price being paid for service rendered on a *quantum meruit* principle. It is applicable to building and engineering contracts where work is not covered by the original contract sum, for example, because of variations or because the contract is in a re-measurement form.

Though an express agreement governs the amount of remuneration in the absence of such an agreement, there is an entitlement to a reasonable sum, the amount of which is a question of fact. Indeed, in order for a contract to become binding on a contractor where he has simply promised to carry out the work without mentioning any price for it, there needs to be some consideration to support it. 'Consideration' being sufficient if the contractor was clearly employed to do the work, there being an implied agreement on the part of the client to pay the contractor a reasonable sum for the work done and the materials supplied. Nevertheless, if a contractor undertakes work of specified dimensions and materials but deviates from them, and the client does not avail himself of the right of rejecting them, the contractor although he cannot claim the price payable under the contract, because it has not been performed, can claim the actual value of the goods supplied. If the contractor brings an action for it, he is said to sue on a *quantum valebant*.

11.2 DUTIES AND OBLIGATIONS

Q. What are my duties and obligations as an architect to my client for the contractor's reasonable workmanship?

The general duty of of an architect when a contract has been signed is towards the client, representing him throughout the contract.

The FAS Form, clause 2.11, gives the architect's obligations as to 'inspect work in progress, certify payments, and deal with his (the client's) part of the contract administration'. In other words, the architect is to direct and supervise the works to ensure that they are carried out to the specified design, dimensions and standard required by the contract and give to the contractor such additional information that he may need to complete the work within the contract time and for the contract sum. The amount of this information can be specifically limited as in the ACA contract. The contract gives two alternatives for the preparation of further drawings:

Alternative 1
Clause 2.1
The Architecct without charge to the Contractor shall supply him with two copies (or a negative) of such drawings or details as are in the Architect's opinion, reasonably necessary either to explain and amplify the Contract Drawings or to enable the Contractor to execute and complete the Works in accordance with this Agreement on the dates shown within the Time Schedule or, where no such date is shown, as and when it is reasonably necessary for the Contractor to receive it.

Alternative 2
Clause 2.1
The Architect without charge to the Contractor shall supply him with two copies (or a negative) of such drawings or details which the Contract Documents expressly state will be prepared by the Architect on the dates shown on the Time Schedule.
Clause 2.2
The contractor shall submit to the Architect two copies (or a negative) of all other drawings, details, documents or information which are:
(a) reasonably necessary from time to time to explain and amplify the Contract Drawings, or
(b) reasonably necessary to enable the Contractor to execute and complete the Works or to comply with any instruction issued by the Architect, or
(c) stated in the Contract Documents to be provided by the Contractor.

11.3 REASONABLE WORKMANSHIP

Q. Does the term 'reasonable workmanship' have any implications as to the type of materials which should be used?

Together with those terms within standard forms which state that work is to be carried out with materials which conform to those specified in the contract documents, there is an implied obligation which has been embodied within the *Sale of Goods and Services Act 1982* that materials would be fit for the purpose for which they were intended, primarily where it was made known to the contractor either expressly within the contract documents or by implication that the purpose for which the materials are to be used may be unusual or peculiar to that particular scheme. It is of little value to the client if the contractor obtains materials which, though they adequately fulfil the functions for which they are normally used, are useless for the client's particular requirements.

The obligation of fitness for purpose is independent of the obligation to provide good workmanship and good materials. Both good workmanship and materials can be provided but there can still be a breach of the third obligation that the structure will be reasonably fit for the purpose required.

Clause 8.1 of JCT 80 may reduce the contractor's liability to ensure that workmanship and materials used are those specified. They are to be used only so far as they are 'procurable'. It is a clause which has been designed to recognize the realities of the building industry. Some things available when the specification was drawn up may no longer be available when the contractor needs them for the Works.

However, nothing may be substituted by the contractor for whatever reason unless written consent is given.

As a general principle, the client does not warrant that the site is fit for the works or that the contractor will be able to build there. Clause 11 of ICE and FIDIC contracts emphasize the contractual duty implicit in most standard forms that the contractor takes full responsibility for the method of construction, that he has examined the site himself and has allowed in his tender for all materials and work necessary for the completion of that contract.

Q. How skilled should a contractor be if he is to carry out the contract with reasonable workmanship?

The term reasonable workmanship assumes that the contractor is capable of carrying out the scheme, that he has the necessary skill and that he is able and competent to complete the work.

The ACA contract, clause 1.2, states that the contractor is required to exercise all the skill, care and diligence to be expected of a properly qualified and competent contractor experienced in carrying out work of a similar scope, nature and size to the Works. By signing such a contract, the contractor represents himself as being competent to carry out the Works. In deciding what degree of skill and competence a builder is required to have, all the circumstances of the contract should be considered including the degree of skill expressly or impliedly professed by the contractor.

At the same time, it is an architect's or engineer's duty to make reasonable enquiries that the contractor is suitable for carrying out the proposed work. Although they may not be liable to warrant either the contractor's insolvency or capability, they are obliged to inform the client of anything known to them about the contractor so as to prevent the client signing a contract with a contractor who is inefficient, incompetent or financially unstable. In other words, they are bound to make reasonable enquiries as to his eligibility.

A comparison of clauses on the contractor's duties and obligations for reasonable workmanship

Clauses 8.1.1/2 of JCT 80 state:

8.1.1   All materials and goods shall so far as procurable, be of the kinds and standards described in the Contract Bills provided that materials and goods shall be to the reasonable satisfaction of the Architect where and to the extent that this is required in accordance with clause 2.1.

8.1.2   All workmanship shall be of the standards described in the Contract Bills, or to the extent that no such standards are described in the Contract Bills, shall be of a standard appropriate to the Works, provided that workmanship shall be to the reasonable satisfaction of the Architect where and to the extent that this is required in accordance with clause 2.1.

Clause 7(1) of GC/Works/1 states:

The Contractor shall carry out and complete the execution of Works to the satisfaction of the SO.

13(1)   All things for incorporation shall be of the receptive kinds described in the Specification and/or Bills of Quantities and/or Drawings and the Contractor shall upon the request of the SO prove to the SO's satisfaction that such things do so conform.

13(4)   The Works shall be executed in a workmanlike manner and to the satisfaction in all respects of the SO. If any

A cautionary tale of what the client can do about the contractor's bad workmanship

In 1979, Mr and Mrs Lawson, employed Supasink Ltd to design, supply and install a fitted kitchen at their home for £1200; the plans were prepared and accepted by Mr and Mrs Lawson. The company's fitter followed an alternative design when installing the units because he regarded the original plan as impractical. After the units had been installed, but before the kitchen was completed, Mr and Mrs Lawson complained about the standard of work and a representative of the company offered to carry out certain rectifications free of charge.

Having taken expert advice, Mr and Mrs Lawson rejected the company's offer and requested the company to refund their deposit and remove the units which had been installed. The company refused.

In County Court proceedings Mr and Mrs Lawson were awarded damages for the difference between the cost of similar units and the contract price less the deposit, as well as £500 damages for inconvenience and loss of use. The trial judge accepted the evidence of Mr and Mrs Lawson's expert that remedial action was out of the question as a consequence of poor design and workmanship, and that it was impossible to achieve an acceptable standard through replacement and making good of the existing units.

The company raised two arguments on appeal. First, the company argued that it had substantially performed the contract and that, subject to a set-off for the costs of remedying any defects, it was entitled to the contract price. This argument traversed well-trodden ground, for the courts have long recognized a contractor's ability to recover the contract price where the cost of remedying the defects is small, having regard to the total contract price. Against this background, and in the light of the trial judge's acceptance of the expert evidence, the company's appeal on this ground was almost bound to fail. The trial judge's findings that the kitchen was not only extemporized, but installed in a shocking and shoddy manner was supported to the hilt by the evidence of the expert. In so far as substantial performance was concerned, the doctrine could hardly be applied where the original work was beyond redemption.

Secondly, the company argued that Mr and Mrs Lawson had failed to mitigate the loss by their rejection of the offer to rectify the defects free of charge. In short, had the Lawsons acted unreasonably in refusing Supasink Ltd's offer of rectification free of charge? The Court of Appeal unanimously said 'no' because, in Shaw, L.J.'s words, 'I do not see how Mr and Mrs Lawson could be required to afford the company a second opportunity of doing properly what they singularly failed to do adequately in the first instance'.

In other words:

1. A client should never repudiate a substantially performed contract for defective workmanship unless he feels sure he can satisfy a court that the defects were not of a minor nature, having regard to the amount of work involved;

2. If the contractor offers to remedy the alleged defects, the offer can be safely refused only if the defects are so serious as to have caused the client to lose confidence in the contractor's ability to perform his part of the agreement;

3. The importance of an inspection of the defective work by a suitably qualified expert cannot be overstated. The decision in *Lawson and Lawson* v. *Supasink Ltd.* was the trial judge's acceptance of the evidence given by the plaintiffs' expert, who examined the kitchen before the offending units had been removed. In such cases, photographs of the defective workmanship should also be taken.

Lawson & Lawson v. *Supasink Ltd.* [1984] 3 Tr.L. 37.

things for incorporation do not accord with the provisions of the Contract or if any workmanship does not so accord the same shall at the cost of the Contractor be replaced, rectified or reconstructed as the case may be, and all such things which are rejected shall be removed from the Site.

Clause 1.1 of the ACA form states:

1.1   In consideration of the payments to be made by the Employer to the Contractor under this Agreement the Contractor shall execute and complete the Works in strict accordance with the Contract Documents and shall comply with and adhere strictly to the Architect's instructions issued under this agreement.

1.2   Without prejudice to any express or implied warranties or conditions the Contractor shall exercise in the performance of his obligations under this Agreement all the skill, care and diligence to be expected of a properly qualified and competent contractor experienced in carrying out work of a similar scope, nature and size to the Works.

Clause 3.1 of the FAS contract states:

Materials and workmanship on all the materials, goods, and workmanship shall be the best of their respective kinds, in accordance with the qualities and details described in the drawings and Specification and Bills of Quantities, and to a standard of finish to the satisfaction of the Architect.

Clause 12.1 of the FAS contract states:

The whole of the materials and workmanship are to be the best of their respective kinds and to the satisfaction of the Architect. The Contractor shall be responsible for the proper and efficient execution of the work according to the true intent and meaning of the drawings and Specification/Bills of Quantities.

Clause 36(1) of the ICE contract states:

All materials and workmanship shall be of the respective kinds described in the Contract and in accordance with the Engineer's

instructions and shall be subjected from time to time to such tests as the Engineer may direct at the place of manufacture or fabrication, or on the Site or such other place or places as may be specified in the Contract.

Clause 8.1 of the FIDIC contract states:

The Contractor shall, with due care and diligence, design (to the extent provided for by the Contract), execute and complete the Works and remedy any defects therein in accordance with the provisions of the Contract. The Contractor shall provide all superintendence, labour, materials, plant, contractor's equipment and all other things, whether of a temporary or permanent nature, required in and for such design, execution, completion and remedying of the defects, so far as the necessity for providing the same is specified in or is reasonably to be inferred from the Contract.

Q. What are the contractor's duties and obligations in respect of reasonable workmanship?

It has been suggested that most construction industry disputes turn on the question of either workmanship or delay, even though the quality of workmanship is the subject of control by statute, common law and contract. Clause 2.1 of JCT 80 indicates the type of clause used within standard forms of building contract to give a clear meaning to the phrase 'reasonable workmanship':

The Contractor shall upon and subject to the Conditions carry out and complete the works shown upon the Contract Drawings and described by or referred to in the Contract Bills and in the Articles of Agreement, the Conditions and the Appendix . . . in compliance therewith using materials and workmanship of the quality and standard therein specified.

Where no specific standard is described in the contract documents, it is implied that the contractor is obliged to supply materials and workmanship compatible with good practice. Indeed, clause 8.1 of the FIDIC contract states that the works are to be executed with 'due care and diligence' (see 'A comparison of clauses on the contractor's duties and obligations for reasonable workmanship'), p. 154).

Q. What is the effect of appointing a clerk of works on liability for reasonable workmanship?

As a general principle, a contractor's liability for defective materials is not negated by the presence of either an architect or a clerk of works. Equally, the fact that a clerk of works is on site does not reduce the duty of an architect to ensure that the design is carried out under proper supervision to a reasonable standard of workmanship.

The ACA form makes no special provision for the appointment of a clerk of works, in other standard forms there is a provision. The terms which cover the scope of the clerk of works' duties varies from the length of GC/Works/1, clauses 16 and 13(1) and (2), to the shortness of FAS, clause 2.6. The FAS contract gives the terms of reference for the appointment by the client of a clerk of works, which are applicable to most building contracts. The clerk of works shall act solely as an inspector on behalf of the employer under the architect's directions.

JCT 80, clause 12, provides that apart from the clerk of works being unable to issue any instructions unless they are covered by those which can be issued by the architect under the contract, those instructions will be of no effect unless they are confirmed in writing by the architect within 2 working days.

Though a clerk of works may owe an implied duty of care similar to an architect's to those who may be affected by his actions under such contracts as JCT 80, a clerk of works is contractually unable to originate anything because of his function as an inspector. Indeed, an architect or engineer cannot use as a defence for his own negligence and lack of reasonable skill and care the incompetence of a clerk of works in carrying out the architect's duties. For example, in *Saunders & Collard* v. *Broadstairs Local Board* [1890] H.B.C. (4th edn, 1914) vol. 2, p. 164 (D.C.), engineers employed by the Board were found negligent in designing and supervising the construction of a combined drainage scheme. As a result of uneven levels, too weak a concrete mix and poor overall design, the sewers deflected causing damage calculated at £4600 in a contract valued at £5000. The clerk of works appointed by the Board to superintend the levels of the sewers was known to the engineers to be incompetent. They pointed this out to the Board. Nevertheless, the engineers relied on the clerk of works to supervise the works. It was found that the engineers were guilty of gross and culpable negligence, for if they did not trust the clerk of works, it was their business to ensure the work was properly carried out.

A comparison of clauses on written instructions

Clause 4.3.1 of JCT 80 states:

> All instructions issued by the Architect shall be in writing.

Clause 7(2) of GC/Works/1 states:

> If any of the SO's instructions issued orally have not been confirmed in writing by him such confirmation shall be given upon a reasonable request by the Contractor made within fourteen days of the issue of such instructions.

A cautionary tale of architects' and contractors' liability to third parties

A complex of large office, shopping and amenity areas, known as Great Oaks House in Basildon, Essex, was built in 1970–1. The building contractor was Thomas Bates & Son. The contract was under a JCT contract. The client under the building contract was EMI Development Holdings Ltd. It was the leaseholder of the land and premises built upon them. The freeholder was Basildon Development Corporation (now part of the New Town Commission). The Corporation architects' department designed the complex.

Sometime prior to completion of the building works EMI agreed to grant the Department of the Environment (DoE) an underlease of part of the complex, and those parts were occupied by the department at the end of 1971 on a 42-year lease.

The complete scheme contained four buildings. There was a low-rise, two-storey building with a flat roof, comprising offices, a Job Centre and a supermarket. At one end of the building abutted an eleven-storey tower block with nine storeys of offices. At the other end a cinema was linked to it. The fourth building was a public house which was adjacent to the tower block and the low-rise building, but separate from them.

The DoE took an underlease of part of the low-rise building, which was used as a Job Centre, with the top nine storeys of the eleven-storey block as offices. EMI kept the main structure of the low-rise building including the roof. The rooflights, ventilators, acoustic ceiling tiles and the depth of the plaster in the ceiling all formed part of the demised premises of the underlease.

The underlease required the DoE to keep the premises in good and substantial repair below 'level 120.50', as marked on the elevation drawing. This excluded the first-floor of the tower below the offices and the flat roof of the low-rise building, which remained the responsibility of EMI under the underlease. However, the underlease required the DoE to pay a percentage of the cost of repairing the structure and exterior below level 120.50 to EMI.

The DoE occupied the premises for more than 7 years. In about March 1979 water began to drip through the ceiling in the Job Centre. Defects in the flat roof were extensive and included defects in construction and design. As to construction, this included poor fixing of Metsec joists to the concrete beams and uneven upper surfaces of both joist and beams, so that they were not flush with each other, and the failure to cut or notch timber firrings to take account of the uneven surface on which they were laid and their poor fixings. The consequent irregularities of the roof led to ponding with long-standing accumulations of water.

So far as design defects were concerned, the architects failed to take into account the deflection caused by the load borne by the firrings, contrary to Code of Practice 144, Part 3 (para. 3.11.1). As a result, some ponding was likely because of the design, though failures in construction rendered the ponding substantially worse than it otherwise would have been.

The remedial works to the flat roof involved extensive use of internal scaffolding, so that it was unreasonable for the DoE employees to continue working in the Job Centre or offices in the low-rise building while work was carried out. Alternative accommodation was found at a cost of £86 000. The remedial works were comprehensive and cost £286 000, and involved not only replacement of the felt and insulation, but also the decking, re-cutting of the firrings, and substantial and noisy operations in rectifying the defects to the Metsec joists and concrete beams.

The DoE sought to recover £63 000 from the contractors. This was intended to reflect the percentage contribution due from them under the underlease, together with interest and costs they had paid in the action in which they had been named as a third party.

Though there was no danger to the safety of the employees and other persons in the department's leased premises, there was an increasing danger to their health and welfare because of the damp conditions.

The DoE also claimed the cost of alternative accommodation – £86 000. It was found that:

(continued)

1. Neither the construction nor the design defects were to that part of the building in which the DoE had any proprietary or possessory interest. But the leaks through the roof had damaged the plaintiff's property. The ceiling was stained and some acoustic tiles were loosened and others fell. However, the remedial costs for these were not claimed in the proceedings.

2. The condition of the roof as a result of the leaks was such that by the summer of 1981 it presented an imminent danger to the health of the DoE employees.

3. The remedial works meant the employees had to move into alternative accommodation. But the remedial scheme adopted was more than strictly necessary and contained an element of improvement. A lesser scheme involving stripping off and replacement of the felt and polystyrene insulation would not have demanded evacuation of the premises and would have cost considerably less.

4. The building contractor was aware that part of the low-rise building was intended for use by the Crown and had the means of knowledge that the occupants were likely to be the DoE.

5. The department could be expected to rely upon the contractor and architect to have taken reasonable care in the construction and design of the building, so that when it was handed over it would for a reasonable period be capable of providing safe and healthy accommodation and not cause physical damage.

6. In so far as the department was under a contractual obligation (by virtue of its underlease) to contribute to the landlord's cost of rectifying faults of construction or design, such obligation on the department was not reasonably foreseeable to the contractor or the architect. However, it was reasonably foreseeable to both that any defect in construction or design likely to cause danger to health or safety or cause physical damage would involve cost to whoever had any proprietary title in the premises, including the cost of repairs necessary to avert the danger.

7. Could the loss be recovered if the repairs were either for: the immediate protection of the health or safety of a subtenant's (i.e. the department's) employees; or the avoidance of threatened damage to the subtenant's premises (those parts comprised in the underlease)? This question raised the issue of whether the contribution to the cost of remedial works could be recovered where expenditure was incurred to avoid imminent (though not actual) danger to health and threatened (though not actual) damage to property.

   The judge found that he could see no necessity or policy that would require a court to draw any distinction between danger to the health of a subtenant occupier and the danger to the health of its employees. He held that the cases of *Anns* v. *London Borough of Merton* and *Batty* v. *Metropolitan Property Realisations Limited*

(1978) formed authority for the proportions that a builder who constructs negligently (and likewise an architect who designs negligently), and so creates a present or imminent danger to health or safety is liable to subsequent owners or lessees for any expense incurred in rendering the building safe and for economic loss due to the unsafe condition of the building. It was enough that the building endangered the health or safety of those lawfully on the premises. Further, the case could still be made that a claim to recover costs incurred for remedial works to prevent leakage that threatened damage to the department's property should not be considered as for purely economic loss.

The duty of care owed by the contractor to the department was also owed by the architect in respect of the design of the low-rise building.

8. The department was not entitled to recover from the contractor moneys paid for alternative accommodation, nor for the department's contractual underlease obligations. This contract obliged the DoE to contribute towards the cost of rectification of the defects, even where such rectification was necessary to correct the falls on the roof. Nor could it claim for the expenses of alternative accommodation.

The duty of care owed by the contractor to the department was also owed by the architect to the department in respect of

(continued)

the design aspects of the low-rise building.

9. Accordingly, the architect was in breach of duty for negligent design and was liable to the contractor to contribute to the contractor's liability in damages to the department in respect of the flat roof.

During the remedial work to the low-rise building it was discovered that certain concrete beams in the building were soft and a series of core tests revealed a weak mix of concrete due to excessive fine aggregate. This led to concern regarding the concrete pillars supporting the various floors in the tower block, with the top nine floors included in the department's underlease. The lower floors were not.

Core samples were taken and extensive ultrasonic pulse velocity testing was carried out on certain supporting pillars between ground- and second-floor levels. The results indicated that certain pillars of the tower block were insufficient to support safely the design load. On the consulting engineer's advice, these pillars were strengthened.

Of the nine pillars treated, three were below first-floor level, so the department's liability for these was to contribute a percentage of the total cost which was the direct responsibility of the landlord. The other six were on or above the first floor and were directly the department's responsibility. The department therefore sought to recover from the contractor the whole cost of the repair of these six pillars. The total cost of strengthening all nine pillars was £95 000, of which the department incurred £71 000.

The remedial works would allow the building to be used up to its design load, but such remedial works were not required if the building was used on a more restricted basis. So the purpose of the department's strengthening of the pillars was not to avert imminent danger to health or safety, nor to avoid physical damage to the tower block. It was to cure a defect which prevented the department from making full use of the building to the extent for which it was designed.

No cracks occurred in the concrete – i.e. no physical damage was suffered – because precautions were taken to ensure that the concrete was not loaded beyond its bearing capacity. The weak concrete did not constitute physical damage. The mere discovery of the defect did not convert the defect into physical damage. Where there was no physical damage and the remedial works were not undertaken to avoid physical damage, but simply to maximize the intended use of the building to its design loading, there was no cause of action in negligence.

Thomson Bates and Son v. *E. M. I. Development Holdings Ltd* (unreported).

Clause 23.1 of the ACA form states:

All certificates, notices, comments, instructions, consents, applications, orders or approvals to be given or made by either party or by the Architect under the terms of this Agreement shall be given in writing (subject to the provisions of Clause 8.3 and shall be served on the Architect and/or Employer and/or Contractor, by sending the same by pre-paid first class post to or delivering the same to the addresses stated in this Agreement (except as otherwise provided in the Contract Documents) and, if so posted, shall be deemed to have been given 2 working days after the date when posted.

For clause 2.3 of the FAS contract, see 'A comparison of clauses on complying with instructions' (p. 163).
Clauses 51(2) and (3) of the ICE contract state:

51(2)   No such variation shall be made by the Contractor without an order by the Engineer. All such orders shall be given in writing provided that if for any reason the Engineer shall find it necessary to give any such order orally in the first instance the Contractor shall comply with such oral order. Such oral order shall be confirmed in writing by the Engineer as soon as is possible in the circumstances. If the Contractor shall confirm in writing

A cautionary tale of butchery on a massive scale

The John Harrison House was to be a home for student nurses at the London Hospital. It was a ten-storey building constructed by McLaughlin & Harvey (builders) in 1962–3. Part of the design involved the use of reinforced concrete at gable ends. These panels required concrete nibs at each floor level, from the first to the tenth floors. These nibs were horizontal projections of reinforced concrete across the face of the panel, the sole purpose of which was to provide support for the brickwork at approximately 2.7 m centres up the face of the concrete panel.

To achieve satisfactory construction, it was necessary for the contractors to construct the panel accurately vertically, at least within permitted tolerances, so that the faces of the nibs were horizontal and 2.7 m apart. It was also necessary for the bricks to be laid such that the brickwork rose at a prescribed rate of 0.3 m for every four courses. In this way, the concrete and the brickwork was designed to fit. Any inaccuracy in setting out the construction could result in a poor fit at the stage where the brickwork was due to meet the nib.

In 1979, 16 years after completion, a bulge of brickwork in one of the lower panels alerted the owners to the possibility of defective work. The brickwork was opened up and it revealed that the concrete nib had been severely hacked back to accommodate the brickwork. As a result, all of the brickwork panels were opened up at nib level, and this disclosed that approximately 90% of the nibs

had been hacked back or butchered. In some instances, it was so severe that the nib was hacked right back, leaving the steel reinforcement sticking out.

Remedial works had to be put in hand to re-form the nibs and erect new brickwork cladding. As a result, the hospital sued the builders and also the architects, both in respect of their own conduct and that of the clerk of works, who was alleged to have been the agent of the architects and consulting engineers. It was alleged that the architects and clerk of works had failed to stop the builders from drilling and hammering the nibs. They failed to inspect the nibs before the bricks were erected. The allegations against the consulting engineers were similar to those against the architect and clerk of works.

In their defence the architects denied that the clerk of works was their servant or agent. They contended that he was the servant of the hospital and that the damage was caused, therefore, wholly or in part by the hospital as a result of the negligence of its clerk of works in failing to detect or prevent the builder from committing the alleged breaches of contract.

In considering the position of the clerk of works it was held that though he had been recommended by the architects and had worked with them on two previous projects, he was nevertheless the employee of the hospital. The clerk of works knew nothing about the butchering of the nibs. The clerk of works was a man of long experience and

sound competence. He was regarded as a strict clerk of works. He had other jobs to inspect, as well as this particular contract. He said that he had never heard the sound of loud or incessant hammering with Kango hammers when he had been on the site. Expert evidence varied as to the time it would take to hack back one of the nibs, but generally it would seem to have taken half a day to hack back one nib, of which there were over 80, and lay the bricks and to cover what had been done.

It was held that the architect was not negligent in not detecting that the nibs were being butchered. As soon as it had been butchered, it would be covered up by brickwork and there would be nothing for the architect to see on his frequent visits to the site. The only possible explanation was that deliberate steps were being taken by the contractor to conceal what was going on from those whose duty it would have been to stop it. It was destruction on a massive scale. Approximately 80 nibs were either hacked back to some extent or hacked right back. No bricklayer or operative acting in that way could fail to know what he was doing was wrong. Accordingly, they must have deliberately concealed it.

The hospital failed to prove that the architect or clerk of works were negligent. As to the clerk of works, not only was he not negligent,

(continued)

he was the employee of the hospital and not an agent of the architect. Furthermore, there was no evidence of any conspiracy between the architect, clerk of works and consulting engineers and the contractor deliberately to conceal the damage to the nibs. The alleged negligence against the consulting engineers was not proved.

As far as the action against the builders was concerned, clearly they were liable. Further, they could not claim that any action against them was statute barred under the *Limitation Act 1980*, in view of the fact that there was fraudulent concealment. Accordingly, by virtue of section 32, the limitation period did not begin to run until the hospital had

discovered the concealment, in this case the bulge in the brickwork which was detected in November 1979.

Gray & Others v. *T.P. Bennett & Son & Others*, (1987) unreported.

to the Engineer any oral order by the Engineer and such confirmation shall not be contradicted in writing by the Engineer forthwith it shall be deemed to be an order in writing by the Engineer. No variation ordered or deemed to be ordered in writing in accordance with sub-clauses (1) and (2) of this Clause shall in any way vitiate or invalidate the Contract but the value (if any) of all such variations shall be taken into account in ascertaining the amount of the Contract Price.

51(3)   No order in writing shall be required for increase or decrease in the quantity of any work where such increase or decrease is not the result of an order given under this Clause but is the result of the quantities exceeding or being less than those stated in the Bill of Quantities.

Clause 2.5 of the FIDIC contract states:

Instructions given by the Engineer shall be in writing, provided that if for any reason the Engineer considers it necessary to give any such instruction orally, the Contractor shall comply with such instruction. Confirmation in writing of such oral instruction given by the Engineer, whether before or after the carrying out of the instruction, shall be deemed to be an instruction within the meaning of this Sub-Clause. Provided further that if the Contractor, within 7 days, confirms in writing to the Engineer any oral instruction of the Engineer and such con-

firmation is not contradicted in writing within 7 days by the Engineer, it shall be deemed to be an instruction of the Engineer.

Q. In general terms, what are the parties' obligations for the issue and compliance with instructions on workmanship?

The extent to which instructions may be issued to the contractor is phrased in much wider terms under clause 13(1) of ICE and FIDIC contracts than in other standard forms apart from ACA. In the former, instructions and directions may be issued to the contractor who shall comply and adhere strictly to them, provided that it is physically and legally possible to do the work. Instructions may be issued on any matter connected with the works, whether or not it is mentioned in the contract.

In JCT 80, GC/Works/1 and FAS, instructions may only be issued on matters expressly set out within the terms of the contract (see 'A comparison of clauses on complying with instructions') p. 163.

The Contractor, under JCT 80, clause 4.1.1, is only obliged to comply with instructions if the architect can

---

A cautionary tale about writing clearly

A firm of London solicitors were ordered by Mr Justice Jupp to pay damages of £95 000 which included interest for giving 'disastrous' advice to their property company client, Socpen Trustees Ltd, which had lost £90 000 rent on offices.

The dispute concerned offices in Rathbone Street, West London, leased to a business by Socpen. A 'get-out' clause allowed either party to break the agreement after 15 years.

A badly worded letter from the solicitors, Wood, Nash & Winters, of Gray's Inn misled Socpen's secretary into thinking the lease could not be terminated and that the tenants could stay on at the same rent for many more years. Mr Justice Jupp remarked that part of the letter was phrased in 'very obscure' English, and it was not surprising that the secretary who was not a lawyer misunderstood the letter which emanated from the solicitor's negligence and which produced such disastrous results for Scopen.

Socpen Trustees Ltd. v. *Wood Nash & Winters*, (1983) *The Times*, 7 October.

---

produce express authority for them in the contract. The contractor's compliance with an instruction is limited where the instruction is one requiring a variation. The contractor need not comply to the extent that he makes reasonable objection in writing to the architect to such compliance. The term arose because of the belief held by the JCT that some measure of protection should be given to the contractor where an instruction would substantially alter the conditions on which the contractor based his tender.

By way of contrast, under ACA, clause 17, the contractor shall not comply with instructions before supplying estimates of the work, its effect on the contract time or sum, when the instruction affects the time or price of the contract.

Standard forms expressly state that instructions are to be given and confirmed in writing (see 'A comparison of clauses on written instructions' p. 157). It follows upon the rule of law that oral promises or instructions cannot add to, vary or contradict a written contract. However, a client may be obliged to honour an architect's oral instruction though it went against an express term of the contract in certain circumstances. The rule of law is riddled with exceptions. A written contract can be varied by agreement for consideration. A written contract could also provide that an oral promise could vary any of its terms.

A comparison of clauses on complying with instructions

Clause 4.1.1 of JCT 80 states:

> The Contractor shall forthwith comply with all instructions issued to him by the Architect in regard to any matter in respect of which the Architect is expressly empowered by the Conditions to issue instructions.

Clause 7(1) of GC/Works/1 states:

> (1) The Contractor shall carry out and complete the execution of the Works to the satisfaction of the SO who may from time to time issue further drawings, details and/or instructions, directions and explanations (all of which are hereafter referred to as 'the SO's instructions') in regard to:

(a) the variation or modification of the design, quality or quantity of the Works or the addition or omission or substitution of any work;

(b) any discrepancy in or between the Specification and/or Bills of Quantities and/or Drawings;

(c) the removal from Site of any things for incoporation which are brought thereon by the Contractor and the substitution therefore of any other such things;

(d) the removal and/or re-execution of any work executed by the Contractor;

(e) the order of execution of the Works or any part thereof;

(f) the hours of working and the extent of overtime or nightwork to be adopted;

(g) the suspension of the execution of the Works or any part thereof;

(h) the replacement of any foreman or person below that grade employed in connection with the Contract;

(i) the opening up for inspection of any work covered up;

(j) the amending and making good of any defects under Condition 32;

(k) the execution in an emergency of work necessary for security;

(l) the use of materials obtained from excavations on the Site;

(m) any other matter as to which it is necessary or expedient for the SO to issue instructions, directions or explanations.

Clause 2.3 of the FAS form states:

The Architect may issue instructions, normally in writing and the Contractor shall comply forthwith with these – if given verbally the Contractor shall confirm them in writing within 7 days (unless already so confirmed by the Architect) to the Architect for him to ratify – the Contractor shall still comply unless the Architect dissents within a further 7 days.

Clause 8 of the ACA form lists a number of specific areas where an architect may issue instructions:

8.1 The Architect shall have authority to issue instructions at any time up to the taking over of the Works and the Contractor shall immediately comply with all instructions issued to him by the Architect in regard to any of the following matters:

(a) the removal from the Site of any work, materials or goods which are not in accordance with this Agreement;

(b) the dismissal from the Works of any person employed on them if, in the opinion of the Architect, such person misconducts himself or is incompetent or negligent in the performance of his duties;

(c) the opening up for inspection of any work covered up or the carrying out of any test of any materials or goods or of any executed work;

(d) the addition, alteration or omission of any obligations or restrictions in regard to any limitations of working space or working hours, access to the Site or use of any parts of the Site;

(e) the alteration or modification of the design, quality or quantity of the Works as described in the Contract Documents, including the addition, omission or substitution of any work, the alteration of any work, the attraction of any kind or standard of materials or goods to be used in the Works and the removal from the Site of any materials or goods brought on to it by the Contractor for the Works;

(f) on any matter connected with the Works;

(g) pursuant to clauses 1.5, 1.6, 1.7, 2.6 (if applicable), 3.5, 9.4, 9.5, 10.2, 11.8, 12.2 and 14.

Clause 13 of the ICE contract states:

13. (1) Save in so far as it is legally or physically impossible the Contractor shall construct, complete and maintain the Works in strict accordance with the Contract

to the satisfaction of the Engineer and shall comply with and adhere strictly to the Engineer's instructions and directions on any matter connected therewith (whether mentioned in the Contract or not). The Contractor shall take instructions and directions only from the Engineer or (subject to the limitations referred to in clause 2) from the Engineer's Representative.

(2) The whole of the materials, plant and labour to be provided by the Contractor under clause 8 and the mode, manner and speed of construction and maintenance of the Works are to be of a kind and conducted in a manner approved of by the Engineer.

(3) If in pursuance of clause 5 or sub-clause (1) of this clause the Engineer shall issue instructions or directions which involve the Contractor in delay or disrupt his arrangements or methods of construction so as to cause him to incur cost beyond that reasonably to have been foreseen by an experienced contractor at the time of tender then the Engineer shall take such delay into account in determining any extension of time to which the Contractor is entitled under Clause 44 and the Contractor shall subject to Clause 52(4) be paid in accordance with Clause 60 the amount of such cost as may be reasonable. If such instructions or directions require any variation to any part of the Works the same shall be deemed to have been given pursuant to Clause 51.

Clause 13.1 of the FIDIC contract states:

Unless it is legally or physically impossible, the Contractor shall execute and complete the Works and remedy any defects therein in strict accordance with the Contract to the satisfaction of the Engineer. The Contractor shall comply with and adhere strictly to the Engineer's instructions on any matter, whether mentioned in the Contract or not, touching or concerning the Works. The Contractor shall take instructions only from the Engineer or, subject to the provisions of Clause 2, from the Engineer's Representative.

Q. What is my liability if I accept a low standard of workmanship?

It is difficult to include in a standard form of contract a precisely worded clause covering the standard of workmanship and the quality of materials to be expected from each contractor every time on all schemes where the contract is used. Forms, therefore, generally allow for some degree of flexibility. The architect may use his discretion on what is, and what is not, acceptable in some circumstances.

For example, JCT 80, clause 2.1, provides that 'where and to the extent that approval of the quality of materials or of the standards of workmanship is a matter for the opinion of the Architect such quality and standards shall be to the reasonable satisfaction of the Architect'.

Where there is a clearly worded term to this effect and there are no contrary clauses, you may take into account the price at which the work is being done to establish whether or not it is adequate. In these circumstances, you may not be liable to the client if you issued instructions accepting a lower standard of work where the price itself is low. However, it does not matter if that price is low, you must still see that the contract is properly carried out.

Q. To what extent should I supervise a contractor to ensure reasonable workmanship?

Your duties of supervision are based upon the ordinary skill and care to be expected from a competent practitioner, judged by the standards prevailing at the time.

A cautionary tale of building down to a price

A building owner entered into a JCT standard form of contract with a builder to construct a house for the admittedly low sum of £1910. Mr Cotton was nominated as the architect.

Two years after the house was completed, the architect brought an action against his client, Mr Wallis, claiming a sum of money, the balance of fees and expenses owed to him. Mr Wallis counter-claimed for damages, alleging that the architect had not exercised due skill and care in supervising the work and ensuring that the house was constructed with proper materials and good workmanship.

The County Court judge, in dismissing both claim and counter-claim, which was upheld by the Court of Appeal, found that while there were a number of items of workmanship and materials which were not as good as they might have been, and while another architect might have required a higher standard, the house was being 'built down to a price', so that the builder could not be expected to execute the work in a perfect manner. Instructions issued by the architect passing defects did not amount to negligence or breach of duty, provided that he used his skill and acted reasonably.

Cotton v. *Wallis*, [1955] 1 W.L.R. 1168.

A cautionary tale of the drains which failed because of their unsuitable design, not because of the contractor's workmanship

In 1972 the Peabody Charity decided to build 245 houses on a hillside at Knights Hill, Lambeth. They retained the firm of Sir Lindsay Parkinson & Co. as building contractors, and Austin Vernon & Partners as the architects.

The architects were to design a suitable drainage system for the site and the contractors were to build it in accordance with their instructions. The architects, rather than adopt a traditional rigid pipe drainage system which would have been unsuitable for the site, designed a drainage system which was flexible and would allow for the subsoil movements of London clay which tends to expand and contract with changing seasons. The London Borough of Lambeth approved the design.

In early 1973 the contractors were ready to start laying the drains. The architects had a trainee architect supervising for them on site. The local authority had appointed an unqualified though experienced drainage inspector to inspect the site works.

The architect and the inspector met and decided that the drains should be constructed in the traditional way, not in the way set out in the design plans deposited with Lambeth LBC. The architect issued instructions for the revised work to the contractor.

During 1975 and 1976, before the development had been completed, testing of the drains revealed that a substantial number of them had failed. As a result, the drainage system had to be reconstructed by the contractors, at an estimated cost of £118 139. The development was delayed for about 3 years. Peabody lost rents which they would otherwise have received. The contractors claimed that under their contract with Peabody they were entitled to be paid substantial additional sums because of the delay. It was found that they were so entitled. It was implied that the architects would have been found negligent had they not already settled Peabody's claim against them.

Peabody Donation Fund v. *Sir Lindsay Parkinson & Co. Ltd. & Others* [1983] 1 W.L.R. 754.

The degree of supervision required must be governed to some extent by your confidence in the contractor. If and when something occurs which should indicate to you a lack of confidence in the contractor, then in the interest of your client the standard of your supervision should be higher.

No one suggests that you are required to tell a contractor how his work is to be done, nor are you responsible for the manner in which the contractor does the work. What your supervisory duty does require of you is to follow the progress of the work and to take steps to see that those works comply with the general requirements of the contract in specification and quality.

It is a very weak argument that when an architect or engineer undertakes and is handsomely paid for supervision, that the limit of his duty is to pay occasional visits at longer or shorter intervals to the site, and that in paying those visits assumes that all is right which he does not observe to be wrong.

Q. In general terms, what are the architect's or engineer's liabilities to a third party for a contractor's reasonable workmanship?

Where there has been defective workmanship on a scheme and a contractor has been sued as a result of it, a defence has sometimes been put forward that the architect or engineer owed a duty of care to the contractor to detect or prevent the defective work. For example, where a party wall collapses during the course of construction. The duty of care which an architect or consulting engineer owes to a third party is limited by the assumption that the contractor who executes the work acts at all times as a competent contractor.

The contractor cannot seek to pass the blame for incom-petent work on to the architect or engineer on the grounds that they failed to intervene to prevent it.

The architect's responsibility is for the design, and his supervisory responsibility is to his client to ensure that the works are carried out in accordance with that design. But, if the design was so faulty that a component contractor in the course of executing the works could not have avoided the resulting damage, then on principle the designer should bear the loss.

11.4 REASONABLE TIME

Q. What is the effect of the term 'reasonable time'?

What is a reasonable time may not depend solely upon the convenience and financial interests of the contractors. No doubt, it is in their interest to have every detail 'cut and dried' on the day a contract is signed, but a contract may not contemplate that. Rather, it may contemplate further drawings and details being provided. The architect or engineer is to have time to provide them which is reasonable having regard to the point of view of him and his staff and the point of view of the client as well, as the point of view of the contractor.

Where the time for completion is not given in the contract documents, the *Supply of Goods and Services Act 1982*, Part 2, section 14(1), provides for a term to be implied that the work will be carried out within a reasonable time. However, if parties to a contract were told by the client the contract completion date because it had been left out of the contract documents, such evidence may not be admitted, particularly where to put in the date would lead to a severe liquidated damages clause being brought into operation. In other words, as a general principle, where a complete blank is left in a material part of the contract evidence is not admissible to fill it.

Q. What duties and obligations arise when a date is given in the contract for possession of the site?

Subject to any provisions to the contrary, the contractor's right to the possession of the site on the date which is entered into the contract is an absolute one. It is fundamental to the contract if the contractor is to complete the works by the completion date. JCT 80, clause 23.1, states, 'On the date of possession, possession of the site shall be given to the Contractor who shall thereupon begin the Works, regularly and diligently proceed with the same and shall complete the same on or before the completion date'. Similar terms are used in ACA, FAS, ICE and FIDIC contracts to grant a licence to the contractor to enter and occupy the site until the works are completed (see 'A comparison of clauses on the commencement and completion of works', this page). By implication the client has an obligation not to withdraw that licence unless the terms of the contract are such as to permit its determination in the particular circumstances (see 'A comparison of clauses, on the determination of a contract because of the contractor's default, p. 172).

A licence is an authority to do something which would otherwise be inoperative, wrongful or illegal – e.g. to enter on land which would otherwise be a trespass. A licence passes no interest, and a mere licence, such as is given to a contractor, is always revocable.

A contract necessarily requires the building owner to give the contractor such possession, occupation and use as is necessary to enable him to perform the contract. But whether in a given case the contractor in law has possession must be dependent at least as much on what is done as on what the contract provides. Unlike other standard form building forms, ICE and FIDIC specifically provide for an extension of time to be granted and the payment of reasonable costs if the client fails to give the contractor possession of the site on the due date (see 'A comparison of clauses on the commencement and completion of works', below).

A comparison of clauses on the commencement and completion of works

Clause 23.1/2 of JCT 80 states:

23.1   On the date of possession, possession of the site shall be given to the contractor who shall thereupon begin the works, regularly and diligently proceed with the same and shall complete the same on or before the completion date.

23.1.2   Where clause 23.1.2 is stated in the Appendix to apply the Employer may defer the giving of possession for a period not exceeding six weeks or such lesser period stated in the Appendix calculated from the date of possession.

Clause 6 of GC/Works/1 states:

Possession of the Site or the order to commence shall be given to the Contractor by notice and the Contractor shall thereupon commence the execution of the Works and shall proceed with diligence and expedition in regular progression or as may be directed by the SO under Condition 7 so that the whole of the Works shall be completed by the date for completion.

Clause 4.1 of FAS states:

Progress, completion – the Contractor shall be given possession of this site and access to it on the date in Agreement item A5.1. He shall proceed diligently and expeditiously with the work, and shall be held responsible for any delays arising out of his failure so to do unless such delays are beyond the contractor's control as

A cautionary tale of what you can and cannot do with time clauses

By 1853 the parish church at Leiston, Suffolk, being in a decayed and ruinous state, Mrs Rose, then the Hon. Mrs Thelusson in conjunction with her mother, who later died, sought to obtain subscriptions for rebuilding the church. An agreement dated 15 April 1853 was made between the two ladies and the minister and churchwardens by which the former agreed 'That with their own monies and what could be raised by subscriptions they would raise the sums of money to be applied in rebuilding the church according to the plans of Mr. Buckton Lamb, architect'.

Prior to the agreement, Mr Lamb had been employed to prepare plans for rebuilding the church at a cost not exceeding £2500. The ladies, wanting to employ the parishioners in the works, instead of advertising, a specification of the proposed works was deposited in the parish schoolroom and certain drawings showing the general elevations were hung up, but there were no detailed working plans exhibited and no copies were allowed to be made of the plans.

Kemp's who were working bricklayers, tendered for the job, and the contract was awarded to them. One of the clauses of the contract which they signed stated:

If any alteration should hereafter be made by order of the said committee or their architect, by varying from the plans or the foregoing specification, either in adding thereto or diminishing therefrom, or otherwise however, such alteration, shall not vacate the contract here entered into, but the value thereof shall be ascertained by the said architect, and added to or deducting from the amount of the contract, as the case may be, nor shall such alterations, either in addition, or diminution, or otherwise supersede the conditions for the completion of the whole of the works, but the contractor or contractors shall, if such alterations, of whatever sort, require it, increase the number of his or their workmen so that the same, as well as the work contained in the foregoing particulars, shall be completely finished and delivered up to said committee on or before the day .... of ....; and in failure thereof, the contractor or contractors shall forfeit and pay to the said committee the sum of £5 for every week that the work shall remain unfinished, out of monies that may be due and owing to the contractor or contractors on account of the said works.

The blank in the contract relating to the completion date was not filled in. Instead each of the contracting parties were told verbally what it was to be. The contract was not a happy one, and numerous complaints were made by Kemp's. One of them was that they had been charged with a sum of £32 as a fine for delay in not completing the building of the church by a certain day.

It was found by the Vice-Chancellor, Sir John Stuart, that it was not enough for the contracting parties merely to be told of the completion date; He said:

Even if the evidence were clear (which it is not), in order to introduce this term into a written contract by parole evidence there must be something very strong in any case. But in this case the introduction is sought in order to inflict a penalty. In all that relates to penalties, the Court exercises a very nice and scrupulous judgment. The evidence as to the substitution of the verbal contract for the blank contained in the written contract is far from clear. On that part of the case I think the decision of Mr. Lamb [to impose a penalty] is wrong. It is a harsh and severe judgment, and cannot be upheld.

It was held that the court would not readily act on parole evidence to fill up a blank in a written contract, where the object of the evidence was to inflict a penalty or forfeiture. The court declared that Kemp's were not to be charged with the sum of £32 or any other sum in respect of the penalty for delay in completing the contract.

Kemp v. *Rose* [1858] I Giff. 258.

Clause 4.4 'Delay, extension of time'. He shall complete the whole of the works on or before the completion date in Agreement item A5.2, subject to the provisions of the afore-mentioned Clause 4.4.

Clauses 41 and 42(1) of the ICE contract state:

4.1   The Contractor shall commence the works on or as soon as is reasonably possible after the date of commencement of the works to be notified by the Engineer in writing which date shall be within a reasonable time after the date of acceptance of the Tender. Thereafter, the Contractor shall proceed with the works with due expedition and without delay in accordance with the Contract.

42(1) save insofar as the Contract may prescribe the extent of portions of the site of which the Contractor is to be given possession from time to time and the order in which such portions shall be made available to him and subject to any requirement in the Contract as to the order in which the works shall be executed the Employer will at the date of commencement of the works notified under Clause 41 give to the Contractor possession of so much of the site as may be required to enable to Contractor to commence and proceed with the construction of the works in accordance with the programme referred to in Clause 14 and will from time to time as the works proceed give to the Contractor possession of such further portions of the site as may be required to enable the Contractor to proceed with the construction of the works with due despatch in accord-ance with the said programme. If the Contractor suffers delay or incurs cost from failure on the part of the Employer to give possession in accordance with the terms of this Clause then the Engineer shall take such delay into account in determining any extension of time to which the Contractor is entitled under Clause 44 and the Contractor shall subject to Clause 52(4) be paid in accordance with Clause 60 the amount of such costs as may be reasonable.

Clauses 41.1 and 42.1 of the FIDIC contract state:

41.1   The Contractor shall commence the works as soon as is reasonably possible after the receipt by him of a notice to this effect from the Engineer, which notice shall be issued within the time stated in the Appendix to Tender after the date of the letter of acceptance. Thereafter, the Contrac-tor shall proceed with the work with due expedition and without delay.

42.1   Save insofar as the Contract may prescribe:
(a) The extent of portions of the site of which the Contractor is to be given possession from time to time;
(b) The order in which such portions shall be made available to the Contractor

and subject to any requirement in the Contract as to the order in which the works shall be executed, the Employer will, with the Engineer's notice to commence the works, give to the Contractor possession of:
(c) So much of the site, and
(d) Such access as, in accordance with the Contract, is to be provided by the Employer

as may be required to enable the Contractor to com-mence and proceed with the execution of the works in accordance with the programme referred to in Clause 14, if any, and otherwise in accordance with such reasonable proposals as the Contractor shall, by notice to the Engineer with a copy to the Employer, make. The Employer will, from time to time as the works proceed, give to the Contractor possession of such further portions of the site as may be required to enable the Contractor to proceed with the execution of the works with due dispatch in accordance with such programme or propo-sals, as the case may be.

A comparison of clauses on the programme of works

Clause 5.3.1.2 of JCT 80 refers to the programme of works in the following manner:

The Contractor without charge to the Employer shall provide the Architect (unless he shall have been previously so provided) with 2 copies of his master programme for the execution of the Works and within 14 days of any decision by the Architect under Clause 25.3.1 or 33.1.3 with 2 copies of any amendments and revisions to take account of that decision. It is noted in footnote (h) that this clause may be deleted if no master programme is required.

Clause 4.11 of FAS states:

Programme, progress chart – the Contractor shall prepare at the outset his detailed programme for completion of the works by the contract completion date, showing proposed starting and finishing dates for each trade, phase and nominated sub-contractor and supplier. He shall submit 2 copies of this to the Architect within 3 weeks of the signing of the contract, for information and comment. The Contractor shall revise it as necessary and keep an up-to-date copy in view in the site agent's office, and shall show progress achieved weekly in each trade and phase.

The Contractor shall constantly organise and progress the work to keep to and improve on the programme. If an extension of time or revisions become necessary, the Architect shall promptly be sent up-to-date revised dated copies, for information.

Clause 14(1) of the ICE contract states:

Within 21 days after the acceptance of his tender the Contractor shall submit to the Engineer for his approval a programme showing the order of procedure in which he proposes to carry out the works and thereafter shall furnish such futher details and information as the Engineer may reasonably require in regard thereto. The Contractor shall at the same time also provide in writing for the information of the Engineer a general description of the arrangements and methods of construction which the Contractor proposes to adopt for the carrying out of the works.

Clause 14.1 of the FIDIC contract states:

The Contractor shall, within the time stated in part II of these Conditions after the date of the letter of acceptance, submit to the Engineer for his consent a programme, in such form and detail as the Engineer shall reasonably prescribe, for the execution of the works. The Contractor shall, whenever required by the Engineer, also provide in writing for his information a general description of the arrangements and methods which the Contractor proposes to adopt for the execution of the works.

Q. What do the standard forms of contract say on commencement and completion dates?

JCT 80, clause 23.1, gives conditions for the commencement and completion of the works which are similar to those contained in other standard forms (see 'A comparison of clauses on the commencement and completion of works', p. 168). On the date of possession, possession of the site shall be given to the contractor who shall thereupon begin the works, regularly and diligently proceed with the same and shall complete the same on or before the completion date.

The measure of acceptable progress is specified in the ACA form, clause C, by making the Time Schedule a contract document. The works are to proceed not only regularly, but also in accordance with the dates set out in the Time Schedule.

In such contracts as JCT, ICE and FIDIC the programme of works, which is the equivalent of the Time Schedule, is not a contract document, but rather a management document (see 'A comparison of clauses on the programme of works', p. 170). Both are of the greatest importance in establishing whether or not the work is on time, whether instructions or variations give rise to extensions of time and, in the case of the ACA form, whether or not information has been prepared and issued on time either by the architect or by the contractor; TS3 of the ACA form 'The Time Schedule: Issue of Information (Clause 2)' requires a description of drawings, details or documents to be supplied by the architect to the contractor or submitted by the contractor to the architect, details of who is to provide the information and the date on which it is to be supplied or submitted.

Q. What is the effect of a time stipulation in a contract?

Stipulations as to time in standard forms of building contract are generally considered to be 'of the essence'. They are 'conditions' which are based on practical expediency, dictated by the experience of businessmen. A 'condition' may be interpreted as meaning a term the failure to perform which entitles the other party to treat the contract as at an end.

The intention of the parties to a building contract is invariably that the work should be started and completed within a specified time for sound financial reasons. The date for handing over the site by the client to the contractor, and the date by which the works will be completed, are specifically written into a building contract and are clear conditions of the standard forms.

Dates of possession and completion are entered into the Appendix of JCT 80, the Time Schedule of the ACA form, A5.1 and A5.2 in the Articles of Agreement of the FAS form, and in the Appendix of the ICE and FIDIC contracts.

There was an early school of thought, however, that the 'normal rule' within building contracts was that time was not of the essence where 'delay was contemplated as a possibility and provisions were made both to overcome it by allowing

for extensions of time and to avoid it by imposing liquidated damages. For example, in the case of *Felton* v. *Wharrie* (1906) H.B.C. (4th edn) vol. 2, pp. 398, 400, Alfred William Felton, a builder, agreed in the summer of 1904 to pull down all houses and buildings on a site in Great Portland Street, London, for Thomas Wharrie within 42 working days from the time when he should be admitted to the site. The contract sum was £75. In the event of the work being delayed, the builder was to pay Wharrie £1 for every working day the work was delayed. The work was delayed. Some time after the contract completion date had passed when Wharrie complained to Felton about his lack of progress, the builder said he could not tell if he would be able to complete the work even in four months. A fortnight later, Wharrie forcibly took possession of the site and employed another builder to complete the work. Felton had paid a £100 bond to Wharrie for the fulfilment of the contract. He brought an action to recover the bond and for damages for breach of contract. It was held that Wharrie had no right to determine the contract and that Felton was entitled to the return of the £100, the contract price and damages for lost profits on the unfinished balance of the contract. Wharrie was not entitled to liquidated damages accruing after the date of his taking possession.

A comparison of clauses on the determination of a contract because of the contractor's default

Clause 27 of JCT 80 gives the reasons by which a client may determine the contractor's employment as:

27.1   Without prejudice to any other rights or remedies which the Employer may possess, if the Contractor shall make default in any one or more of the following respects, that is to say:

27.1.1   If without reasonable cause he wholly suspends the carrying out of the works before completion thereof; or

27.1.2   If he fails to proceed regularly and diligently with the works; or

27.1.3   If he refuses or neglects to comply with a written notice from the Architect requiring him to remove defective work or improper materials or goods and by such refusal or neglect the works are materially affected; or

27.1.4   If he fails to comply with the provisions of either Clause 19 or 19A . . .

27.2   In the event of the Contractor becoming bankrupt . . .

27.3   . . . If the Contractor shall have offered or given or agreed to give to any person any gift or consideration of any kind as an inducement or reward for doing or forbearing to do or for having done or forborne to do any action in relation to the obtaining or execution of this or any other contract with the Employer . . .

Clause 45 of GC/Works/1 states:

The Authority may without prejudice to the provisions contained in Condition 46 and without prejudice to his rights against the Contractor in respect of any delay or inferior workmanship or otherwise, or to any claim for damage in respect of any breaches of the Contract and whether the date for completion has not elapsed, by notice absolutely determine the contract in any of the following cases, additional to those mentioned in Condition 55 (Corrupt gifts and payments of commission) hereof:

(a) If the Contractor, having been given by the SO a notice to rectify, reconstruct or replace any defective work or a notice that the work is being performed in an inefficient or otherwise improper manner, shall fail to comply with the requirements of such notice within seven days from the service thereof, or if the Contractor shall delay or suspend the execution of the works so that either in the judgment of the SO he will be unable to secure the completion of the works by the date for completion or he has already failed to complete the works by that date;

(b) (i) If the Contractor, being an individual, or where the Contractor is a firm, any partner in that firm shall at any time become bankrupt . . .

     (ii) If the Contractor, being a company shall pass a resolution, or if the Court shall make an order, that the company shall be wound up . . .

(c) In a case where the Contractor has failed to comply with Condition 56 (admission to the site), if the Authority (whose decision on this matter shall be final and conclusive) shall decide that such failure is prejudicial to the interests of the State.

Clause 20.1 of the ACA form states that the client may determine the contract:

Upon the happening of one or more of the following events, namely if the Contractor:

(a) Without reasonable cause (and subject always to Clause 21 of this Agreement) substantially suspends the execution of the works or any section before the taking over of the same;

(b) Fails or neglects to comply with his obligations under Clause 9.1 or 9.2 of this Agreement;

(c) Without reasonable cause fails to proceed regularly and diligently with the works or any section;

(d) Refuses or neglects to comply with any instruction which the Architect is empowered by this Agreement to give;

(e) Shall otherwise be in breach of this Agreement.

Clause 9 of the FAS form states:

9.1   Default by Contractor – the Contractor shall be considered in default if he:

9.11   Fails to proceed with the work regularly and with reasonable diligence, or wholly suspends the work before completion without reasonable cause;

9.12   Refuses or neglects persistently to replace defective work, materials, or goods, or to comply with instructions given to him by the Architect;

9.13   Commits any act of bankruptcy, or, being a company,

has a receiver appointed, or enters into liquidation (except for the purposes of reconstruction of the company);

9.14   Determination by Employer – in any of the aforementioned defaults the following rules shall apply:

(a)   in either of the 9.11 or 9.12 events the Architect shall send to the Contractor a written notice (by recorded delivery or registered post) pointing out such defaults, and the risk of determination if they persist;

(b)   if the Contractor continues the default for 14 days or more after receiving such notice, the Architect shall again inform the Contractor in writing that determination may be enforced if he continues to default;

(c)   if the Contractor still persists in the default the Employer may determine (but not vexatiously or unreasonably) by recorded delivery or registered post the Contractor's employment under the contract;

(d)   in any of the 9.13 events the Contractor's employment shall be determined automatically, but may be reinstated if the Employer and the Contractor or the liquidator, receiver, or manager so agree.

Clause 63(1) of the ICE contract states the reasons whereby a client may determine the contract in similar terms:

If the Contractor shall become bankrupt or have a receiving order made against him or shall present his petition in bankruptcy or shall make an arrangement with or assignment in favour of his creditors or shall agree to carry out the Contract under a committee of inspection of his creditors or (being a corporation) shall go into liquidation (other than voluntary liquidation for the purposes of amalgamation or reconstruction) or if the Contractor shall assign the Contract without the consent in writing of the employer first obtained or shall have an execution levied on his goods or if the Engineer shall certify in writing to the Employer that in his opinion the Contractor:

(a)   has abandoned the Contract; or

(b)   without reasonable excuse has failed to commence the works in accordance with Clause 41 or has suspended the progress of the works for 14 days after receiving from the Engineer written notice to proceed; or

(c)   has failed to remove goods or materials from the Site or to pull down and replace work for 14 days after receiving from the Engineer written notice that the said goods materials or work have been condemned and rejected by the Engineer; or

(d)   despite previous warning by the Engineer in writing is failing to proceed with the works with due diligence or is otherwise persistently or fundamentally in breach of his obligations under the Contract; or

(e)   has to the detriment of good workmanship or in defiance of the Engineer's instruction to the contrary sublet any part of the Contract:

then the Employer may give 7 days (14 days in FIDIC contract) notice in writing to the Contractor enter upon the site and the works and expel the Contractor therefrom.

Clause 63.1 of the FIDIC contract states:

If the Contractor is deemed by law unable to pay his debts as they fall due, or enters into voluntary or involuntary bankruptcy, liquidation or dissolution (other than a voluntary liquidation for the purposes of amalgamation or reconstruction), or becomes insolvent, or makes an arrangement with, or assignment in favour of, his creditors, or agrees to carry out the Contract under a committee of inspection of his creditors, or if a receiver, administrator, trustee or liquidator is appointed over any substantial part of his assets, or if, under any law or regulation relating to reorganization, arrangement or re-adjustment of debts, proceedings are commenced against the Contractor or resolutions passed in connection with dissolution or liquidation or if any steps are taken to enforce any security interest over a substantial part of the assets of the Contractor, or if any act is done or event occurs with respect to the Contractor or his assets which, under any applicable law has a substantially similar effect to any of the foregoing acts or events, or if the Contractor has contravened Sub-Clause 3.1, or has an execution levied on his goods, or if the Engineer certifies to the Employer, with a copy to the Contractor, that, in his opinion, the Contractor:

(a)   has repudiated the Contract; or
(b)   without reasonable excuse has failed
      (i)   to commence the Works in accordance with Sub-Clause 41.1; or
      (ii) to proceed with the Works, or any Section thereof, within 28 days after receiving notice pursuant to Sub-Clause 46.1; or
(c)   has failed to comply with a notice issued pursuant to Sub-Clause 37.4 or an instruction issued pursuant to Sub-Clause 39.1 within 29 days after having received it; or
(d)   despite previous warning from the Engineer, in writing, is otherwise persistently or flagrantly neglecting to comply with any of his obligations under the Contract; or
(e)   has contravened Sub-Clause 4.1,

then the Employer may, after giving 14 days' notice to the Contractor, enter upon the Site and the Works and terminate the employment of the Contractor without thereby releasing the Contractor from any of his obligations or liabilities under the Contract, or affecting the rights and authorities conferred on the Employer or the Engineer by the Contract, and may himself complete the works or may employ any other contractor to complete the works. The Employer or such other contractor may use for such completion so much of the Contractor's equipment, temporary works and materials as he or they may think proper.

Q. What is the effect of delay on the contract?

Contracts are made to be performed and not to be avoided.

There are terms to be implied within standard forms, if they are not clearly stated, that the client and the architect as much as the contractor will do nothing to prevent completion. Where such an obligation exists, it will be fulfilled if one has neither acted negligently nor unreasonably even though the contract may have been subject to protracted delay, provided that that delay is attributable to causes beyond one's control.

Delay on the contract completion date may be made the subject of an extension of time granted retrospectively. On principle, though there is a distinction between cases where the cause of delay is due to some act or default of the client such as not giving possession of the site in due time, or ordering extras or something of that kind. When such things happen, the contract time may well cease to bind the contractor because the client cannot insist on a condition if it is his own fault that the condition has not been fulfilled.

The completion date of the works is that date which is written into either the articles of agreement or the appendix of a contract. Practical completion of the works is simply given in clause 17.1 of JCT 80 as occurring when it is reached in the opinion of the architect. Whereas clause 4.2 of FAS states practical completion shall mean when the works are finished fit and ready for handover to and use by the employer with only acceptable minor items to be completed.

In the ACA form, clause 12.1, the phrase 'taking over' is used rather than practical completion i.e. the client takes over possession of the works, though the principle is the same as in clauses 48.1 of FIDIC. It will occur when the works are 'fit and ready' in the opinion of the contractor to be taken over by the client subject to the completion of any outstanding items. In other words, a practical completion certificate may be issued when, owing to latent defects, the works do not fulfil the contract requirements and that under the contract the works can be completed despite the presence of such defects.

Taking possession is not a mere question of fact; a formal act is needed to bring it about, namely the issuing of a practical completion certificate.

A cautionary tale about practical completion certificates

A fire in Hartlepool, Cleveland, gutted much of a new factory and caused damage estimated at £250 000; the question arose whether the contractors' or the client's insurance company should cover the loss. In February 1969 the contractors George Wimpey & Co. Ltd agreed with English Industrial Estates Corporation, a statutory body, to build large extensions to the existing factory which they owned. It was leased to and occupied by Reed Corrugated Cases Ltd, manufacturers of corrugated cardboard.

The contract was in the sum of £687 860 and was carried out under the JCT Standard Form of Building Contract Local Authorities Edition with Quantities (1968 revision). It was amended to allow work to be carried on and use made of parts nearing completion by Reed's, who wanted to continue making corrugated cardboard while the extensions were being built.

In September 1969 the Corporation's architect issued a practical completion certificate for the car-park. No other practical completion certificates were issued for four parts of the works in which equipment had been installed and which were being occupied by Reed when, on 18 January 1970, they were destroyed by fire. Had the certificates been issued, maintenance of the fire insurance cover for the works would have passed from Wimpey's to the Corporation.

It was found that the words to 'take possession of part of the works must be so interpreted as to give precision to the time of taking possession and accuracy in defining the part, which can only be achieved by the issuing of a practical completion certificate and all which it entails.

English Industrial Estates Corp. v. *George Wimpey & Co. Ltd.* [1973] 1 Ll. Rep. 118.

Q. What do the standard forms of contract say about extensions of time?

The obligation of the contractor to complete the works by the date given in the contract, and the liabilities which arise if they are not, is modified by clauses within the standard forms which allow an extension of time to be granted. They vary greatly in the detail and number of causes for which an extension may be granted (see 'A comparison of clauses on extensions of time, p. 177). FAS used to simply provide for the architect to grant an extension of time in writing at his absolute discretion after due consideration of circumstances which might warrant such an extension.

However, in the new clause 4.45, a list of admissible causes of delay is given. Generally the contractor is required to give within a specified time details of his claim for assessment by the architect. A claim under ICE and FIDIC, clause 44.1, may be made, among other causes of delay referred to in other parts of the contracts, against a variation order, increased quantities, exceptionally adverse weather conditions or other special circumstances of any kind whatsoever which may occur such as fairly to entitle the contractor to an extension of time. JCT 80 clause 25.4 gives thirteen 'relevant' events which may form the grounds for an extension of time.

By contrast, ACA gives two alternatives which can be deleted as appropriate. The first entitles the contractor to an an extension of time only where there is any act, instruction, default or omission by the architect or client which prevents the works from being taken over. The second adds to this four other grounds; *force majeure*, events arising from an insurance clause, war and other forms of civil disorder and delays of a statutory body.

Should the progress of work be such that the contractor is generally ahead of programme, the architect may not be obliged to allow an extension of time for one particular delay. The architect is generally required to make an extension of time only if the works are likely to be, or have been, delayed beyond the original completion date or any extended time previously fixed. If a contractor is well ahead with his work and is than delayed, the architect may reach the conclusion that completion of the work is not likely to be delayed beyond the date of completion. The contractor is under a double obligation. On being given possession of the site, he must begin the works and proceed regularly and diligently with them. He must also complete the works on or before the date for completion. If a delay occurs when two-thirds of the work has been completed in half the time, the contractor on resuming full work is not entitled to slow down so as to last out the time until the new date for completion where an extension of time is granted. He is thereby failing to proceed regularly and diligently with the work.

A comparison of clauses on extensions of time

Clause 25 of JCT 80 states:

25.2.1.1   If and whenever it becomes reasonably apparent that the progress of the works is being or is likely to be delayed the Contractor shall forthwith give written notice to the Architect of the material circumstances including the cause or causes of the delay and identify in such notice any event which in his opinion is a relevant event.

25.4   The following are the relevant events referred to in Clause 25:

25.4.1   Force majeure;

25.4.2   Exceptionally adverse weather conditions;

25.4.3   Loss or damage occasioned by any one or more of the specified perils;

25.4.4   Civil commotion, local combination of workmen, strike or lock-out affecting any of the trades employed upon the works or any of the trades engaged in the preparation, manufacture or transportation of any of the goods or materials required for the works;

25.4.5   Compliance with the Architect's instructions;

25.4.5.1   Under Clauses 2.3, 14.2, 14.3, 23.2, 34, 35 or 36; or

25.4.5.2   In regard to opening up for inspection of any work covered up or the testing of any of the work, materials or goods in accordance with Clause 8.3 (including making good in consequence of such opening up or testing) unless the inspection or test showed that the work, materials or goods were not in accordance with this Contract;

25.4.6   The Contractor not having received in due time necessary instructions, drawings, details or levels from the Architect for which he specifically applied in writing provided that such application was made on a date which having regard to the Completion Date was neither unreasonably distant from nor unreasonably close to the date on which it was necessary for him to receive the same;

25.4.7   Delay on the part of Nominated Sub-Contractors or Nominated Suppliers which the Contractor has taken all practicable steps to avoid or reduce;

25.4.8.1   The execution of work not forming part of this Contract by the Employer himself or by persons employed or otherwise engaged by the Employer as referred to in Clause 29 of the failure to execute such work;

25.4.8.2   The supply by the Employer of materials and goods which the employer has agreed to provide for the works or the failure so to supply;

25.4.9   The exercise after the date of tender by the United Kingdom Government of any statutory power which directly affects the execution of the works by restricting the availability or use of labour which is essential to the proper carrying out of the works or preventing the Contractor from, or delaying the Contractor in, securing such goods or materials or such fuel or energy as are essential to the proper carrying out of the works;

25.4.10.1   The Contractor's inability for reasons beyond his control and which he could not reasonably have foreseen at the date of tender to secure such labour as is essential to the proper carrying out of the works; or

25.4.10.2   The Contractors's inability for reasons beyond his control and which he could not reasonably have foreseen at the date of tender to secure such goods or materials as are essential to the proper carrying out of the works;

25.4.11   The carrying out by a local authority or statutory undertaker of work in pursuance of its statutory obligations in relation to the works, or the failure to carry out such work;

25.4.12   Failure of the Employer to give in due time ingress to or egress from the site of the works or any part thereof through or over any land, buildings, way or passage adjoining or connected with the site and in the possession and control of the Employer, in accordance with the Contract Bills and/or the Contract Drawings, after receipt by the Architect of such notice, if any, as the Contractor is required to give, or failure of the Employer to give such ingress or egress as otherwise agreed between the Architect and the Contractor;

25.4.13   By reason of the execution of work whose quantity was not reasonably accurately forecast in the Contract Bills.

Clause 28(2) of GC/Works/1 states:

28(2)   The Contractor shall be allowed by the Authority a reasonable extension of time for the completion of the works in respect of any delay in such completion which has been caused or which the Authority is satisfied will be caused by any of the following circumstances:

(a) the execution of any modified or additional work;

(b) weather conditions which make continuance of work impracticable;

(c) any act or default of the Authority;

(d) strikes or lock-outs of workpeople employed in any of the building, civil engineering or analogous trades in the district in which the works are being executed or employed elsewhere in the preparation or manufacture of things for incorporation;

(e) any of the accepted risks; or

(f) any other circumstance which is wholly beyond the control of the Contractor.

Provided that:

(i) except as so far as the Authority shall otherwise decide, it shall be a condition upon the observance of which the Contractor's right to any such extension of time shall depend that the Contractor shall, immediately upon becoming aware that any such delay has been or will be caused, give notice to the SO specifying therein the circumstances causing or likely to cause the delay and the actual or estimated extent of the delay caused or likely to be caused thereby;

(ii) the Contractor shall not be entitled to any extension of time in respect of a delay caused by any circumstance mentioned in sub-paragraph (2)(f) of this Condition if he could reasonably be expected to have foreseen at the date of the Contract that a delay caused by that circumstance would, or was likely to, occur;

(iii) in determining what extension of time the Contractor is entitled to the Authority shall be entitled to take into account the effect of any authorised omission from the works;

(iv) it shall be the duty of the Contractor at all times to use his best endeavours to prevent any delay being caused by any of the above-mentioned circumstances and to minimise any such delay as may be caused thereby and to do all that may reasonably be required, to the satisfaction of the SO, to proceed with the works; and

(v) the Contractor shall not be entitled to an extension of time if any such delay is attributable to any negligence, default or improper conduct on his part.

Clause 11.5, alternative 1 of the ACA form states:

Subject to Clauses 11.8 and 25.2 (where applicable) no extension of time shall be granted to the Contractor except in the case of any act, instruction, default or omission of the Employer, or of the Architect on his behalf, whether authorised by or in breach of this Agreement, which in the reasonable opinion of the Architect causes the taking-over of the works or of any section by the date or dates for taking-over stated in the Time Schedule to be prevented . . .

Clause 11.5, alternative 2, of the ACA form states:

Subject to Clauses 11.8 and 25.2 (where applicable) no extension of time shall be granted to the Contractor except in the case of:

(a) force majeure;

(b) the occurrence of one or more of the contingencies referred to in Clause 6.4;

(c) war, hostilities (whether war be declared or not), invasion, act of foreign enemies, rebellion, revolution, insurrection, military or usurped power, civil war, riot, commotion or disorder;

(d) delay or default by a governmental agency, local authority or statutory undertaker in carrying out work in pursuance of its statutory obligations in relation to the works or the exercise after the date of this Agreement of any statutory power which restricts the availability or use of labour or prevents or delays the contractor obtaining goods, materials, fuels or energy;

(e) any act, instruction, default or omission of the Employer, or of the Architect on his behalf, whether authorised by or in breach of this Agreement;

and only then to the extent that the Contractor shall prove to the satisfaction of the Architect that the taking-over of the Works or of any Section by the date or dates stated in the Time Schedule is prevented . . .

Clauses 4.44 and 4.45 of the FAS contract states:

4.44 extension of time – the Architect shall consider any notice of delay and claim, and shall, in his absolute discretion, grant appropriate extensions of time in writing as and if warranted by the circumstances. He may make interim awards, and may defer final decisions until after practical completion when the full position is apparent. The Architect shall give his decisions, in writing, to the Contractor as soon as practicable;

4.45 causes of delay – the admissible causes of delay are defined as follows:

(a) exceptionally adverse weather conditions;

(b) significant delays by nominated sub-contractors and/or nominated suppliers;

(c) significant delays by an authority and/or statutory undertaker in connection with their statutory obligations, or failure to do work;

(d) inability to obtain labour, materials, or goods, which could not have been foreseen at the date of tender;

(e) any direct or significant effect on the work relating to labour, materials, or goods, caused after the date of tender by government acts or controls;

(f) significant delays by civil commotion, strikes, or lock-out directly affecting the work;

(g) significant delays due to any loss or damage defined under the insurance provisions in clause 8.6 'Policies, perils';

(h) significant delays or frustration caused by the Employer over access to the site or any part thereof, or in the execution of work or supply of materials and/or goods which the Employer was to undertake;

(i)   significant delays arising from variation orders, including postponement; or in the issue of Architect's instructions or variation orders or drawings, or information requested in writing by the Contractor after allowing fair and reasonable time for its formulation and preparation;

(j)   significant delays due to opening up and/or testing required by the Architect, but not if faults were found or any materials or workmanship or items/goods were not in accordance with the contract documents;

(k)   delays due to the discovery of objects of artistic or archeological interest as clause 3.8 'Antiquities';

(l)   force majeure – the definition in the *Concise Oxford Dictionary* shall apply – 'irresistible compulsion or coercion, unforeseeable course of events excusing from "fulfilment of contract" '.

Clause 44(1) of the ICE contract states:

Should any variation ordered under Clause 51(1) or increased quantities referred to in Clause 51(3) or any other cause of delay referred to in these Conditions or exceptional adverse weather conditions or other special circumstances of any kind whatsoever which may occur be such as fairly to entitle the Contractor to an extension of time of the completion of the works or (where different periods for completion of different sections are provided for in the Appendix to the Form of Tender) of the relevant section the Contractor shall within 28 days after the cause of the delay has arisen or as soon thereafter as is reasonable in all the circumstances deliver to the Engineer full and detailed particulars of any claim to extension of time to which he may consider himself entitled in order that such claim may be investigated at the time.

Clause 44.1 of the FIDIC contract states:

In the event of:

(a)   the amount or nature of extra or additional work; or

(b)   any cause of delay referred to in these Conditions; or

(c)   exceptionally adverse climatic conditions; or

(d)   any delay, impediment or prevention by the Employer, or

(e)   other special circumstances which may occur, other than through a default of or breach of contract by the Contractor or for which he is responsible,

being such as fairly to entitle the Contractor to an extension of the time for completion of the works, or any section or part thereof, the Engineer shall, after due consultation with the Employer and the Contractor, determine the amount of such extension and shall notify the Contractor accordingly, with a copy to the Employer.

Q. What are my duties and liabilities when issuing an interim certificate?

The issuing of interim certificates follows upon inspection or examination of the works to ensure that they are properly carried out (see 'A comparison of clauses on access to the works for inspection or examination, p. 182).

As a general rule, you should not certify your work which has been incorrectly done. In discharging your function of issuing interim certificates, you are primarily acting in the protection of your client's interests by determining what payment can properly be made on account. Such determination is based on your assessment of the value of the work properly carried out. That assessment, in turn, is made as a result of your professional skill for which the client has engaged you.

It is part of the duty of care you owe to your client when carrying out an inspection to see that the value of work properly executed and only that is included in the valuation for the purpose of an interim certificate. Otherwise you may be liable to your client for any damage attributable to such default.

A cautionary tale about considering contractors' claims

Pacific Associates were dredging contractors. They entered into a contract with the ruler of Dubai (the employer) to carry out dredging and reclamation works in Dubai Creek Lagoon in the Persian Gulf for £20 million. The contract between them was in the FIDIC Standard Form (1969 edition). Halcrow International Partnership were appointed engineers under the contract. Pacific subcontracted the works to RB Construction.

A claim was made by RB Construction against Pacific and consequentially by Pacific against the employer, under clause 12 of the FIDIC contract. The claim was over 'hard materials' which RB Construction encountered and which it alleged could not reasonably be foreseen. It also alleged breach of warranty or representation as it had been led to expect a much lower percentage of hard material by the information supplied by the employer, on which it had relied when entering into the contract. The hard materials claim was for £31 million plus interest.

As a claim under the FIDIC contract, Pacific had first to submit it to Halcrow for interim certification under clause 60 of the contract. If rejected, the contract then allowed Pacific to submit the consequential dispute to Halcrow again, this time for their decision as engineers under clause 67 of the contract which is a prerequisite to a request for arbitration. In this case, Halcrow consistently refused to certify Pacific's claim for extra payment and also rejected the claim by their clause 67 decision.

Accordingly, Pacific sought arbitration.

The claim in arbitration was subsequently settled when the employer paid Pacific £10 million with all parties meeting their own costs. Pacific was authorized to accept this sum for itself and RB Construction, and it was agreed that such payment constituted full and final settlement of both contractors' claims against the employer.

Subsequently Pacific and RB Construction sued Halcrow in their capacity as administrators of the contract, alleging breach of their duties to use due care and to act impartially in certifying under clause 60 and in making decisions under clause 67. Pacific and RB Construction alleged that Halcrow had failed to act with reasonable care and skill, fairness and impartiality in considering the claim in respect of hard materials. In Halcrow's view, the hard materials should have been foreseen by Pacific and RB Construction.

The total claim against Halcrow was for £45 million, made up as follows: entitlement which they should have received under the FIDIC contract, £31 million; interest, £22 million; arbitration costs, £2 million; less credit for amount recovered, £10 million.

On behalf of Halcrow it was claimed, first, that no cause of action was disclosed against them, and secondly, that the action was unconscionable and an abuse of the process of the court.

Of particular relevance were some specific contract conditions (in addition to the general standard printed conditions), of which the most important was specific condition 86:

Neither any member of the employer's staff nor the engineer nor any of his staff, nor the engineer's representative shall be in any way personally liable for their acts or obligation under the contract, or answerable for any default or omission on the part of the employer in the observance or performance of any of the acts, matters or things which are herein contained.

So far as the general conditions of the FIDIC contract are concerned, the most important point to note is that any disputed certificate or decision by the engineers can always be made the subject of review by an arbitrator. So the certificates and decisions of the engineers do not bind the contractor unless he chooses to accept them by not challenging them.

The crucial question was whether Halcrow as engineers under the FIDIC contract, including in this case the specific conditions, owed a duty of care in tort to the contractor. This point was taken as a preliminary issue and, for the purposes of the argument in law as to whether or not a duty of care existed, it was assumed that the factual allegations of negligence against Halcrow were well-founded. Halcrow were appointed by the employer to act as engineers for the purposes of the contract, and as such were the agents of the employer.

(continued)

The scope of this agency was to be found by considering the functions and duties of the engineers under the contract. It followed that short of fraud or dishonesty, the employer would be liable for the acts of the engineers.

In deciding whether Halcrow owed a duty of care in tort to the contractor, the judge said: 'The essential question is whether in the particular circumstances of the case it is just and reasonable and in accordance with sound commonsense that the law should impose a duty of care on the defendant.' In the judge's view, the question of liability depended upon the terms of the contract which brought the engineers into relationship with the contractor. The overriding intention of the contract was to put the engineers beyond the reach of legal responsibility for their acts by denuding them of any attributes which might give rise to liability.

Accordingly, it was held that there was no duty of care owed by Halcrow to Pacific or RB Construction. The hard materials claim, the interest claim and the arbitration costs claim were all dealt with as part of a settlement and could not, as a matter of causation, be laid at the door of the engineers.

As the arbitration settlement was in full and final settlement of all claims against the employer, it was held to be an abuse of the process of court and unconscionable to allow Pacific and RB Construction to pursue the same claim against the engineers who were acting as agents of the employer.

Pacific Associates and R.B. Construction v. *Halcrow International Partnership & Others*, (1988) unreported.

A comparison of clauses on access to the Works for inspection or examination

Clause 3.10 of the RIBA Architect's Appointment states:

The architect will visit the site at intervals appropriate to the stage of construction to inspect the progress and the quality of the works and to determine that they are being executed generally in accordance with the contract documents. The architect will not be required to make frequent or constant inspections.

Clauses 8.3 and 11 of JCT 80 state:

8.3   The Architect may issue instructions requiring the Contractor to open up for inspection any work covered up or to arrange for or carry out any test of any materials or goods (whether or not already incorporated in the Works) or of any executed work . . .

11   The Architect and his representatives shall at all reasonable times have accesss to the Works and to the workshops or other places of the Contractor where work is being prepared for this Contract and when work is to be so prepared in workshops or other places of a Domestic Sub-Contractor or a Nominated Sub-Contractor the Contractor shall by a term in the sub-contract so far as possible secure a similar right of access to those workshops or places for the Architect and his representatives and shall do all things reasonably necessary to make such right effective.

Access in accordance with clause 11 may be subject to such reasonable restrictions of the Contractor or any Domestic Sub-Contractor or any Nominated Sub-Contractor as are necessary to protect any proprietary right of the Contractor or of any Domestic or Nominated Sub-Contractor in the work referred to in Clause 11.

Clause 13.2 of GC/Works/1 states:

The SO and his representative shall have power at any time to inspect and examine any part of the Works or any thing for incorporation either on the Site or at any factory or workshop or other place where any such part or thing is being constructed or manufactured at any place where it is lying or from which it is being obtained, and the Contractor shall give all such facilities as the SO or his representative may require to be given for such inspection and examination.

Clauses 4.1/2 of the ACA form state:

4.1 The Contractor shall give and shall procure that any of his servants, agents, suppliers or sub-contractors give to the Architect and his representatives full access to the works and to the workshops or other places where design of work is being prepared or goods or materials are being manufactured for the works so that the Architect and his representatives may test, inspect or examine the same.

4.2 The Architect may, if he so wishes, visit the site and the workshops and other places referred to in Clause 4.1 from time to time or as may be specified in the Contract documents and the Contractor shall do all things necessary to assist the Architect and his representatives during the course of such visits.

Clause 1.81 of the FAS contract states:

The Architect or any person authorised by him shall at all times have free access to the works and all other places where work is being prepared for this contract.

Clause 37 of the ICE contract states:

37 The Engineer and any person authorised by him shall at all times have access to the works and to the site and to all workshops and places where work is being prepared or whence materials manufactured articles and machinery are being obtained for the works and the Contractor shall afford every facility for and every assistance in or in obtaining the right to such access.

Clause 37 of the FIDIC contract states:

37.1 The Engineer, and any person authorised by him, shall at all reasonable times have access to the site and to all workshops and places where materials or plant are being manufactured, fabricated or prepared for the works and the Contractor shall afford every facility for and every assistance in obtaining the right to such access.

37.2 The Engineer shall be entitled, during manufacture, fabrication or preparation to inspect and test the materials and plant to be supplied under the Contract. If materials or plant are being manufactured, fabricated or prepared in workshops or places other than those of the Contractor, the Contractor shall obtain permission for the Engineer to carry out such inspection and testing in those workshops or places. Such inspection or testing shall not release the Contractor from any obligations under the Contract.

37.3 The Contractor shall agree with the Engineer on the time and place for the inspection or testing of any materials or plant as provided in the Contract. The Engineer shall give the Contractor not less than 24 hours' notice of his intention to carry out the inspection or to attend the test. If the Engineer, or his duly authorised representative, does not attend on the date agreed, the Contractor may, unless otherwise instructed by the Engineer, proceed with the tests, which shall be deemed to have been made in the presence of the Engineer. The Contractor shall forthwith forward to the Engineer duly certified copies of the test readings. If the Engineer has not attended the tests, he shall accept the said readings as accurate.

37.4 If, at the time and place agreed in accordance with Sub-Clause 37.3, the materials or plant are not ready for inspection or testing or if, as a result of the inspection or testing referred to in this Clause, the Engineer determines that the materials or plant are defective or otherwise not in accordance with the Contract, he may reject the materials or plant and shall notify the Contractor thereof immediately. The notice shall state the Engineeer's objections with reasons. The Contractor shall then promptly make good the defect or ensure that rejected materials or plant comply with the Contract. If the

---

A cautionary tale about the perils of not giving possession of the site on time

Rapid Building Group Ltd entered into a JCT 63 form of building contract with Ealing Family Housing Association for the construction of 101 dwellings.

By clause 21, possession of the site was required to be given to the contractor in order for him to commence work. The appendix entry to the contract required Ealing to give possession by a date in June 1980. In breach of this requirement, Ealing delayed the hand-over of the site for a considerable time due to problems with evicting squatters. The archi-tect purported to extend time in connection with this delay.

The contractor contended that there was no provision in clause 23 of the contract (dealing with extensions of time) to extend time for this particular cause of delay (i.e. late posses-sion), and that therefore the architect's certifi-cate under clause 22 that the Works ought to have been completed by the extended com-pletion date was invalid and with that invalidity the employer's right to liquidated damages disappeared.

The Court of Appeal upheld the contractor's contention and Ealing lost its right to claim liquidated damages. However, the court also held that Ealing could still sue for general damages for breach of contract for delay in respect of any delays which were the re-sponsibility of the contractor but, in the ab-sence of a liquidated damages provision, the losses would have to be proved.

Rapid Building Group Ltd v. *Ealing Family Housing Association* (1984) *24 B.L.R.S, C.A.*

Engineer so requests, the test of rejected materials or Plant shall be made or repeated under the same terms and conditions. All costs incurred by the Employer by the repetition of the tests shall, after due consultation with the Employer and the Contractor, be determined by the Engineer and shall be recoverable from the Contractor by the Employer and may be deducted from any monies due or to become due to the Contractor and the Engineer shall notify the Contractor accordingly, with a copy to the Employer.

11.5 REASONABLE PRICE

Q. What is the importance of a reasonable price?

A reasonable price and a steady cash flow are the life-blood of the building industry. They are vital to the contractor; delay in paying him for the work he does may result in his being short of working capital, having to borrow capital to pay wages and hire charges, and locking up in plant, labour and materials capital which he could have invested elsewhere.

There is an implied contractual term at common law which was merely codified by the *Supply of Goods and Services Act 1982*, Part II, section 15, that where consideration for a service is not determined by the contract, a reasonable price will be made for services rendered. A contractor is entitled to be paid a reasonable price which he may, subject to the terms

A cautionary tale about the all-seeing clerk of works

It is a truism that everybody knows that an architect or engineer cannot be on-site all the time, and everybody knows that the clerk of works is appointed to protect the interests of the employer against the builder mainly because the architect or engineer cannot be there. The clerk of works is to see to matters of detail, whereas the architect or engineer is personally responsible to see that his design is carried out.

Trollope was an architect appointed by the Leicester Board of Guardians to design and supervise the building of an infirmary under a contract which was of the usual character. The Board employed a clerk of works who, unknown to the architect, fraudulently colluded with the contractors, allowing them to deviate from the design by laying ground floor timbers directly on to the earth without the specified precautions against damp. The Board claimed damages against the architect for breach of contract to superintend the work.

Channel, J. held that if the architect had taken steps to see that the first block of buildings was done all right, and then he had left the next block of buildings to the clerk of the works to see that it was done in the second block in the same way as in the first, he should have had some doubt whether he would have been liable if the clerk of works had neglected that and allowed it to be done in a different way in the other part. But here there was nothing done at all to see that the design was complied with.

Leicester Board of Guardians v. *Trollope* (1911) 75 J.P. 197.

---

of the contract, be entitled to demand from time to time, for his labour and materials where the contract sum has not been fixed or the contract sum is yet to be agreed.

Q. What is the 'contract sum'? Is it a reasonable price?

The 'contract sum' is defined by clause B of the ACA contract in terms similar to those in other lump-sum standard forms of contract. It is the sum written into the articles of agreement for which the contractor has offered to execute, complete and maintain the works, together with such additions, or deductions as may be made under the provisions of the contract and which the client has undertaken to pay.

By contrast, in clause 1(1)i of the ICE contract, which is a re-measurement contract, the contract price is to be ascertained. The final price paid to the contractor need not be the original tender price, it will be found by the total re-measurement of the works, whether or not there has been any variation to the contract.

Under the standard forms an obligation is clearly placed upon the contractor that his tender price will be sufficient to carry out and complete the works. Clause 11(2) in the ICE form illustrates the point:

> The Contractor shall be deemed to have satisfied himself before submitting his tender as to the correctness and sufficiency of the rates and prices stated by him in the priced Bill of Quantities which shall (except in so far as it is otherwise provided in the Contract) cover all his obligations under the Contract.

Bills of Quantity may be defined as putting into words every obligation or service which will be required in carrying out the building project. However, a client may be under no obligation to pay for goods and materials which though not included in the bill of quantities were generally understood to be necessary and to be done by the contractor in order to complete the works.

For example, in *Williams* v. *Fitzmaurice* [1858] 3 Hurl. & Norm. 844, a fixed-price contract to build a house left out any mention of the floorboards in the specification. It was held that the contractor was not entitled to extra payment for the floorboards because it was evident from the contract documents that he was to do the flooring.

Q. What is the purpose of interim certificates?

The entire purpose of interim certificates is to give the contractor the proper amount of money which is due to him in agreed instalments, usually monthly, so that there is always a cash flow on which he can rely (see 'A comparison of clauses on interim certificates', p. 191).

An architect or engineer in issuing an interim certificate must honestly reflect on that certificate the true value of the work properly carried out, this can only be achieved by giving reasonable supervision to, or inspection of, the works. The duty to supervise or inspect the works is a clear requirement to follow its progress, and to take steps to see that the works comply with the general requirements of the contract both in specification and quality. The degree of supervision must be governed, to some extent, by confidence in the contractor. If and when something occurs which should indicate a lack of competence in the contractor, then in the interest of the client the standard of supervision should be higher. No one suggests that the architect or engineer is required either to tell a contractor how his work is to be done, or is responsible for the manner in which the contractor does the work.

Q. What is my liability if I do not tell my client that the works have not been completed on time?

An obligation may be placed on the architect or engineer to notify the client that the contractor has failed to complete the works by the agreed time after all extensions to the contract date have been taken into account.

The notification is important, for it determines from what date liquidated damages are to be recovered; it should be remembered in some cases where there is a contractual power to grant extensions of time if it is not properly exercised, for example, on account of delay caused by the client, then time for completion may become 'at large'; the effect is that they may be exonerated from liability to pay liquidated damages for delay.

You may be liable to your client if by your actions you lose the client's right to liquidated damages. Indeed, if an extension of time is not granted where it should have been, depending on the terms of the contract, liquidated damages may be recovered by the contractor. In other words, where the power to extend the time for delays caused by the client has not been exercised either at all or within the time expressly or impliedly set by the contract, it may follow (unless the contractor has agreed to complete by the original contract date notwithstanding such delays) that the client has lost the benefit of the clause. In such cases, the contract time has ceased to be applicable, there is no date from which liquidated damages can be assessed; therefore, no liquidated damages can be recovered.

A cautionary tale about who pays for, and who owns, materials

W. Hanson (Harrow) Ltd was a supplier of timber and timber products. Usborne Developments was a development company and was engaged in developing residential sites in London. The building contractor was Rapid Civil Engineering Ltd.

Hanson had been a supplier to Rapid since 1979. The terms of business had always been the same. They were set out on all of the documentation – i.e. consignment notes, delivery notes and invoices. One of those terms, condition 10, dealt with the retention of title:

Transfer of property:
(a) The property in the goods shall not pass to you until payment in full of the price to us;
(b) The above condition may be waived at our discretion where goods or any part of them have been incorporated in building or constructional works.

Rapid and Hanson carried on business on a running account. Rapid was a slow payer. To assist Rapid with its cash flow, Usborne made more frequent payments against the contract price by including valuations of goods on-site, as well as for work done.

On 16 August 1984, Hanson made a delivery to one of the residential sites; shortly afterwards it found out that Rapid had gone into receivership on 15 August. Hanson demanded payment or return of the goods but both were refused by the receivers, although the receivers permitted Hanson to enter the site on 17 August to make inventories, which included the goods delivered on 16 August and also other goods on-site delivered since the end of April 1984 and which had not been paid for. Hanson marked the goods so as to identify them.

Hanson reminded the receivers of its contract with Rapid and, in particular, the retention of title provision and enclosed lists of the goods stating its intention to collect them. Hanson also notified Usborne of its claim to retention of title to the goods and reserved its right to claim damages against Usborne for conversion if it used the goods. Hanson failed to get an assurance from Usborne that Usborne would not use the goods.

Usborne claimed to be protected by section 25 of the *Sale of Goods Act 1979*. Section 25 of the Act provides that where a person has bought, or agreed to buy, goods and obtains, with the consent of the seller, possession of the goods, the delivery or transfer by that person under any sale or pledge or other disposition to any person receiving the same in good faith has the same effect as if the person making the delivery or transfer was a mercantile agent in possession of the goods with the consent of the owner.

It was held that there was no delivery or transfer of the goods on-site by Rapid to Usborne by way of any sale or other disposition under section 25 of the *Sale of Goods Act 1979*.

The contract between Rapid and Usborne provided for monthly payments of 97% of the value of the work executed, including the value of all materials on-site; the contract further provided that the property in the goods supplied should not pass to Usborne until payment of the instalment in which the supply was contained.

The judge referred to section 2 of the *Sale of Goods Act 1979*:

(a) A contract of sale of goods is one by which the seller transfers property in the goods;

(b) Where, under such a contract of sale, the property in the goods is transferred from the seller to the buyer the contract is called a sale; and
(c) Where, under such a contract of sale, the transfer of the property in the goods is to take place at a future time or subject to some condition to be fulfilled, then the contract is called an agreement to sell.

Section 25 only applies to delivery or transfer of goods under a 'sale or other disposition'. An agreement to sell only becomes a sale when any conditions are fulfilled, subject to which the property in the goods is to be transferred. As between Rapid and Usborne the building contract between them only operated to create a sale within the meaning of section 25 when any conditions subject to which the property in the goods was to be transferred were fulfilled. In this case, it meant that payment of the valuation in which the supply of materials was contained was required before any sale took place. Until then there was only an agreement to sell, not a sale. Accordingly, Usborne did not obtain any title to the goods and the claim to title of Hanson was not defeated by the operation of section 25 of the *Sale of Goods Act 1979*.

Hanson had effectively retained title to the goods as permitted by section 19 of the Act, and the title in those goods did not pass to Usborne. In so far as Usborne used them, it had wrongly converted them to its own use.

W. Hanson (Harrow) Ltd. v. *Rapid Civil Engineering Ltd. & Usborne Developments*, (1987) unreported.

A cautionary tale of paying for delay

A nominated piling subcontractor had departed from site without having completed the piling work and leaving behind him defective piles.

There appeared to be a clear breach of the JCT 80 contract by the nominated subcontractor under his contract with the main contractor. This amounted, at least technically, to a breach by the main contractor of his obligations in relation to workmanship under his JCT 80 contract with the client.

As a result of these defects being discovered, it was necessary to carry out redesign work in connection with the piling. The main contractor's next operation, work on the ground beams, had to be postponed. Clause 28 of JCT 80 provided that the contractor may determine his own employment and recover from the client any loss or damage suffered, if the carrying out of the works was suspended for a continuous period of at least one month because of a postponement instruction, unless caused by some negligence or default of the contractor.

The client challenged the contractor's claim to recover loss caused by the delay, on the basis that the defective work of the nominated subcontractor was also the responsibility of the main contractor under the main contract. Therefore, the contractor was in default and could not rely upon the determination provision.

It was held that the contractor could rely upon the determination provision as the default mentioned in clause 28.1.3.4 had to relate to actual default rather than a mere technical breach of contract on the part of the contractor.

The Court of Appeal supported the trial judge's findings with only slight variations. The court stressed that clause 28.1.3.4 made no reference to breach of contract as such, and that it was surprising if the existence of a breach of contract is what determined the contractor's right or lack of right to rely upon a subclause. Bingham, L.J. said:

> In my view the language of the sub-clause is directed to a much more practical question: Whose fault is it that the architect's instruction to postpone the work was given? If it was the fault of the contractor, his servants or agents, then the contractor cannot rely upon the suspension of work, as a ground for determining the contract. If it was not the fault of the contractor, his servants or agents, he can [determine his employment]. He does not lose the right because a nominated sub-contractor chosen by the employer has failed to perform his contract.

John Jervis Ltd. v. *Rockdale Housing Association, Building Design,* (1987) 3 const. L.J. 24.

Q. What do the standard forms of contract say about liquidated damages?

Clauses within standard forms of building contract which allow the architect to extend the completion date of the contract are, as as matter of course, closely associated with those which can be used to impose liquidated damages.

As a general principle, the main contractor is bound to complete the works by the date for completion stated in the contract. If he fails to do so, he will be liable for liquidated damages to the client. Yet payment of such damages does not relieve the contractor of his obligation to complete the works.

The FAS form epitomizes the principle of liquidated damages in the single clause 4.5: 'if the contractor fails to complete the work by the contract completion date or by any

A cautionary tale about how to make a client upset

Mr Miller was a builder who traded under the name of Mears Brothers. He entered into a contract valued at £18 263 3s 7d with London County Council to carry out alterations to Deptford Pumping Station. The whole of the work, carried out in three phases, was to be completed within 7 months from the date of the local authority's engineer's order to commence. That date was 15 November 1931.

There were delays, some such as the ordering of extra work for which the contractor was not responsible. The works were not completed in November, but on 25 July 1932.

The engineer, Thomas Peirson Frank, issued a certificate granting an extension of time to 7 February 1932 and certifying the amount due to the local authority as liquidated damages in respect of the period between 7 February and 25 July 1932.

The contract provided for it to 'be lawful for the engineer if he shall think fit, to grant from time to time and at any time or times by writing under his hand such extension of time for completion of the work and that either prospectively or retrospectively, and to assign such other times for completion as to him may seem reasonable'.

It was held that the words 'either pros-pectively or retrospectively' did not confer on the engineer a right to fix the extension of time *ex post factor* when the work was completed. They empowered him to wait until the cause of delay ceased to operate and then retro-spectively with regard to the causes of delay assign to the contractor a new date to work to. The extension admittedly proper not having been granted in time, no liquidated damages were payable.

Miller v. *London County Council* [1934] I.S.I. Law Reports, 425.

extension granted under the previous clauses, the Contractor shall pay or allow to the Employer the liquidated damages for the period of delay assessed and confirmed in writing by the Architect to the Employer and to the Contractor.' Clause 47(3) of the ICE contract emphasizes that such sums are not to be paid as a penalty for delay. Liquidated damages must be a genuine estimate of the financial loss which the client will suffer if the works are not completed on time. By contrast, only clause 47.3, Part II, of the FIDIC form provides within its terms for a bonus to be paid to the contractor when work is completed ahead of schedule.

The majority of building contracts give the amount of liquidated and ascertained damages in an appendix or in articles of agreement in a manner which leaves no room for alteration. The advantage of this system is that it is inserted by the client for his own protection. It enables him to recover a fixed sum as compensation for delay instead of facing the difficulty and expense of proving the actual damage which the delay may have caused him. Sometimes it is impossible for an estimate to be made of the damages.

ACA has adopted a more flexible approach, giving within clause 11.3 two alternatives for recovering damages for delay. One alternative follows the common formula of allowing the client to deduct liquidated and ascertained damages at rates stated in the contract. The other alternative makes clear allowance where no rates are given for the client to deduct from moneys owing to the contractor such amount as will cover the damage, loss or expense suffered by him because of the contractor's failure to meet the dates written into the Time Schedule.

Q. As an architect, must I accept the quantity surveyor's valuation for an interim certificate?

When certifying sums for payment, you may not be bound to accept a quantity surveryor's opinion or valuation of them. At that point, you remain master in your own field.

The duties of the quantity surveyor are set out in clause 15.3 of the ACA form, which is similar to those contained in other standard forms:

> The Quantity Surveyor may carry out only such duties assigned to the Architect . . . as the Architect shall instruct and which relate to the ascertainment or agreement of any cost or any damage, loss and/or expense or the valuation of any work, materials or goods (but not to the issue of any instruction or certificate . . .) and the Quantity Surveyor shall advise the Architect of all sums so ascertained, agreed or valued.

Though in JCT 80, if clause 40 is used relating to the price adjustment formula, the contract makes the valuation a mandatory requirement before the issue of an interim certificate. It overrides clause 30.1.2, which states that 'Interim valuations shall be made by the Quantity Surveyor for the purpose of ascertaining the amount to be stated as due in an Interim Certificate'.

You are duty-bound to notify the quantity surveyor in advance of any work which you classify as not properly executed so as to give the quantity surveyor the opportunity of excluding it from his valuation. In other words, it is the architect who finally decides the value of the contractor's work, though it may be possible in some cases that you would not be negligent or failing in your professional duties in accepting the quantity surveyor's valuation. However, it should be borne in mind that a quantity surveyor is not infallible. He may make negligent valuations and be liable for them.

Q. To what extent can the client withhold moneys from the contractor?

Although the moneys in an interim certificate may be adjusted by a later interim certificate or the final certificate (see 'A comparison of clauses on interim certificates' and 'Amending interim certificates' pp. 191, 194), the original interim certificate provided it is a properly executed certificate under the terms of the contract must be honoured to its full face value by the client within the time stipulated in the contract. An interim certificate may not be refused or dishonoured unless it could be said that the certificate was 'not in accordance with the contract conditions'.

The client cannot withhold moneys unless it is specifically provided for in the contract (e.g. retention), nor must he interfere with or obstruct the issue of any certificate. If the client does so, the courts may adopt a robust approach against the client should an 'Order 14' action be taken by the contractor to obtain the sum certified. The basis of an 'Order 14' action for summary judgment is that the contractor can show an unanswerable case against the client. The courts may not allow the whole payment to be withheld because part of the certified moneys are in dispute, rather they may order the indisputably due money to be paid and refer the amount which is disputed to arbitration.

For example, in *Frederick Mark Ltd* v. *Schield* (1971) *The Times* 21 October 1971, a house was built under a JCT contract. The client was not satisfied with some of the work, claiming it was defective. He set off the value of the defective work against the sums certified in two interim certificates. The Court of Appeal ordered him to pay the contractor the full amount of money certified in the certificate. Again, in *Kilby and Gayford Ltd.* v. *Selincourt Ltd*, (1976) 3 Building Law Reports, 104, a JCT form of contract was used for alteration works. The client challenged the sixth interim

A cautionary tale about loss and expense

The contractor Croudace Ltd received from Lambeth's Chief Architect an extension of time of 31 weeks and 3 days, due to variations and late instructions. The contractor made a claim for re-imbursement of loss and expense under clauses 11(a) of JCT 63 (dealing with the variations) and clause 24 (dealing with the late instructions).

The Chief Architect retired without having ascertained or having instructed the quantity surveyors to ascertain the amount of loss and expense; no one was appointed in his place. The contractor brought an action for loss and expense without a certificate; or alternatively, for damages for breach of contract.

It was held that Lambeth as employer was in breach of its contract with the contractor on two grounds:

1. If the Chief Architect was regarded as a corporation sole, anyone within his department could have acted as such despite his retirement and could and should therefore have complied with the obligation to ascertain the loss and expense; since that was not done, the employer was liable for the failing of the architect or the Architects Department on the basis that he or they acted as the employer's agents;
2. If the Chief Architect was regarded as an individual, then Lambeth had failed to comply with what was regarded as an obligation within the contract for the employer to appoint a replacement architect upon the retirement of the one originally named.

Loss and expense could be recovered without a certificate in these circumstances, but any amount recovered under such a claim would be equal to or subsumed in any respect of Lambeth's breach of contract. The architect's failure to certify amounted to a breach of contract by the employer.

Croudace Ltd. v. *London Borough of Lambeth* (1984) C.I.L.L. 136.

---

certificate contending that no written variation orders had been issued for some work. He withheld payment. The Court of Appeal found in favour of the contractor because in the absence of evidence that the variations were not properly ordered, the interim certificate must be honoured in full, pending practical completion. Lord Denning remarked:

So long as the certificate is good on the face of it and is within the authority given by the contract then it is in accordance with the conditions. It must be honoured. I do not think that it is open to employers of the contractor to challenge an interim certificate by saying that is is too much or too little or includes this or omits that or that the extras were not sanctioned in writing. Such matters must be left until after practical completion of the work.

A comparison of clauses on interim certificates

Clause 30.1.1.1 of JCT 80 states:

The Architect shall from time to time issue Interim Certificates stating the amount due to the Contractor from the Employer and the Contractor shall be entitled to payment therefore within 14 days from the date of issue of each Interim Certificate.

Clause 40(1) of GC/Works/1 states:

The Contractor shall be entitled to be paid during the progress of the execution of the works 97% of the value of the work executed on the site to the satisfaction of the SO and the Authority shall accumulate the balance as a reserve.

Clause 16.2 of the ACA form states:

Within 10 working days of receipt by the Architect of the application and documents referred to in Clause 16.1, the Architect shall issue an interim certificate stating the amount due to the Contractor from the Employer which shall, subject to adjustment under Clause 18, if applicable, be:

(a) the total value of work properly executed calculated in accordance with the Schedule of Rates (excluding, but without limitation, the value of any work which in the reasonable opinion of this Architect shall not have been executed in accordance with this Agreement); and

(b) the total value of any goods and materials intended for but not incorporated into the works where the contract documents expressly provide that payment shall be made for such goods and materials before incorporation into the works (excluding the value of any such goods and materials where the Architect is not satisfied on the basis of the documents referred to in Clause 16.1 that property in such goods and materials is vested in the contractor and the conditions for payment set out in the contract documents have been complied with); and

(c) the amount of any adjustments to the contract sum agreed or certified or otherwise ascertained under this agreement to the extent that such adjustment is in respect of work already executed or damage, loss and/or expense already incurred:

up to and including a date not more than 10 working days before the date of the said certificate, less all amounts previously stated as due under Clause 16.2.

Clauses 6.2/3 of the FAS contract state:

6.2   Interim Payments – interim certificates for payment will be issued at monthly intervals or as stated in Agreement item A.5.5.

6.3   Certificates – the Architect will issue the certificates – the following rules shall apply:

6.3.1   valuation – the Quantity Surveyor shall make a valuation for each certificate – if there is no Quantity Surveyor, the Contractor shall apply to the Architect for each certificate 14 days before issue is due, supported by his statement showing in suitable detail his valuation of work done, including that by nominated sub-contractors and suppliers, also of materials and goods properly on site, with any further particulars needed, for checking by the Architect;

6.3.2   amount – the amount certified shall be the approved gross value of work done, including that of nominated sub-contractors and suppliers, also allowable fluctuations, and other items approved by the Architect and materials and goods properly on site (but subject to clause 6.34 'materials and goods', and only if adequately stored and protected), excluding premature deliveries – less the retention and amounts previously paid;

6.3.3   issue, payment – all certificates shall be issued to the Employer, and at the same time a copy to the Contractor and to the Quantity Surveyor (if any) – after practical completion (as clause 4.2 'practical completion') interim certificates shall be issued when further amounts are due and/or ascertained, but not more often than monthly.

The Employer shall pay to the Contractor the amount certified within 14 days of the date of the certificate, subject to any deductions and set-offs due under the contract;

6.3.4   materials and goods – the materials and goods when paid for under a certificate shall become the Employers' property, but the Contractor is responsible for loss or damage to them – receipts of payment for materials and/or goods shall be produced to prove ownership, if required by the Architect;

6.3.5   additions, deductions – any additions or deductions, such as variations, fluctuations, and claims, due under these contract conditions shall, as soon as quantified in whole or part and approved by the Architect, be included in the next certificate valuation for interim certifying, and in the final account and set against the appropriate provisional sum, if any, in the specification or bills of quantities;

6.3.6 qualifications – certificates are issued for financial purposes only, and shall not be construed as approval of the work done by the Contractor and/or Sub-Contractors;

6.3.7 Quantity Surveyor's function – the Quantity Surveyor shall be responsible for the preparation of certificate valuations, and for the final account for the contract work, including nominated Sub-Contractors.

Clause 60(1)/(2) of the ICE contract state:

60(1) The Contractor shall submit to the Engineer after the end of each month a statement (in such form if any as may be prescribed in the Specification) showing:
(a) the estimated contract value of the permanent works executed up to the end of that month;
(b) a list of any goods or materials delivered to the site for but not yet incorporated in the permanent works and their value;
(c) a list of any goods or materials listed in the Appendix to the Form of Tender which have not yet been delivered to the site but of which the property has vested in the Employer pursuant to Clause 54 and their value;
(d) the estimated amounts to which the Contractor considers himself entitled in connection with all other matters for which provision is made under the Contract including any temporary works or constructional plant for which separate amounts are included in the Bill of Quantities;
unless in the opinion of the Contractor such values and amount together will not justify the issue of an interim certificate.

Amounts payable in respect of Nominated Sub-Contractors are to be listed separately.

(2) Within 28 days of the date of delivery to the Engineer or Engineer's representative in accordance with sub-clause

(1) of this Clause of the Contractor's monthly statement the Engineer shall certify and the Employer shall pay to the Contractor (after deducting any previous payments on account):
(a) the amount which in the opinion of the Engineer on the basis of the monthly statement is due to the Contractor on account of sub-clause 1(a) and (d) of this Clause less a retention as provided in sub-clause (4) of this Clause;
(b) such amounts (if any) as the Engineer may consider proper (but in no case exceeding the percentage of the value stated in the Appendix to the Form of Tender) in respect of (b) and (c) of sub-clause (1) of this Clause which amounts shall not be subject to a retention under sub-clause (4) of this Clause.

The amounts certified in respect of Nominated Sub-Contractors shall be shown separately in the certificate. The Engineer shall not be bound to issue an interim certificate for a sum less than that named in the Appendix to the Form of Tender.

Clauses 60.1/2 of the FIDIC contract state:

60.1 The Contractor shall submit to the Engineer after the end of each month six copies, each signed by the Contractor's representative approved by the Engineer in accordance with Sub-Clause 15.1, of a statement, in such form as the Engineer may from time to time prescribe, showing the amounts to which the Contractor considers himself to be entitled up to the end of the month in respect of:
(a) the value of the permanent works executed
(b) any other items in the Bill of Quantities including those for Contractor's equipment, temporary works, dayworks and the like;
(c) the percentage of the invoice value of listed materials, all as stated in the Appendix to Tender, and plant delivered by the Contractor on the site for incorporation in the permanent works but not incorporated in such works;
(d) adjustment under Clause 70;

(e) any other sum to which the Contractor may be entitled under the Contract.

60.2 The Engineer shall, within 28 days of receiving such statement, certify to the Employer the amount of payment to the Contractor which he considers due and payable in respect thereof, subject:

(a) firstly, to the retention of the amount calculated by applying the percentage of retention stated in the Appendix to Tender, to the amount to which the Contractor is entitled under paragraphs (a), (b), (c) and (e) of Sub-Clause 60.1 until the amount so retained reaches the limit of retention money stated in the Appendix to Tender; and

(b) secondly, to the deduction, other than pursuant to Clause 47, of any sums which may have become due and payable by the Contractor to the Employer.

Provided that the Engineer shall not be bound to certify any payment under this Sub-Clause if the net amount thereof, after all retentions and deductions, would be less than the minimum amount of interim certificates stated in the Appendix to Tender. Notwithstanding the terms of this Clause or any other Clause of the Contract no amount will be certified by the Engineer for payment until the performance security, if required under the Contract, has been provided by the Contractor and approved by the Employer.

A comparison of clauses on amending interim certificates

Clause 30.6.1.2 of JCT 80 states:

30.6.1.2 Not later than 3 months after receipt by the Architect or Quantity Surveyor of the documents referred to in clause 30.6.1.1.

30.6.1.2.1 The Architect, or, if the Architect has so instructed, the Quantity Surveyor shall ascertain (unless previously ascertained) any loss and for expense under clauses 26.1, 26.4.1, and 34.3, and

30.6.1.2.2 The Quantity Surveyor shall prepare a statement of all adjustments to be made to the Contract Sum as referred to in clause 30.6.2 other than any to which clause 30.6.1.2.1 applies.

and the Architect shall forthwith send a copy of any ascertainment to which clause 30.6.1.2.1 refers and of the statement prepared in compliance with clause 30.6.1.2.2 to the contractor and the relevant extract therefrom to each Nominated Sub-Contractor.

Clause 42(2) of GC/Works/1 states:

Any interim certificate relating to payment for work done or things for incorporation delivered may be modified or corrected by any subsequent interim certificate or by the final certificate for payment, and no interim certificate of the SO shall of itself be conclusive evidence that any form or things to which it relates are in accordance with the Contract.

Clause 19.5 of the ACA form states:

No certificate (including the final certificate) issued by the Architect under this Agreement shall relieve the Contractor from any liability arising out of or in connection with this Agreement. The Architect may by any certificate delete, correct or modify any sum previously certified by him.

Clause 60(7) of the ICE contract states:

The Engineer shall have power to omit from any certificate the value of any work done, goods or materials supplied or services rendered with which he may for the time being be dissatisfied and for that purpose or for any other reason which to him may seem proper may by any certificate delete, correct or modify any sum previously certified by him.

Clause 60.4 of the FIDIC contract states:

60.4   The Engineer may by any interim certificate make any correction or modification in any previous certificate which shall have been issued by him and shall have authority, if any work is not being carried out to his satisfaction, to omit or reduce the value of such works in any interim certificate.

Q. To what extent am I liable if I over-certify?

You may be liable for any loss borne by your client where a sum has been negligently over-certified on an interim certificate.

Equally, you may be liable to the contractor when you negligently under-certify on an interim certificate, and indeed to any other person such as subcontractors whose payment depends on the issue of a certificate. It should be noted that in *Lubenham Fidelity and Investment Co. v. South Pembrokshire District Council*, (1986) 33 B.L.R., the Court of Appeal held that the client was not liable under the JCT contract where architects negligently under-certified payments to the contractor.

Q. What do the standard forms of contract say on the contractor's recovering direct loss and expense?

The FAS contract previously made little mention of the recovery of direct loss and expense by the contractor. Now, however, clause 9.4 states that if a claim does arise, it is for the architect to consider and assess. Nevertheless, a positive duty is placed upon the contractor to avoid and reduce such event and costs.

In contrast, clause 26 of JCT considers the matter in exhaustive detail (see 'A comparison of clauses on recovering direct loss and expense', this page). The general purpose of this and similar clauses within other building contracts is to re-imburse the contractor for his direct loss and expense where the regular progress of the works has been or is likely to be delayed for reasons which he is not responsible for. Indeed contractors are generally entitled to recover as direct loss and expense those sums of money which they would have made if the contract had been performed, less the money which had been saved to them because of the disappearance of their contractual obligation.

Within JCT 80 a claim can only arise from one or more of seven reasons all of which stem from either an act or default on the part of the client or the architect. The principle of the seven reasons is followed in the ACA form but with the added rider, in clause 7.1, that claims for loss and expense suffered by the contractor shall apply to any act, omission, default or negligence of the employer or of the architect which disrupts the regular progress of the works or of any section or delays the execution of them in accordance with the dates stated in the Time Schedule.

The ICE contract, in a similar manner to JCT 80, clearly lists those items which may give rise to a claim for extra moneys over and above that allowed for by the contract sum. Yet emphasis is placed on a claim being considered only if the delay or cost was beyond that which could have reasonably been foreseen by an experienced contractor at the time of tender. But a contractor may only recover such damages for loss and expense which is 'reasonably foreseen' to result from that particular breach of the contract.

A comparison of clauses on recovering direct loss and expense

Clause 26.2 of JCT 80 gives the list of matters which may result in claims for loss and expense:

26.2.1   the Contractor not having received in due time necessary instructions, drawings, details, or levels from the Architect for which he specifically applied in writing provided that such application was made on a date which having regard to the completion date was neither unreasonably distant from nor unreasonably close to the date on which it was necessary for him to receive the same;

26.2.2   the opening up for inspection of any work covered up or the testing of any of the work, materials or goods in accordance with Clause 8.3 (including making good in consequence of such opening up or testing), unless the inspection or test showed that the work, materials or goods were not in accordance with this Contract;

26.2.3   any discrepancy or divergence as is referred to in clause 2.3;

26.2.4   the execution of work not forming part of this Contract by the Employer himself or by persons employed or otherwise engaged by the Employer as referred to in Clause 29 or the failure to execute such work;

26.2.4.1   the supply by the Employer of materials and goods which the Employer has agreed to provide for the works or the failure so to supply;

26.2.5   Architect's instructions under Clause 23.2 issued in regard to the postponement of any work to be executed under the provisions of this Contract;

26.2.6   failure of the Employer to give in due time ingress to or egress from the site of the works, or any part thereof through or over any land, buildings, way or passage adjoining or connected with the site and in the possession and control of the Employer, in accordance with the contract bills and/or contract drawings, after receipt by the Architect of such notice, if any, as the Contractor is required to give, or failure of the Employer to give such ingress or egress as otherwise agreed between the Architect and the Contractor;

26.2.7   Architect's instructions issued under Clause 14.2 requiring a variation or under Clause 14.3 in regard to the expenditure of provisional sums (other than work to which Clause 14.4.2 refers).

Clause 53 of GC/Works/1 states:

53(1)   If:
      (a) complying with any of the SO's instructions;
      (b) the making good of loss or damage falling within Condition 26(2);
      (c) the execution of works pursuant to Condition 50; or
      (d) delay in the provision of any of the items specified in paragraph (2) of this Condition

unavoidably results in the regular progress of the works or of any part thereof being materially disrupted or prolonged and in consequence of such disruption or prolongation the Contractor properly and directly incurs any expense in performing the Contract which he would not otherwise have incurred and which is beyond that otherwise provided for in or reasonably contemplated by the Contract, the contract sum shall, subject to paragraph (3) of this Condition and to Condition 23, be increased by the amount of that expense as ascertained by the Quantity Surveyor.

Provided that there shall be no such increase in respect of expense incurred in consequences of the making good of loss or damage falling within Condition 26(2) except where the Contractor is entitled to payment under that provision and where his entitlement to payment under that provision is limited to a proportionate sum any such increase in respect of expense so incurred shall be limited in like manner.

(2) The items referred to in sub-paragraph (1)(d) of this Condition are:

(a) any drawings, schedules, levels or other design information to be provided by the SO and to be prepared otherwise than by the Contractor or any of his sub-contractors;

(b) any work the execution of which, or thing the supplying of which, is to be undertaken by the Authority or is to be ordered direct by him otherwise than from the Contractor and is to be so undertaken or ordered otherwise than in consequence of any default on the part of the Contractor; and

(c) any direction from the Authority or the SO regarding the nomination or appointment of any person, or any instruction of the SO or consent of the Authority, to be given under Condition 38(4).

(3) It shall be a condition precedent to the contract sum being increased under paragraph (1) of this Condition:

(a) in the case of expense incurred in consequence of an SO's instruction, that the instruction shall have been given or confirmed in writing and shall not have been rendered necessary as a result of any default on the part of the Contractor;

(b) in the case of expense incurred in consequence of delay in the provision of any of the items specified in paragraph (2) of this Condition, that, except where a date for the provision of the relevant item was agreed with the SO, the Contractor shall, neither unreasonably early nor unreasonably late, have given notice to the SO specifying that item and the date by which it was reasonably required; and

(c) in any case that:

(i) the Contractor, immediately upon becoming aware that the regular progress of the works or of any part thereof has been or is likely to be disrupted or prolonged as aforesaid, shall have given notice to the SO specifying the circumstances causing or expected to cause that disruption or prolongation and stating that he is or expects to be entitled to an increase in the contract sum under that paragraph;

(ii) as soon as reasonably practicable after incurring the expense the Contractor shall have provided such documents and information in respect of the expense as he is required to provide under Condition 37(2).

Clause 7 of the ACA form states:

7.1 Save in the case of Architect's instructions (to which the provisions of Clause 17 shall apply), if any act, omission, default or negligence of the Employer or of the Architect disrupts the regular progress of the works or of any section or delays the execution of them in accordance with the dates stated in the Time Schedule and, in consequence of such disruption or delay, the Contractor suffers or incurs damage, loss and/or expense, he shall be entitled to recover the same in accordance with the provisions of this Clause 7.

7.2 Upon it becoming reasonably apparent that any event giving rise to a claim under Clause 7.1 is likely to occur or has occurred, the Contractor shall immediately give notice to the Architect of such event and shall, on presentation of his interim application pursuant to Clause 16.1 next following the giving of such notice, submit to the Architect an estimate of the adjustment to the Contract Sum which the Contractor requires to take account of such damage, loss and/or expense suffered or incurred by him in consequence of such event prior to the date of submission of his estimate.

7.3 Following the submission of an estimate under Clause 7.2, the Contractor shall, for so long as the Contractor suffers or incurs damage, loss and/or expense in consequence of such event, on presentation of each interim application pursuant to Clause 16.1, submit to the Architect an estimate of the adjustment to the contract sum which the Contractor requires to take account of such damage, loss and/or expense suffered or incurred by him since the submission of his previous estimate.

7.4   Any estimate submitted by the Contractor pursuant to Clause 7.2 or 7.3 shall be supported by such documents, vouchers and receipts as shall be necessary for computing the same or as may be required by the Architect. Within 20 working days of receipt of any such estimate duly supported as aforesaid, the Architect shall either give notice that he accepts it or he shall give notice of his wish to negotiate the adjustment to the contract sum. Upon agreement being reached as to the amount of damage, loss and/or expense, the contract sum shall be adjusted accordingly and no further or other additions or payments shall be made in respect of the damage, loss and/or expense suffered or incurred by the Contractor during the period and in consequence of the event to which such agreement relates.

7.5   If the Contractor fails to comply with the provisions of Clause 7.2 or 7.3, then the Architect shall have no power or authority to make, and the Contractor shall not be entitled to any adjustment to the contract sum in respect of the damage, loss and/or expense to which such failure relates on any certificate issued under this Agreement prior to the final certificate. Such adjustment shall not in such event include an addition in respect of loss of interest or financing charges suffered or incurred by the Contractor between the date of the Contractor's failure so to comply and the date of the final certificate.

7.6   If agreement cannot be reached within 20 working days after the Architect's notice under Clause 7.4, either party may refer the Contractor's estimates to the Adjudicator for his decision under Clause 25.

Clause 9.4 of the FAS contract states:

9.4   Claims, direct loss or expense – any claim by the Contractor, and/or a nominated Sub-Contractor, for direct loss and/or expense arising under this Contract, for which he would not be paid under any other provisions in the Contract, may be submitted in writing to the Architect to consider.

If the loss or expense is due to disruption of the regular progress of the work by any of the causes listed in Clause 9.42 a claim shall, if valid, be considered and assessed by the Architect.

The Contractor shall use all possible means to avoid and reduce such events and cost, and the Architect may require evidence of this in considering a claim.

All the above is subject to the following rules:

9.4.1   Claim notice, submission – as and when such loss and/or expense becomes apparent, the Contractor shall at once give written notice to the Architect with relevant particulars. The Contractor shall, unless the Architect rejects the notice as invalid, submit as soon as practicable his quantified claim, in duplicate, to the Architect, with relevant contract clause numbers, financial details, vouchers, receipts, and a reasoned case in support.

If several claims are made, the Contractor shall, at or near practical completion and not later than 4 weeks thereafter, submit to the Architect a summary case (in duplicate) for the total claimed. He shall supply to the Architect, and to the Quantity Surveyor, where acting, any further information and details required;

9.4.2   Causes – the admissible causes, which may effect progress as aforementioned, are defined as follows:

(a)   discrepancy between the contract drawings and/or other drawings and/or the specification/bills of quantities;

(b)   delay or frustration by the Employer over access to the site, or in the execution of work or supply of materials and/or goods which the Employer was to undertake;

(c)   delays arising from variations or variation orders or Architect's instructions;

(d)   the postponement of any work under a variation order;

(e) delay in the issuing of Architect's instructions or variation orders or drawings or information requested in writing by the Contractor, after allowing fair and reasonable time for its formulation and preparation;

(f) opening up and/or testing required by the Architect, but not if faults were found or the materials or workmanship or items/goods were not in accordance with the contract;

9.4.4 Claims by nominated sub-contractors – claims for direct loss and/or expense by nominated sub-contractors which conform to the aforementioned rules, received and checked as to these rules by the Contractor, shall be submitted by him to the Architect for consideration – the sub-contractor shall supply and further information or details required;

9.4.5 Assessment – if the basis of the notices and claims is valid under Clause 9.4 and these rules, the claim assessments shall be considered by the Architect, and the Quantity Surveyor where acting – the appropriate amount approved by the Architect shall be notified to the Contractor and nominated sub-contractors where concerned, and be included for certifying and in the final account, as Clause 6.35 'additions, deductions';

9.4.6 Other rights – the provisions, in Clauses 9.4 and 9.45, are to be without prejudice to any other rights possessed by the parties (Employer or Contractor).

The following clauses of the ICE contract state the items which may give rise to a claim for loss and expense:

7(3)   Delay in issue of contract documents, drawings.
12(3)   Adverse physical conditions.
13(3)   Engineer's instructions.
14(6)   Approval of construction methods and design criteria.
27(6)   Variations in street works.
31(2)   Other contractors.
52(4)   Notice of claims.

59B(4) Nominated sub-contractors.
60   Payment.

Clause 53 of the FIDIC contract states:

53.1 Notwithstanding any other provision of the Contract, if the Contractor intends to claim any additional payment pursuant to any Clause of these Conditions or otherwise, he shall give notice of his intention to the Engineer, with a copy to the Employer, within 28 days after the event giving rise to the claim has first arisen.

53.2 Upon the happening of the event referred to in Sub-Clause 53.1, the Contractor shall keep such contemporary records as may reasonably be necessary to support any claim he may subsequently wish to make. Without necessarily admitting the Employer's liability, the Engineer shall, on receipt of a notice under Sub-Clause 53.1, inspect such contemporary records and may instruct the Contractor to keep any further contemporary records as are reasonable and may be material to the claim of which notice has been given. The Contractor shall permit the Engineer to inspect all records kept pursuant to this Sub-Clause and shall supply him with copies thereof as and when the Engineer so instructs.

53.3 Within 28 days, or such other reasonable time as may be agreed by the Engineer, of giving notice under Sub-Clause 53.1, the Contractor shall send to the Engineer an account giving detailed particulars of the amount claimed and the grounds upon which the claim is based. Where the event giving rise to the claim has a continuing effect, such account shall be considered to be an interim account and the Contractor shall, at such intervals as the Engineer may reasonably require, send further interim accounts giving the accumulated amount of the claim and any further grounds upon which it is based. In cases where interim accounts are sent to the Engineer, the Contractor shall send a final account within 28 days of the end of the effects resulting from the event. The Contractor shall, if required by the Engineer so to do,

A cautionary tale about delay leading to loss and expense

In 1969 a firm of builders by the name of Wates submitted a competitive tender to the Greater London Council (GLC). The tender was for building an estate of 1807 houses at Graham Park in the London Borough of Barnet. The tender was accepted.

Work began in January 1970; the retrospective contract was signed on 22 June 1970. Difficulties arose because of the extraordinary spiralling inflation which occurred soon after, which could not have been foreseen by either party.

By clause 31 of the contract, which had been adapted by the GLC from the JCT form, provision was made for fluctuations in the price of labour and materials to be taken into account in the contract price and interim payments payable under the contract that provided for no additional profit, overhead or other expenses should be allowed to Wates in any adjustment.

By 1972 problems had occurred. Delay by the GLC in complying with the obligations under the contract to provide timely instructions had caused Wates considerable loss. Further, the price fluctuations contained in clause 31 were inadequate to deal with inflation which increased, not at a trot or canter but a gallop. The work being done by Wates was being seriously undervalued. Wates were not receiving a substantial measure of protection against cost inflation.

On 23 January 1974, Wates formally requested payment in respect of matters in dispute to the value of £421 000. The GLC did not accept liability and did not pay any sums in excess of certificate sums.

Wates stopped work and withdrew from the site on 22 February 1974. The GLC wrote that it accepted the withdrawal as being repudiatory breach by Wates which brought the contract to an end.

Wates brought an action against the GLC. The High Court held that Wates had wrongfully repudiated the contract. Wates appealed; however, the Court of Appeal dismissed their appeal. In dismissing the appeal, Purchas, L.J. said:

while having considerable sympathy with Wates because they undoubtedly suffered damages as a result of the postponement of proper adjustment of the certified sum and would, had the contract been fully executed still have suffered damage, it was not possible to say that the terms of the contract did not in fact as a matter of law cover all the eventualities including those which occurred.

Wates v. *Greater London Council,* (1984) 25 B.L.R. 1, C.A.

copy to the Employer all accounts sent to the Engineer pursuant to this Sub-Clause.

53.4 If the Contractor fails to comply with any of the provisions of this Clause in respect of any claim which he seeks to make, his entitlement to payment in respect thereof shall not exceed such amount as the Engineer or any arbitrator or arbitrators appointed pursuant to Sub-Clause 67.3 assessing the claim considers to be verified by contemporary records (whether or not such records were brought to the Engineer's notice as required under Sub-Clauses 53.2 and 53.3).

53.5 The Contractor shall be entitled to have included in any interim payment certified by the Engineer pursuant to Clause 60 such amount in respect of any claim as the Engineer, after due consultation with the Employer and the Contractor, may consider due to the Contractor provided that the Contractor has supplied sufficient particulars to enable the Engineer to determine the amount due. If such particulars are insufficient to substantiate the whole of the claim, the Contractor shall be entitled to payment in respect of such part of the claim as such particulars may substantiate to the satisfaction of the Engineer. The Engineer shall notify the Contractor of any determination made under this Sub-Clause, with a copy to the Employer.

Q. In general terms, what are the mechanics of evaluating a claim?

Under most standard forms of contract the architect or engineer is obliged to form an opinion of whether or not the claim is valid and then to make an assessment of the amount of the contractor's loss and expense, or under clause 26.1 of JCT 80 instruct the quantity surveyor so to do.

That evaluation can only be made, and indeed only considered, in several contracts if the contractor has given notice within a specified time that a claim for loss and expense has occurred, or is likely to occur, and that claim is supported by such documents and vouchers or receipts, or as clause 51(4)(a)–(f) of the ICE contract puts it, such 'contemporary records', as are necessary.

An assessment of a claim for loss and expense may be an invitation for the architect or engineer to condemn his own actions, leaving him open for a claim for damages from his client where, for example, drawings, instructions or certificates have not been issued in sufficient time to prevent the contractor suffering loss and expense.

Q. What is the effect of the contractor not giving information on which to base an assessment for loss and expense?

Should the contractor not supply the necessary information for the architect or engineer to reach a decision as to what is a reasonable sum for the contractor's claim for direct loss and expense, or fail to comply with the procedures laid down in the contract thus interfering with his assessment, sanctions may be brought to bear on the contractor. Under the ACA form, clause 7.5, his entitlement to an adjustment to the contract sum may be removed until the final certificate.

In comparison, in the ICE contract, clause 52(4)(E), the contractor may be entitled only to such payment as the engineer can make which has not been prevented or substantially prejudiced by the actions of the contractor during his investigations of the contractor's claim.

TWELVE

How do I effectively argue

the limitations of

my liability?

12.1 ARBITRATION

Q. What does arbitration mean?

The word 'arbitration' has been used to describe many different types of agreement or procedure which may not all in fact be arbitration. These range from agreements which are designed to prevent disputes arising in the future to agreements to be bound by the result of a valuation, even though there may be no hearing or submission of evidence, or an agreement to take the opinion of counsel though it is not binding on the parties. Indeed, clause 25.3 of the ACA form notes that an 'adjudicator' appointed by the parties to the contract to determine certain disputes referred to him acts merely as an expert and not as an arbitrator.

Arbitration means the process whereby two or more parties who are in dispute agree in writing to settle their disagreement privately by referring the question not to a court of law, but to an independent person, or persons, as the case may be – namely, to an arbitrator. The dispute must be essentially civil in nature and one which can be settled by accord and satisfaction.

The award, or decision of the arbitrator, is made after the evidence of all parties has been heard in a judicial manner, following the directions prescribed by such statutes as the *Arbitration Act 1979*. In certain circumstances, the arbitrator's award may be reviewed by the courts.

Q. When does an arbitration agreement exist?

An arbitration agreement so long as it is in writing can take several forms, as is illustrated by the number of ways in which the standard forms of building and engineering contracts containing such agreements can be executed, namely:

1. mutual bonds;
2. deed;
3. simple contract;
4. sealed by one party but signed by another.

However, to be binding on all parties to a contract the arbitration agreement should be brought to the attention of each, particularly where the contract refers to certain provisions which are then set out in another document. Indeed, as a matter of good practice, this should be done even where the detailed arbitration provisions are included in the main contract.

Where an arbitration agreement is entered into by an agent who is duly authorized, it will be binding on his principal. Likewise, if it is signed by a partner in the usual course of the partnership business, the arbitration agreement will bind both the partnership and his partners. Furthermore, should one of the parties to the contract become bankrupt, the arbitration agreement may be enforced by or against the trustee in bankruptcy if he adopts the contract.

Q. I am the personal representative of a small builder who recently died in the middle of a contract. How does this affect the arbitration agreement?

The arbitration agreement may not be discharged by the death of the contractor, or indeed any other party to the contract. You, as the personal representative may enforce it. Equally, it may be enforced against you.

Q. Should a particular form of words be used for an arbitration clause to be valid?

An arbitration clause need not be in any particular form, provided the form it does take is not ambiguous. If the words are ambiguous, they may be regarded as a nullity.

You may use whatever words you believe to be appropriate to the particular contract you are undertaking. An arbitration clause which is as short and succinct as 'Arbitration to be settled in London' may be upheld as much as such all-embracing clauses as refer to arbitration in 'any dispute or difference which arises or occurs between the parties in relation to any thing or matter arising out of or under this agreement'. Indeed, article 5 of JCT 80 clearly states:

5.1   In case any dispute or difference shall arise between the Employer or the Architect on his behalf and the Contractor, either during the progress or after the completion or abandonment of the works, as to;

5.1.1   The construction of this Contract, or;

5.1.2   Any matter or thing of whatsoever nature arising hereunder or in connection herewith including any matter or thing left by this Contract to the discretion of the Architect or the withholding by the Architect of any certificate to which the Contractor may claim to be entitled or the adjustment of the Contract Sum under clause 30.6.2 or the rights and liabilities of the parties under clauses 27, 28, 32 or 33 or unreasonable withholding of consent or agreement by the Employer or the Architect on his behalf or by the Contractor . . .

then such dispute or difference shall be and is hereby referred to the arbitration and final decision of a person to be agreed between the parties to act as Arbitrator . . .

If certain terms are not expressly included in an arbitration clause, they may be implied unless you have agreed otherwise and that agreement is included in the contract or can be implied from it. For example, a term is generally implied that any arbitration will be decided in accordance with the ordinary law. A fundamental principle of this is that the arbitrator will hear both parties. However, you can agree if you so wish, to dispense with oral evidence and agreement, submissions being entirely in writing. For example, clause 10.5 of the FAS contract gives a shortened procedure for arbitration:

> 10.3   Shortened procedure – if arbitration becomes necessary the parties may hereby decide together, or the Arbitrator shall have powers so to direct, to shorten settlement of certain disputes by one of the following methods and rules therefore, under the control of the Arbitrator;
> 1.   A written statement of case and supporting evidence by each party to be submitted to the Arbitrator at the times and in the manner decided by him, with a copy for him to send to each party concurrently – within 2 weeks of this each party shall give to him their representations – he shall then request submissions within another 2 weeks of any further information he requires – he shall then make his award or findings within a further 3 weeks.

In other words, you and the other parties to the arbitration may choose your own rules of procedure. They will be upheld, provided that they are not repugnant to the courts; if they are repugnant, the arbitrators' award will not be enforced.

Under clause 66(5)(a) of the ICE contract any reference to arbitration shall be conducted in accordance with the Institution of Civil Engineers' Arbitration Procedure (1983); while under clause 67.3 of the FIDIC contract arbitration, it will be settled under the Rules of Conciliation and Arbitration of the International Chamber of Commerce.

Q. We are involved in an international engineering contract abroad. Whose law governs the arbitration?

The law which governs a contract carried out abroad and which will be used to interpret its clauses, determining the rights and obligations of yourselves and the other parties to the contract, is quite simply the law you have agreed and intended should apply to the contract. This is commonly termed the 'proper law of the contract'.

Arbitration clauses such as those contained in FIDIC, clause 67.3, recognize:

1.   Arbitration may be held in a different country from the one in which the contract is being undertaken;
2.   The procedure governing the arbitration may be the same as that of the country in which the arbitration is being held;
3.   The proper law of the contract may be different from that which governs the procedure of the arbitration.

For example, a contract may be undertaken in Nigeria. It is agreed that any arbitration which arises from the contract will be heard in Zurich. The arbitration procedure will be determined by Swiss law. The law governing the interpretation of the contract will be English law.

If no mention has been made as to the proper law of the contract, it may reasonably be inferred that where you agree that an arbitration is to be held in a particular country, then the law of that country will be applied to interpret the

---

A cautionary tale about a question of whose law

An English client retained a Scottish contractor to build a factory in Scotland. The architect was English. The contract was JCT 63. The agreement was made in Scotland.

The Scottish contractor began proceedings in the English courts. The English client applied for a stay which was granted by the courts. The Scottish contractor applied to the president of the Royal Institute of British Architects (RIBA) for the appointment of an arbitrator. A Scottish arbitrator was appointed.

The Scottish arbitrator began the arbitration.

He refused to state a case for the opinion of the English courts. He was of the opinion that Scottish law governed the procedure of the arbitration.

The Court of Appeal and the House of Lords held by a majority that while the general facts of the contract might point to Scottish law as the proper law of the contract, the use of the English JCT form of contract with its many references to and dependency on English substantive and procedural law, pointed to a contrary intention, which was reinforced by

the subsequent conduct of the parties. However, the House of Lords, overruling the Court of Appeal held that the procedural law could be different from the proper law. The conduct of the parties after the appointment showed acceptance that the proceedings should be governed by the law of Scotland. Consequently, the arbitrator's award was final.

James Miller & Partners v. *Whitworth Street Estates* [1970] 2 W.L.R. 728.

---

contract. However, this may not invariably be the case. All the relevant circumstances must be considered including the other terms of the contract.

Q. What is the effect on my liability of an arbitration clause in a standard form of contract?

If you have agreed to settle any dispute by arbitration by signing a written contract, whether or not an arbitrator is named within the contract, then it is binding on all parties.

If you then break the arbitration clause, you may be liable in damages as the breach gives the other party a right to an action for damages. (Indeed, the same principle applies if the agreement had been purely oral.)

Q. Who chooses the arbitrator?

The choice is yours. Initially you and the other parties to the contract may select your own arbitrator, whether it be a single arbitrator or two or more arbitrators either with or without an umpire.

It is a principle which is embodied in the standard forms of building and engineering contracts. Article 5.1.3 of JCT 80 makes provision for the nomination of a single arbitrator, as do GC/Works/1 clause 61(1), the ACA form clause 25.3, the FAS contract clause 10.2 and ICE clause 66(3)(b)(ii). In contrast, under clause 67.3 of the FIDIC contract more than one arbitrator may be appointed.

Where the contract does not direct the manner in which an arbitrator is to be selected, then the way in which you choose one is entirely a matter for you to decide. For example, you may choose an arbitrator by lot or any other method which appears appropriate and it is generally your own affair, if as a result, you selected someone who is unfit or incompetent. If you cannot agree upon an arbitrator, the standard building and engineering contracts provide for some other independent person to appoint him. In the case of article 5 of JCT 80, this includes the President or Vice-President of the RIBA.

The appointment of an arbitrator becomes effective or valid when the following conditions are fulfilled:

1. The arbitrator is notified of the appointment;
2. The arbitrator consents to act;
3. The name of the arbitrator and the fact of his appointment are communicated to all parties;
4. Any time stipulations within the contract for the arbitrator's appointment are complied with.

Q. After an arbitrator has been chosen, are we stuck with him? How can an arbitrator be changed?

You may not be obliged to stick with an arbitrator you have deliberately chosen in certain circumstances.

The authority of an arbitrator may be revoked, that is he may be removed from conducting the arbitration, by the High Court if:

1. The arbitrator is not, or may not be, impartial because, for instance, he may have some interest in the result of the arbitration (particularly important where you did not know certain facts which make the arbitrator biased at the time of his appointment);
2. The arbitrator does not use all reasonable dispatch either

in starting on, proceeding with or making an award in the arbitration;
3. The arbitrator misconducts himself; for example, by receiving gifts or hospitality his mind is influenced;
4. The arbitrator misconducts the proceedings;
5. The dispute includes an issue as to whether or not one of the parties to the contract has acted fraudently and should therefore be determined by the High Court.

Where an arbitrator has been removed, the court may appoint another arbitrator.

The ICE contract contains a most useful clause, namely clause 66(4)(b), which recognizes the problems which can arise when an arbitrator ceases to act; it provides for them in the following manner;

> If an arbitrator declines the appointment or after appointment is removed by order of a competent court or is incapable of acting or dies and the parties do not within one calendar month of the vacancy arising fill the vacancy then either party may apply to the President for the time being of the Institution of Civil Engineers to appoint another arbitrator to fill the vacancy.

Q. Are there any rules as to the number of arbitrators to be chosen and who they are?

Where a contract simply refers to arbitration in broad and sweeping terms, it will generally be inferred that that arbitration will be conducted by a single person. However, if the contract expressly states that you and the other parties to it should select two arbitrators, then as a corollary to that clause it may be implied (unless the contrary intention is expressed), that the arbitrators after they have been appointed should themselves nominate a third person to act as an umpire. The umpire will enter upon the arbitration as if he were a sole arbitrator if the two arbitrators cannot agree and they have indicated as much in writing either to yourself, to the other parties to the contract or the umpire.

Generally any person whom you believe is suitable because of his experience, his expertise or for some other reason may be appointed as an arbitrator. Indeed, a judge could be chosen as an arbitrator, if he agrees to act outside the scope of his judicial duties.

Q. Must an arbitration claim be brought within a particular time?

The statutory limitation periods in which an arbitration should be brought to prevent it being statute barred are set out in the limitation acts discussed earlier. The limitation period stops running when an arbitration is begun. This occurs when one party serves a notice on the other, either personally or by registered/recorded delivery, requiring them to:

1. appoint an arbitrator;
2. agree to an arbitrator's appointment;
3. submit the dispute to an arbitrator who has already been named by the contract.

Under the ACA form, clause 25.3, the notice must be given within 20 working days, unless some other time is agreed, of the architect's initial decision on the dispute.

Generally there is no reason why an agreement cannot be reached at the very beginning of a contract that arbitration proceedings will not be brought after a stated period of time, that period being different from the one which is given in the limitation acts.

Likewise, it may be agreed that an arbitration award must be made before either party can begin litigation in the courts. The award is a condition precedent to litigation. The clause is commonly known as a 'Scott v. Avery clause'. As a corollary to this it should be noted that some standard-form contracts state that arbitration proceedings must not start until the contract itself is completed; for example, clause 61(2) of GC/Works/1 states:

> Unless the parties otherwise agree, such reference (to arbitration) shall not take place until after the completion, alleged completion or abandonment of the works or the determination of the contract.

Q. What are the powers of an arbitrator?

In broad terms, the power of an arbitrator is to decide the dispute between the parties and as a result of his decision to make an award. To this power must be added any other additional powers which the parties may agree to give the arbitrator. Equally, an arbitrator's powers may be limited by the parties.

In other words, the power of an arbitrator is based upon whatever agreement is reached between the parties. The arbitrator cannot ignore or disregard it, nor can he delegate that power which the agreement has given to him. However, he may consider whether or not he has, as a result of the agreement, jurisdiction to act upon the particular dispute to decide if it is worth while to continue with the arbitration.

Certain of the arbitrator's powers may be implied where the agreement either does not expressly refer to them or where no contrary intention appears in it; these are:

1. To make an interim award;

A cautionary tale about how to remove an arbitrator

C. Miskin & Sons Ltd were main contractors employed by Bedfordshire County Council to build a police station at Luton. Modern Engineering (Bristol) Ltd were nominated subcontractors who were to provide and erect the steelwork.

The subcontract between Miskin and Modern Engineering was in the NFBTE/FASS standard form commonly known as the 'green form', clause 8(a) of which provided:

1. The Sub-Contractor shall commence the Sub-Contract works within an agreed time or, if none is agreed, then within a reasonable time after the receipt by him of an order in writing under this Sub-Contract from the Contractor to that effect and shall proceed with the same with due expedition.

   The Sub-Contractor shall complete the Sub-Contract works and each section thereof within the period specified in Part II of the Appendix to this Sub-Contract or within such extended period or periods as may be granted pursuant to the provisions hereinafter contained.

   If the Sub-Contractor fails to complete the Sub-Contract or any section thereof within the period or periods as hereinafter provided, he shall pay or allow to the Contractor a sum equivalent to any loss or damage suffered or incurred by the Contractor and caused by the failure of the Sub-Contractor as aforesaid. The Contractor shall at the earliest opportunity give reasonable notice to the Sub-Contractor that loss or damage as aforesaid is being or has been suffered or incurred.

   Provided that the Contractor shall not be entitled to claim any loss or damage under this clause unless the Architect shall have issued to the Contractor (with a duplicate copy to the Sub-Contractor) a certificate in writing stating that in his opinion the Sub-Contract works or the relevant section thereof ought reasonably to have been completed within the specified period or within any extended period or periods as the case may be.

Modern Engineering carried out the subcontract works and completed them by 7 February 1973. The architect certified that in his opinion the subcontract works ought reasonably to have been completed by 7 February 1973.

Miskins made a claim against Modern Engineering for damages for delay and defective work. The claim was disputed. The dispute was referred to arbitration. The President of the Royal Institute of Chartered Surveyors appointed an arbitrator. In due course the hearing of the matter was commenced. On the first day of the hearing counsel for Miskins began to open his client's case. He told the arbitrator that one issue which arose concerned the legal effect of the architect's certificate. It was Miskins's case that the certificate in question could be opened up, reviewed and revised by the arbitrator. It was Modern Engineering's pleaded case that the certificate was not subject to review and that its existence defeated Miskins's delay claim.

Counsel appearing for Modern Engineering was invited to, and did, confirm that the pleaded case would be maintained, and he briefly stated what were the propositions for which he would be contending, Miskins's counsel then proceeded to develop his argument on that particular point. He concluded that part of his opening by mentioning to the arbitrator that he might wish to take independent legal advice upon that disputed point of law and urging him to feel free to do so. He then moved on to deal with other matters. The opening continued for the remainder of that first day (Monday) and for the whole of Tuesday. The arbitrator did not sit on Wednesday and the hearing was resumed on Thursday. Immediately the hearing resumed on Thursday, the arbitrator handed to the parties his 'Award' which stated that in his opinion he was empowered to open up, review or revise the certificate.

Modern Engineering considered what the arbitrator had done and decided that they would seek from the High Court an order under section 23(1) of the *Arbitration Act 1950* that the arbitrator should be removed; section

(continued)

23(1) provides: 'Where an arbitrator . . . has misconducted himself or the proceedings, the High Court may remove him.' The arbitration was adjourned to enable them to do so.

Both parties agreed that the arbitrator had acted wrongly in preparing and publishing his 'Award' without having heard the arguments which Modern Engineering wished to put before him. Accordingly, Miskins conceded that the 'Award' should be set aside, but opposed the application for the arbitrator's removal.

The arbitrator did not seek to justify or explain his conduct to the court. He neither swore an affidavit setting out the circumstances and the reasons which had led him to make the 'Award', nor did he write a letter to the parties for them to place before the court.

Robert Goff, J. refused to order the arbitrator's removal. In his judgment the test to be applied when considering the section 23(1) power was to consider whether the circumstances were such that the arbitrator had demonstrated he was not a fit and proper person to continue to conduct the arbitration proceedings. Although the arbitrator had made a 'serious error', the learned judge was not persuaded that he ought to be removed. In the course of his judgment, Robert Goff, J. expressed regret that he had not had any explanation from the arbitrator.

Modern Engineering appealed. The appeal was allowed, and it was held that:

1. It was clear that the arbitrator had misconducted the proceedings, so that the court had power to remove him;

2. The proper test to apply when considering whether to order removal was to ask whether the arbitrator's conduct was such as to destroy the confidence of the parties, or either of them, in his ability to come to a fair and just conclusion;

3. Applying that test to the facts of this particular case, the removal of the arbitrator should be ordered;

4. The Court of Appeal entirely agreed with the observations of Robert Goff, J., that it was a matter of regret that there was no explanation of his conduct from the arbitrator.

Modern Engineering (Bristol) Ltd. v. *C. Miskin & Son Ltd.* (1980) 15 B.L.R. 82.

2. To examine all parties to the arbitration including each of their witnesses either on oath or affirmation;
3. To give directions on costs;
4. To award interest on any sum found due to one of the parties by the other, from the date when the cause of action arose to the date of the award or any part of it;
5. To correct any clerical mistake or error in the award;
6. The award will be final and binding on all the parties to the arbitration.

Under Rule 6 of the ICE Arbitration Procedure (1983) which is used in conjunction with clause 66 of the ICE contract for settlement of disputes by arbitration, the arbitrator is given power to order certain 'protection measures'; they are:

6.1(a) To give directions for the detention, storage, sale or disposal of the whole or any part of the subject matter of the dispute at the expense of one or both parties;

(b) To give directions for the preservation of any document or thing which is or may become evidence in the arbitration;

(c) To order the deposit of money or other security to secure the whole or any part of the amount(s) in dispute;

(d) To make an order for security for costs in favour of one or more of the parties;

(e) To order his own costs to be secured.

6.2 Money ordered to be paid under this Rule shall be paid without delay into a separate bank account in the name of a stake holder to be appointed by and subject to the directions of the Arbitrator.

A cautionary tale about appointing arbitrators

A acted for the South Devon Railway Co. as their agent. He made an offer to E for some land which the railway company wanted to buy under their powers of compulsory purchase. The railway company and E could not agree a suitable price, therefore, they went to arbitration to settle the matter.

The railway company appointed A as their arbitrator. E appointed B as his arbitrator. An umpire, C, was chosen by B from a list which had been given to him by A. B was, unknown to E, a surveyor of and a shareholder in a company which was itself interested in the success of the railway company's undertaking. C was also unknown to E; he too was a surveyor employed by the same company as B.

It was held that E by appointing his own arbitrator had waived any objection to the appointment of A, and that the facts as to B and C did not afford any judicial grounds for setting aside the award.

Re Elliott, ex parte South Devon Railway (1848) 12 Jur. (O.S.) 445.

Q. What is the procedure in an arbitration?

Having selected an arbitrator who had accepted the appointment, the arbitrator will consult the parties in order to arrange convenient times, dates and places of meetings, after which he will notify them of the details and may give orders about the exchange of pleadings, discovery and inspection of documents and interrogatories.

At meetings both parties must be present as the arbitrator cannot hear one if the other is not there. However, he may hear one party alone if the other clearly refuses to attend, even though they are fully aware of the meeting and can give no reasonable excuse to explain their absence.

The arbitrator may not without sufficient reason exclude anyone from the meeting whom one of the parties wishes to be present to assist in the arbitration. For example, if one party wishes to be represented by leading counsel and the other party does not as yet have such representation rather than exclude counsel, the arbitrator should give the other party the opportunity of also having counsel.

The arbitrator in conducting the arbitration procedure must follow not only whatever directions have been agreed between the parties, but also the rules of court wherever practicable. Each party and their witness may be required to:

1. take an oath or affirmation;
2. be examined by the arbitrator;
3. produce all relevant documents in his possession;
4. do all other things which the arbitrator may ask of him in order to decide the dispute.

The normal procedure is:

1. Claimant presents his case to the arbitrator;
2. Claimant calls and examines his witnesses;
3. Respondent cross-examines the claimants witnesses;
4. Claimant re-examines his witnesses;
5. Arbitrator questions claimant's witnesses;
6. Respondent presents his case to the arbitrator;
7. Respondent calls and examines his witnesses;
8. Claimant cross-examines the respondent's witnesses;

9. Respondent re-examines his witnesses;
10. Arbitrator questions respondent's witnesses;
11. Respondent addresses the arbitrator;
12. Arbitrator discusses any issues upon which he requires further guidance from the respondent;
13. Claimant addresses the arbitrator;
14. Arbitrator discusses any issues upon which he requires further guidance from the respondent;
15. Arbitrator indicates that he will make his award in due course.

Should the arbitrator wish to adopt a procedure which is different from the norm, then the agreement of all parties is necessary. The arbitrator himself takes a note, possibly in longhand supported by his own tape recording of each party's case, to assist him in preparing his award. However, a shorthand note of the arbitration may be made if the parties agree.

If the arbitrator, having expert knowledge on a particular matter, tends from that knowledge to disagree with a submission made by one of the parties, he should make that point known, in order to hear submissions on it (see Fig. 12.1, p. 216).

Q. Must an award be made in a particular time?

As a general principle, an award may be made by an arbitrator at any time. However, there are a number of provisos and exceptions to this principle; these are:

1. The arbitrator should not delay giving the award. He must use all reasonable dispatch. If he does not, the court may remove him and the parties to the arbitration need not pay him;
2. Time in which an award should be made may be limited by statute. For example, under clause 22(2) of the *Arbitration Act 1950* where an award is remitted by the court, the new award must be made within 3 months of the order unless the order directs otherwise;
3. The parties may expressly agree that the award should be made within a particular time. For example, clauses 10.3.1/2 of the FAS contract state that where the shortened procedure for arbitration is used, the arbitrator should make his award within 3 weeks of receiving information or hearing the parties. Similar provision is made in the ICE rules for arbitration;
4. Where the time in which an award should have been given and is not, then the time period can be extended either by the courts or by the written agreement of the parties.

Q. Who pays the arbitrator, and how much?

The arbitrator's fees may be set in a number of ways:

1. The arbitrator may himself set a fee which may be included in his award;
2. Where an umpire makes an award, following the disagreement of the arbitrators, his fees together with those of the arbitrators may be included in his award;
3. The arbitration fees may be agreed by the parties beforehand;
4. Where there is no agreement, it will be implied that the arbitrator is entitled to a reasonable fee;
5. Where an award does not include either the arbitrator's or if appropriate umpire's fees, then their charges may be taken, on application of the party liable to pay those fees.

The arbitrator may direct who is to pay not only the award, but also the costs of the arbitration, which costs are taxable in the High Court. They include the preparation of a party's case, its submission to the arbitrator and the costs of the actual proceedings before the arbitrator.

Terms to this effect may be implied into all arbitration contracts unless the parties agree otherwise. However, even if an agreement (unless it is to refer a dispute which has already arisen) is reached before arbitration that each party shall pay their own costs, it will be treated as void.

Nevertheless, Rule 21.1 of the ICE Arbitration Procedure (1983), Part F (short procedure), notes that unless the parties otherwise agree, the arbitrator shall have no power to award costs to either party and his own fees and charges shall be paid in equal shares by the parties.

Q. Does the arbitrator have to be paid before we hear of his award?

Yes. Usually the arbitrator will let you know when his award is ready and, at the same time, indicate what his fees are. He may not release his award to you until his fees have first been paid.

The reason for this is that the arbitrator has a lien on the arbitration agreement and the award for the value of his fees. In other words, the arbitrator has a right by which he is entitled to obtain satisfaction of a debt, namely his fees, by means of property, the agreement and award, belonging to you and the other parties to the arbitration who are indebted to him.

If the arbitrator refuses to release his award to you until his fees have been paid, and there has been no prior agreement on the subject, then you or any other party to the arbitration may apply to the court for an order that the arbitrator deliver the award to you upon your paying the amount demanded by the arbitrator as fees into court. The arbitrator's fees will then be taxed by the court. Such amount which is found to be reasonable will be paid to him from the moneys in court, and what is left, if any, will be returned to you.

Q. What is the effect and scope of an arbitrator's award?

It is not necessary for an award to be in any particular form for it to be effective. However, it will not be effective and will not be enforced if it is either ambiguous, uncertain or does not decide the issues which the parties placed before the arbitrator. Furthermore, as the scope of the award should be final and binding in determining the issues between the parties, one which is conditional, that is it gives an alternative award if a condition is not met will not be effective.

The award may, in certain circumstances, act as a bar to any party bringing an action on such matters as are decided by the award. In other words, it gives rise to an estoppel.

Interest may be payable on an award, if it is for a sum to be paid by one party to another, from the date of the award until such time as it is paid. The rate of interest may be the same as for a judgment debt, but not higher, though the arbitrator could direct that a lower rate should be paid.

Q. How can an arbitration award be enforced?

If an arbitration goes against you, you cannot be compelled to comply with the arbitrator's decision purely on the basis of the award.

An arbitration award must be enforced by a court which has competent jurisdiction either by leave of the High Court to enforce the award as a judgment or by bringing an action on the award.

A cautionary tale of a builder who was asked for £75

A builder was sued for defects which were valued at approximately £75. In his defence the builder claimed:

1. Lateness of a notice under a defects clause;
2. He was ready and willing at all material times to make good defects;
3. The client refused to allow one of the builder's workmen to carry out remedial work;
4. The client offered later dates for access which were either impracticable or were of too short a notice;
5. The client refused to suggest later dates for access.

The builder denied that the client was entitled to a damages award; furthermore, he asked for his own costs to be paid by the client.

The arbitrator awarded £45 to the client but with costs against him. An appeal was made against the award.

The Court of Appeal held that:

1. There was a settled practice of the courts that in the absence of special circumstances a successful litigant should receive his costs;
2. It was for the party seeking to justify an order which departed from this principle to show that there was material justifying such a departure;
3. On the facts no such material existed in the present case;
4. The award should be set aside and the builder ordered to pay the client's costs.

Dineen v. *Walpole* [1969] 1. Ll. Rep. 261.

An application is made to the court for an order to enforce the award. Where the application is successful and leave is granted, then the court judgment is entered in the same terms as the award. Leave is granted unless there are some real grounds for doubting the validity of the award if an application to remit or set it aside has not been made within 6 weeks of the award. After that time, the award is final and binding on all parties.

Should leave be refused, an action on the award should be brought in order to enforce it. To succeed in an action, it is necessary to prove:

1. The making of the contract;
2. The dispute arose within its terms;
3. Arbitrators were appointed in accordance with the contract's arbitration clause;
4. The making of the award;
5. The amount awarded has not been paid.

Q. If I sign an arbitration agreement, will this prevent me from going to court if a dispute arises?

An arbitration agreement cannot be used against you by acting as a bar or defence to any litigation proceedings which could be brought by you in respect of the particular dispute in question. Indeed, any such agreement would be illegal and void as it would essentially oust the jurisdiction of the court.

For example, phrases to the effect that the arbitrator's award is to be final and binding on the parties which may be found in article 5.4 of JCT 80 does not oust the court's jurisdiction. It would add nothing even if the clause included a term that it was accepted as such by all parties. Likewise, the courts' jurisdiction will not be excluded where a clause expressly states that the arbitrator's award, 'shall be final and binding upon the parties who covenant that their disputes shall be so decided by arbitration alone and not by recourse to any court by way of action at law'.

Even where arbitration is a condition precedent to litigation, in certain circumstances this may not prevent an action if no arbitration has taken place should the court order that the clause itself is ineffective.

Q. When can an appeal to the courts be made against an arbitrator's award?

An appeal can be made against an arbitrator's decision on a point of law. However, an appeal cannot be made on a question of fact. The arbitrator is the sole judge of the facts. His award, in so far as it deals with the fact, is final and binding on the parties to the arbitration. Nevertheless, whether or not there is sufficient evidence to support a finding of fact by an arbitrator may itself be a question of law and therefore open to appeal. Because of this, the arbitrator should give reasons for his award which cover all important issues.

An appeal may be made either if:

1. All parties to the arbitration consent;
2. The High Court grants leave to appeal.

The nature of the contract may affect the question of whether or not leave to appeal is granted, that is whether it is a one-off contract especially drawn up for the parties or whether it is a standard form of contract in general use. The criteria for granting leave to appeal have been set out in *The Nema* [1981] 2 All E.R. 1030.

On a one-off contract the criterion is:

That it is apparent to the judge upon a mere perusal of the reasoned award itself without the benefit of adversary argument that the meaning ascribed to the clause by the arbitrator is obviously wrong, but if on such perusal it appears to the judge that it is possible that argument might persuade him, despite first impression to the contrary, that the arbitrator might be right, he should not grant leave.

On standard form contracts the criteria is:

If the decision of the question of construction in the circumstances of the particular case would add significantly to the clarity and certainty of English commercial law it would be proper to give leave. But leave should not be given in such a case, unless the judge considered that there was a strong prima facie case and that there had been a doubt that the arbitrator had been wrong in his construction; and when the events to which the standard clause fell to be applied in the particular arbitration were themselves one off events, stricter criteria, should be applied on the same lines as those that are appropriate to one off clauses.

It is open to the court when granting leave to appeal to attach conditions to the grant, for example, the party who wishes to lodge an appeal must first pay into court the amount of the arbitrator's award.

Q. When can an award be remitted to an arbitrator by a court?

The court has a general discretion to remit or return an award to an arbitrator for reconsideration by him if:

1. there is a clear defect or error on the face of the award, for example, it is not consistent with the terms of the arbitration clause, is ambiguous or uncertain;

2. the arbitrator recognizes that he has made a mistake in the award, for example, the principle on which he based the award was wrong, and he therefore asks for it to be returned to him for correction;
3. new evidence has been brought forward which is material to the dispute and was not available at the arbitration; the evidence could not have been discovered at the time of the arbitration, even with the use of reasonable diligence;
4. the arbitrator has misconducted himself.

Q. When can the court set aside an arbitrator's award?

The award of an arbitrator may be set aside either if:

1. there is an error of law on the face of the award;
2. the arbitration has been improperly procured, for example, if the arbitrator has been deceived;
3. the award has been improperly procured, for example, material evidence has been fraudulently concealed;
4. the arbitrator has misconducted himself, for example, by not deciding all matters which were referred to him;
5. the arbitrator has misconducted the proceedings, for example, where he has refused to hear the evidence of a material witness;
6. there is either wholly or partially a want of jurisdiction, for example, where the arbitrator is not qualified to act.

It should be noted that an order of the High Court to set aside an arbitrator's award may be appealed against by application to the Court of Appeal, and thence to the House of Lords, either with the leave of the Court of Appeal or of the House of Lords.

12.2 LITIGATION

Q. What must I do to prepare my case if I were to begin legal proceedings?

As a matter of general practice, try to make sure that:

1. Everything is in writing from the memo of a five-minute telephone conversation, to the minutes of a three-hour meeting. Make sure it is correct and you understand it;
2. All correspondence and relevant documentation on a scheme is filed in a logical and simple way. This includes the envelopes in which correspondence is received. Never throw them away. Staple them to the back of letters, taking great care not to damage the date stamp – it could be important, for example, where the date of a contract or instructions are in question;
3. Query everything which you are not clear on immediately. Do not leave it until later;
4. Keep accurate time records; they could be vital if you are going to try to recover fees charged on a time basis. Do not be tempted to adjust times you have spent on a job by deducting time from one scheme and giving it to another for whatever reason;
5. Maintain a comprehensive and clear photographic record of the scheme from the virgin site to the completed building. Make sure you include in that record all boundary walls and any adjoining property. Time, date and identify each photograph with a short description of location and matters of interest.

Decide whom you will appoint as expert witnesses. Give them all relevant documents, information and any other assistance that may be required, such as inspecting the site, in

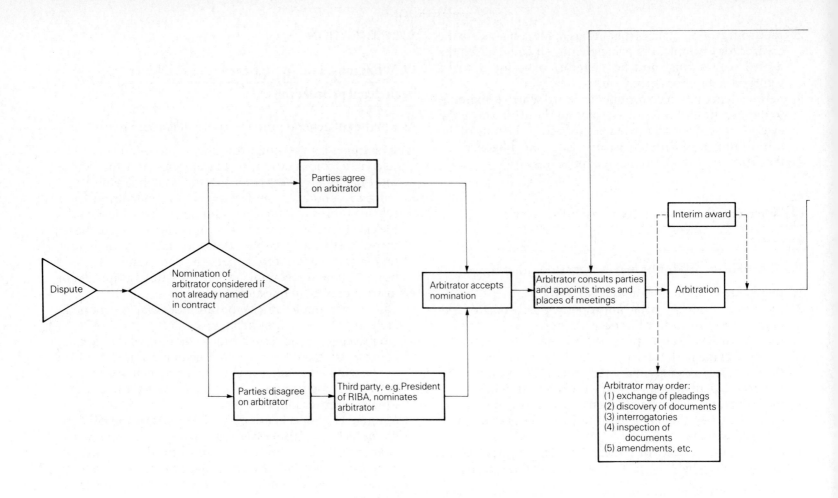

Fig. 12.1 Procedure in arbitration

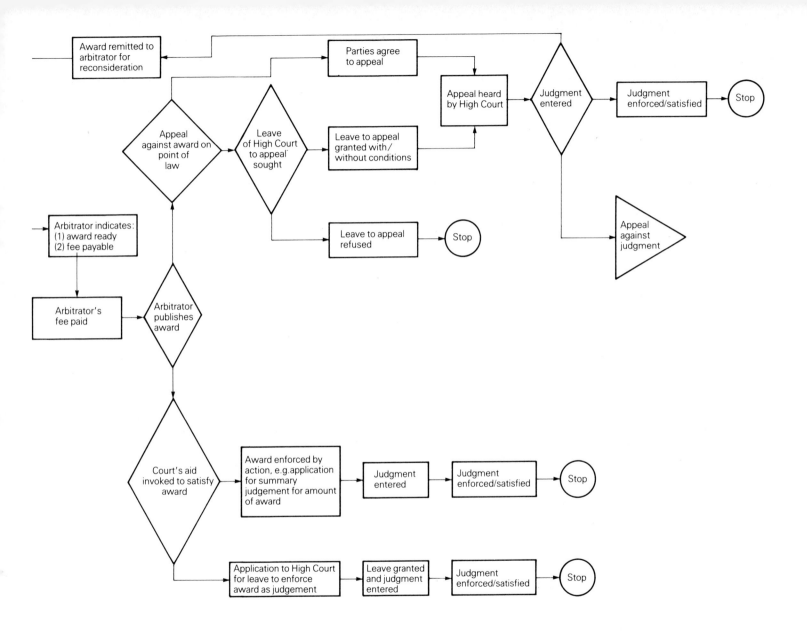

Award remitted to arbitrator for reconsideration

Parties agree to appeal

Appeal heard by High Court

Judgment entered

Judgment enforced/satisfied

Stop

Appeal against award on point of law

Leave of High Court to appeal sought

Leave to appeal granted with/without conditions

Leave to appeal refused

Stop

Appeal against judgment

Arbitrator indicates:
(1) award ready
(2) fee payable

Arbitrator's fee paid

Arbitrator publishes award

Court's aid invoked to satisfy award

Award enforced by action, e.g.application for summary judgement for amount of award

Judgment entered

Judgment enforced/satisfied

Stop

Application to High Court for leave to enforce award as judgement

Leave granted and judgment entered

Judgment enforced/satisfied

Stop

Table 12.1 Scott Schedule

No.	Work specified in contract	Plaintiff's comments			Defendants comments		Column for official referee
		Work Supplied	Work Required	Estimate of Loss	Work Supplied	Estimate of Loss	
1	2	3	4	5	6	7	8
1	Supply and fix external door D12 to be solid oak 4-panelled with solid ogee mouldings and painted with 4 coats external quality polyurethene varnish	External door D12 was supplied and fixed as a hardwood faced flush door painted with 3 coats external quality varnish	Take down and remove hardwood faced door D12; make good to doorframe; supply and fix solid 4-panelled door with solid ogee mouldings and painted with 4 coats external quality polyure-thene varnish	£500	External hard-wood faced flush door D12 painted 3 coats external quality varnish was supplied and fixed upon Architect's Instruc-tion 2001 to omit door D12 as specified in original contract documents	Nil	

order for them to prepare an accurate, comprehensive yet impartial expert witness report. The report may be used not only as the basis for the expert witness's proof of evidence, but also for extracting vital information to enter into a Scott Schedule (Table 12.1).

Decide whether or not you are going to conduct the case yourself, or whether you will want to be legally represented. If the latter, consult a solicitor who may, in turn, arrange a conference with counsel to discuss the case and/or prepare a written advice covering such points as the merits of the case, liability quantum of damages and tactics. (See Figs 12.2–12.4.)

Q. Which court should I bring an action in?

The choice for bringing a civil action lies between the County Court and the High Court. It depends upon the value and nature of the claim as the courts have different jurisdictions. The County Court has a limited jurisdiction, whereas the High Court has a general jurisdiction to hear and determine all classes of claim whatever their nature or amount unless a statute directs otherwise. For example, the County Court can hear actions in debt, contract or tort where the sum claimed is not more than £5000. If the sum exceeds £5000, the claim must be brought in the High Court.

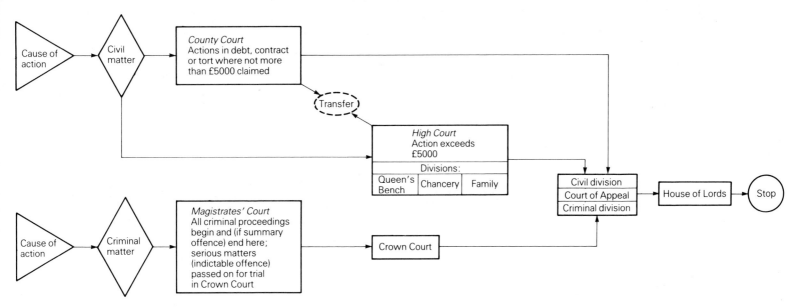

Fig. 12.2 The courts

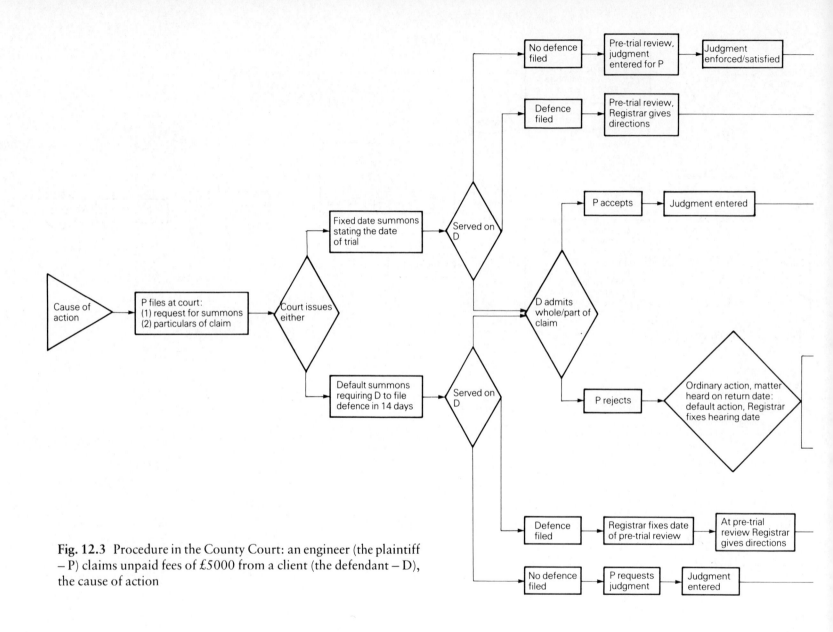

Fig. 12.3 Procedure in the County Court: an engineer (the plaintiff – P) claims unpaid fees of £5000 from a client (the defendant – D), the cause of action

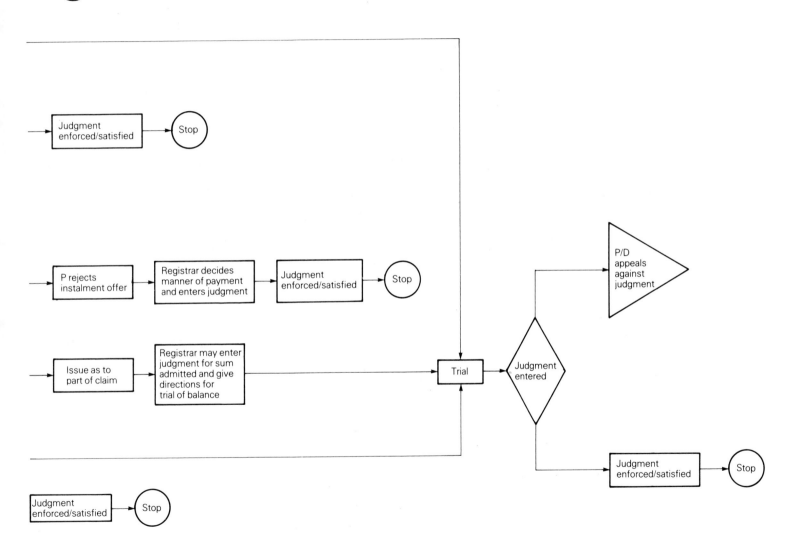

Stop

Judgment enforced/satisfied → Stop

P rejects instalment offer → Registrar decides manner of payment and enters judgment → Judgment enforced/satisfied → Stop

Issue as to part of claim → Registrar may enter judgment for sum admitted and give directions for trial of balance → Trial → Judgment entered

P/D appeals against judgment

Judgment enforced/satisfied → Stop

Judgment enforced/satisfied → Stop

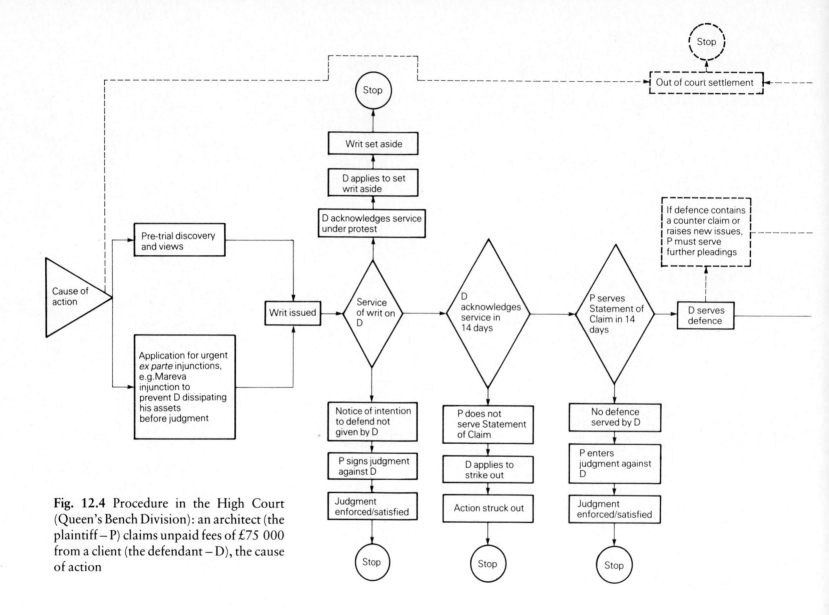

Fig. 12.4 Procedure in the High Court (Queen's Bench Division): an architect (the plaintiff – P) claims unpaid fees of £75 000 from a client (the defendant – D), the cause of action

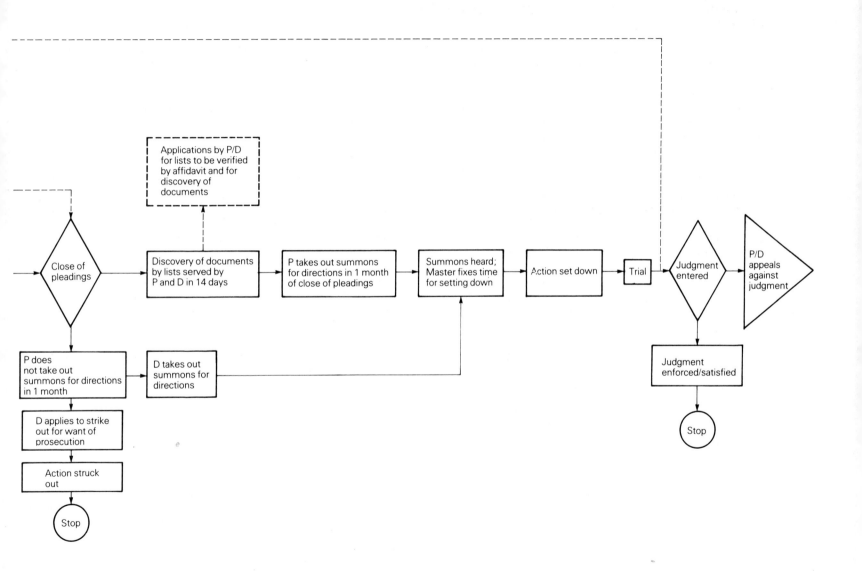

Applications by P/D
for lists to be verified
by affidavit and for
discovery of
documents

Close of
pleadings

Discovery of documents
by lists served by
P and D in 14 days

P takes out summons
for directions in 1 month
of close of pleadings

Summons heard;
Master fixes time
for setting down

Action set down

Trial

Judgment
entered

P/D
appeals
against
judgment

P does
not take out
summons for directions
in 1 month

D takes out
summons for
directions

Judgment
enforced/satisfied

D applies to strike
out for want of
prosecution

Action struck
out

Stop

Stop

Stop

A cautionary tale about making sure that what you ask for is correct

Where a plaintiff claimed repayment of sums which he alleged had been overcharged on a number of invoices and pleaded particulars of the alleged overcharging, it was not permissible for him to claim further sums allegedly overcharged on other invoices, of which overcharging he could neither give particulars nor adduce specific evidence, on the basis that it could be inferred that the level of overcharging on the latter invoices was the same as the average level of overcharging on the invoices in respect of which particulars had been given.

The British Coal Corporation (BCC) had employed Dennis Rye Ltd to make good damage caused by subsidence due to mining, which fell into two categories: repairing fissures in land, and building work. BCC's claim was for money had and received, misrepresentation and fraud: it alleged that it had been overcharged on 192 invoices in respect of fissure work and 242 invoices in respect of building work.

The amended statement of claim gave particulars of the alleged overcharging in respect of 130 of the fissure invoices and 127 of the building invoices. Paragraphs 92 and 93 added claims in respect of the other invoices but gave no particulars. Instead BCC sought to extrapolate from the average amount overcharged on the invoices for which particulars were given, which was 82.73% on the fissure invoices and 33.11% on the building invoices. However, the amount of overcharging of which particulars were given varied considerably: 27–97% on the fissure invoices, and between 2–66% on the building invoices.

The pleading failed to comply with the rules requiring the particularization of allegations of misrepresentation or fraud in Order 18, rule 12, of the Rules of the Supreme Court, and did not give Dennis Rye the information which they needed in order to know what case they had to meet and prepare for trial. That was wrong in principle, and the remedy of striking out was available.

BCC's case on the unparticularized invoices was that Dennis Rye had operated a system of overcharging and that the amount overcharged on those invoices could be established by proving as similar facts the amounts overcharged on the particularized ones. There were two difficulties with that: the pleadings did not adequately allege a consistent system of overcharging, and the amount of the loss could not be proved by reference to the similar facts in relation to the particularized claim, because the average percentage overcharged was not logically probative of the loss for which no particulars were available since the rate of overcharging varied so much between the different invoices.

It was therefore held to be oppressive and unfair to Dennis Rye to allow paragraphs 92 and 93 to stand, and since BCC was unable to give any particulars in respect of those claims, they should be struck out.

British Coal Corporation v. *Dennis Rye Ltd. & Another*, (1988) *The Times*, 7 March.

Though, at first sight, it may appear that you should bring an action in the High Court where, say, you wish to claim in contract recovery of £7000 in unpaid fees, an action may still be brought in the County Court if:

1. you are prepared expressly to limit the claim to £5000 within the Statement of Claim;
2. the claim is abandoned, in so far as it exceeds £5000;
3. you and the other parties to the case expressly agree in writing, though the claim exceeds £5000, to give the County Court jurisdiction to hear the claim if it does not involve substantial issues of fact, or law or where a speedy trial is needed and costs to be saved;
4. the proceedings are transferred to the County Court from the High Court, either by the consent of all parties or by

the application of one of them, or by the High Court of its own motion.

Conversely, an action may be brought in the High Court, even though it initially appears that it should be brought in the County Court; for example:

1. there is some good reason for bringing the case in the High Court, though the sum involved is less than £5000, as where it is an important test case;
2. there are reasonable grounds for supposing the amount which would be recovered will be more than the County Court limit of £5000;
3. though the claim is less than £5000 you, as the plaintiff, want to obtain summary judgment as you consider there to be no defence to your claim and you want to use the High Court machinery for enforcement of the judgment as it is generally more efficient that that of the County Court.

If an action is brought in the High Court if in fact the County Court is the proper court formal sanction may be imposed by the Court. For example, if an action in contract or tort is brought in the High Court and the damages recovered are less than £600, the plaintiff may receive no costs; while if the damages are less than £3000, only costs on the appropriate County Court scale may be awarded.

In deciding which court to bring an action where a choice does exist the following points should be considered:

1. *Complexity* – where difficult and complex questions of law or fact are in issue, the claim would be better heard in the High Court before a judge who is more experienced in such matters; if the questions to be decided are relatively straightforward, then the procedure in the County Court may have an advantage especially as it is less formal than in the High Court;

2. *Convenience* – there are more County Courts than there are High Courts; the former are thus in many cases easier to reach with a consequent saving in time and cost spent on travelling;
3. *Cost* – the costs of bringing an action in the High Court are more than in the County Court; there must be some degree of certainty that the damages which will be recovered in the High Court will be at least £600 and preferably not less than £5000 for the reasons indicated above, otherwise the economics of the exercise may become wholly unbalanced: You will be spending more than you can recover; however, the question of whether or not to go ahead simply on a matter of principle may play an important part at this stage;
4. *Time* – the time taken for proceedings to be brought, heard, judgment to be given, then enforced and settled is frequently longer in the High Court than the County Court.

Statement of claim by client against an architect for damages for negligence and breach of contract

In the High Court of Justice   1989. D.No. 007
Queen's Bench Division
between: Miffe de   *Plaintiff*
                          and
                    Caul M.E. Godde   *Defendant*

Statement of claim

1. The Plaintiff is and was at all material times the owner and occupier of Ty Pensaer, Dinas Cawdl ['the house'] and the Defendant is a chartered architect.

2. By a contract made on or about 1 April 1986 between the Plaintiff and the Defendant, the Plaintiff engaged the Defendant to act as architect for reward in connection with the house. The contract was made in writing and is contained in and evidenced by the Plaintiff's letter to the Defendant, dated 1 April 1986, and the Defendant's letter to the Plaintiff, dated 6 April 1986.

3. It was an implied term of the contract that the Defendant would exercise all due professional skill and care in the performance of his services thereunder.

4. Further or alternatively, the Defendant owed the Plaintiff a duty of care in performing his services as architect.

5. The Defendant performed services as architect for the Plaintiff between about 1 April 1986 and 25 December 1987 in connection with the carrying out of building works at the house.

6. Negligently and in breach of contract, the Defendant failed to exercise all due professional skill and care in the performance of his services.

Particulars

The Defendant, his servants or agents were negligent, in that they:

(a) failed to place the building contract for the carrying out of the works with a competent contractor on terms which afforded reasonable protection to the Plaintiff;

(b) failed to administer the building contract so as to achieve speedy and economical completion of the works;

(c) certified moneys as due to the contractor, Knockitup Ltd, without exercising any of any reasonable skill and care to ascertain the value of the works carried out and materials supplied;

(d) failed to inspect the works properly or at all, allowing the laying of the damp courses to be omitted or improperly carried out and the cavities to be fouled with mortar droppings resulting in water penetration.

7. The Plaintiff has thereby suffered loss and damage.

Particulars

(a) The works purportedly completed by Knockitup Ltd were in fact incomplete and contained the defects referred to in subparagraph (d) above. The Plaintiff has had to incur the cost of employing another contractor to carry out remedial works of £75 000;

(b) The Defendant certified the total value of the Works as £150 000. The total value of the Works was in fact £100 000. The balance, £50 000, is irrecoverable from Knockitup Ltd, who went into liquidation on 1 May 1988;

(c) The works should have been completed by 1 April 1987, but were not completed until 25 December 1987 and the Plaintiff and his family have thereby suffered distress and inconvenience.

8. Further, the Plaintiff is entitled to and claims interest pursuant to section 35 of the *Supreme Court Act 1981* on the amount found to be due to the Plaintiff at such rate and for such period as the Court thinks fit.
and the Plaintiff claims:

(a) damages for breach of contract;

(b) damages for negligence;

(c) the aforesaid interest pursuant to section 35A of the *Supreme Court Act 1981* to be assessed.

Served, etc.   I. V. DUNIT

A defence to a claim of damages for delay and failure to carry out works made by main contractors against sub-contractors who counterclaim for unpaid moneys

In the High Court of Justice   1988. S. No. 177
Queen's Bench Division
Between: S. C. Arem   *Plaintiffs*
     and
     H. I. Flyers   *Defendants*

Defence and Counter-claim Defence

1. Paragraph 1 of the Statement of Claim is admitted.
2. As to paragraph 2 of the Statement of Claim, it is admitted that the Defendants carried on business as structural steelwork contractors at Ddranep, Glamorgan. It is admitted that as from May 1984, the Defendants knew that the Plaintiffs were employed by TWP Ltd on the Pwll Project in Ddranep Marina. Save as aforesaid, paragraph 2 is not admitted.
3. Paragraph 3 of the Statement of Claim is denied. It is denied that there was, at any time, any binding agreement between the Defendants and the Plaintiffs as alleged or at all, save, as hereinafter pleaded, in respect purely of preparatory work.
4. Paragraph 5 of the Statement of Claim is denied. There was no contract as alleged. The Defendants were not prepared to proceed with the erection of the steelworks which was the subject-matter of their quotation of 1 May 1984 not only because there was no contract between the parties for the same, but also because in the intervening period between August and October the work to be done and the programme and the period for the same had been substantially revised by the Plaintiffs.
5. Paragraph 6 of the Statement of Claim and the Particulars of Loss and Damage are denied.
6. The Defendants will seek to set-off their counter-claim in diminution of the Plaintiffs' claim.
7. Paragraph 7 of the Statement of Claim is not admitted. It is denied that the Plaintiffs are entitled to the relief claimed or to any relief.

Counter-claim

8. The Defence is repeated.
9. Pursuant to the agreement referred to in Paragraph 3 of the Defence, the Defendants carried out the said preparatory work for which they are entitled to be paid the sum of £50 955.01 being the reasonable cost thereof. Particulars of the said sum are given in the Schedule served herewith. Alternatively to their claim in contract, the Defendants claim the said sum on a *quantum meruit* as the reasonable value for services provided at the request of the Plaintiffs. *and* the defendants' Counter-claim:

(a) £150 955.01.
(b) interest pursuant to section 35(A) of the *Supreme Court Act 1981* at such rate and for such period as the Court thinks fit.

Served, etc.   W. H. T. WIGGE

A reply made by the plaintiffs fo a defence raised by the first of two defendants who alleged that the plaintiffs' contract was made not with themselves as project managers, but with the second defendants, who were developers and for whom they acted as agents

In the High Court of Justice   1988. S. No. 111.
Queen's Bench Division
Between: Steppe Lightly Lift Engineers   *Plaintiffs*
                  Limited
                  and
          (1) D. R. Martins Management   *Defendants*
                  Limited
          (2) Boothes Property Developers

Reply to the Defence of the First Defendants

1. Save in so far as the same consists of admissions, the Plaintiffs join issue with the First Defendants upon their Defence.
2. As to paragraph 3 of the Defence which is denied, it is expressly denied that the First Defendants acted as agent for the Second Defendants, to the Plaintiffs' knowledge or otherwise. The First Defendants at no time either held themselves out as agents for the Second Defendants or informed the Plaintiffs of any such agency. Furthermore, the terms of the subcontract between the Plaintiffs and the First Defendants are inconsistent with any such agency.
3. Paragraph 4 of the Statement of Claim is denied. There was, in any event, a contract between the parties whereby the Plaintiffs undertook to carry out the specified work and the First Defendants agreed to pay therefor.

Served, etc.   WILES GILES

Further and better particulars, explaining queries that were raised by defendants about certain things within the plaintiffs' statement of claim

In the High Court of Justice   1988. R. No. 1012.
Queen's Bench Division
Between: Ruff Builders   *Plaintiffs*
                  and
                  P. C. Plumbing   *Defendants*

Further and Better Particulars of the Statement of Claim Served Pursuant to Defendants' Request, dated the 17th Day of November 1988

Under paragraph 3(b)
Of:
The draft subcontract enclosed with such letter.
Request
Please produce a copy of the draft subcontract pursuant to R.S.C.O.24 r. 10.
Answer
Pursuant to R.S.C. O24 r. 10 the draft subcontract may be inspected at the offices of Batterem & Co. during office hours, upon notice.

Under paragraph 4(e)
Of:
The allegation that the Defendants warranted . . .

Request
Please set out in relation to the two allegations in this subparagraph of warranty by the Defendants all matters that will be relied upon by the Defendants in support of the allegation that on its proper construction the Defendants gave such warranties.

Answer
The Plaintiffs' case is properly pleaded. The said warranty was given, upon the proper construction of Clause 101 taking into account all the Clauses of the subcontract, and in particular Clause 150 which stated that nothing in the subcontract should create any privity of contract between the Plaintiffs and the Defendants or any other subcontractor.

Served, etc.   T. O. RIGHTE

Q. What is the procedure in court?

While you, as a litigant, may represent yourself and have a right of audience in the courts, if you chose to be legally represented, then barristers alone have the right of audience in the High Court. However, they should appear properly instructed. In other words, a barrister's instructing solicitors (those whom you have retained) must attend.

Procedure in the High Court if you are legally represented is as follows:

1. Generally plaintiff's counsel will make an opening speech. However, if the defence bears the burden of proof, then defence counsel may open. The purpose of an opening speech is to outline the case to the court by reading aloud the pleadings and relevant documents summarizing what all the witnesses he is calling may say and how the party making the opening speech views the issue;

2. The plaintiff's witnesses, including experts, are called and examined in chief in order to adduce evidence supporting the plaintiff's case;
3. The defendant's counsel will cross-examine each of the plaintiff's witnesses not only to discredit the evidence they have given, but also to obtain evidence which is favourable to the defendant's case;
4. Plaintiff's counsel re-examines each of his witnesses to repair what damage may have been done to the plaintiff's case during the defendant's cross-examination of the witness;
5. The judge may ask questions of the plaintiff's witnesses;
6. Defence counsel may make a submission of 'no case to answer', that is the plaintiff has not proved his case against the defendant to the required standard of proof, which with only rare exceptions, is on the balance of probabilities. Should the defendant's submission be upheld and the plaintiff's case dismissed, the plaintiff may appeal to the Court of Appeal, and if it grants the plaintiff's appeal, the defendant may ask that the case be remitted to the trial judge for him to hear their evidence;
7. Defence counsel opens his case and calls the defendant's witnesses and experts to be examined in chief;
8. The plaintiff may cross-examine the defendant's witnesses;
9. Defence counsel may re-examine his witnesses;
10. The judge may ask questions of the defendant's witnesses;
11. The judge may, after the evidence has been heard or indeed at any time during the trial, view the site, building or place in question;
12. Defence counsel may make a closing speech and give submissions on points of law;
13. Plaintiff's counsel likewise makes a closing speech and gives submissions on points of law unless the judge has

indicated that counsel need not do so as he will find for the plaintiff on all points;

14. The judge gives a reasoned judgment on every relevant issue;
15. After an oral judgment has been given, the successful party's counsel will formally ask the court for judgment, together with interest on the award and costs where appropriate.

12.3 AWARD, TAXATION AND PAYMENT

Q. What are the different types of award for damages?

The damages which you have claimed as a plaintiff may be awarded in full if it is found that the other party, the defendant, is wholly liable.

However, if there has been an element of contributory negligence on your part, that is you have not exercised ordinary care to avoid the consequence of the other party's negligence, then the award may be reduced in the same proportion as your contributory negligence. For example, if the potential award for damages is £100 000 but you are found to be 25% contributory negligent, then the award is reduced by 25% to £75 000.

Where appropriate, interest may be awarded on the damages. The purpose is to compensate you for the fact that you have been kept out of your money while the action has been proceeding. The amount of interest may be:

1. that which is set in a contract under whose terms you have brought the action;
2. as set by a relevant statute;
3. at such rate and for such period as the court thinks fit.

A little history on economic loss

A useful starting point for considering the way in which the principles of recovering economic loss has developed is in the case of *Spartan Steel & Alloys Ltd* v. *Martin & Co. (Contractors) Ltd* [1973] 1 Q.B.27.

A steelworks was operated 24 hours a day. The power supply cable to the steelworks was cut, negligently, by a building contractor. The result was that a furnace unexpectedly cooled down and it had to be emptied of the melt which was being fabricated. The value of the metal emptied out of the furnace depreciated. The steelworks lost the profit it would have made on the melt had it been treated. Until the damage had been repaired the furnaces could not be operated and so further production and profit was lost. The building contractors said they were liable only for the loss in value of the metal which had been poured out of the furnaces and not for the lost profits either of that metal or of further lost production because these were *only* or *pure* economic loss. However, Edmund Davies L.J. concluded that an action lay in negligence for damages in respect of pure economic loss, provided, as here, it was a reasonably foreseeable and direct consequence of failure in a duty of care.

In 1983 the case of *Junior Books* v. *Veitchi Co. Ltd* [1983] A.C. 520 was decided by the House of Lords. That case is authority for the principle that there was, in Junior Books, sufficient proximity between the parties for the defendant to owe the plaintiff a duty of care, and the duty of care included a duty not to cause economic loss. Lord Roskill was of the opinion that if a duty of care were shown, and if there were a breach of that duty, then in *all* cases economic loss would be recoverable.

The principle was refined by Slade L.J. two years later in *Investors in Industry* v. *South Bedfordshire District Council* [1985] 32 B.L.R. 1. He said 'the purpose for which the legislature has confirmed the supervisory powers over building operations on local authorities is to protect occupiers of buildings built in the local authority's area and also members of the public generally against dangers to health or personal safety. It is not to safeguard the building developer himself against economic loss incurred in the course of a building project or indeed anyone else against purely economic loss'.

The case appears to preserve the distinction between economic and non-economic loss. Nevertheless, it indicates that the real issue is not whether the loss is purely economic and, therefore, irrecoverable, but whether the duty is such that it extends to economic loss or loss of this kind whether economic or not.

The Junior Books case was described in *Muirhead* v. *Industrial Tank Specialities Ltd* [1986] 1 Q.B. 507 as a case, decided on its own very special facts. However, the principle which emerged was the same. In any particular case the relevant question is not did the Plaintiff foresee damage to the Defendant but did the Plaintiff foresee damage to the Defendant of this type?

In *Leigh & Sullivan Ltd* v. *Aliakman Shipping Co Ltd* [1986] A.C. 785, H.L. it was found that for a plaintiff to have a right to claim in negligence for loss caused to him by reason of loss or damages to property, he had to have either the legal ownership or possessing title to the property concerned at the time that the loss or damage occurred. It did not suffice merely to have contracted rights in relation thereto which had been adversely affected by loss or damage.

The question of recovery for economic loss was considered by His Honour Judge Smout Q.C. in *D.O.E.* v. *Thomas Bates* [1987] 36 B.L.R., 109. He said 'given that a builder and an architect have by defects of construction and design respectively caused loss to a sub-tenant occupier, can that loss be recovered insofar as it arises from either:

(a) a contractual obligation of the sub-tenant occupier to contribute to repairs of defects in property which he does not own or occupy, where such repairs exceed what is necessary either for the protection of his own property or for the protection of the health or safety of his employees;

or

(b) the expense of alternative accommodation for his employees whilst such repairs are undertaken?

The answers to such a double-headed question are covered by direct authority. As a matter of over-riding policy such loss cannot be recovered in either case. If loss is not proved to have arisen from actual or perhaps threatened injury to person or to the plaintiff's, it is purely economic loss and as such cannot be recoverable.

In *Simaan General Contracting Co* v. *Pilkington Glass Ltd* [1988] 1 A.L.L.E.R. 791 C.A. it was accepted by Bingham L.J. that a claim may lie in negligence for recovery of economic loss alone. However, it was not accepted that *Hedley Byrne & Co Ltd* v. *Heller & Partners Ltd* [1964] A.C. 465, and such authorities as *Ross* v. *Caunters* [1980] Ch. 297, established a general rule that claims in negligence may succeed on proof of foreseeable economic loss caused by the defendant even where no damage to property and no proprietary or possessory interest is shown.

The Court of Appeal in *Greater Nottingham Co-operative Society* v. *Cementation Piling & Foundation Ltd & Others* [1988] 41 B.L.R. used the Junior Books case as the parameter against which to measure whether or not the plaintiff could recover from the defendant what was clearly a purely financial or economic loss. The crucial determining consideration was that there existed between the plaintiff and the defendant, who were respectively employer and subcontractor, a direct warranty agreement and that that direct warranty agreement had not dealt with the subject matter of the plaintiff's claim. This negatized the existence of the exceptional circumstances needed for there to exist liability for economic loss and on that basis the Junior Books case was distinguished.

Q. What are the different types of costs which can be awarded by a court?

As a general principle, costs follow the event. In other words, if you have succeeded in your case, then the court may order that those costs or expenses which you have incurred in the course of litigation should be paid for by the party who has lost. The different types of costs which may be ordered include:

1. Plaintiff's (or defendant's) costs in cause – the named party will get his costs of this application if he wins;
2. The plaintiff's costs in any event – whether the plaintiff wins or loses the action, he will recover the costs of the application from the defendant;
3. Costs thrown away – such an order is made where costs have been wasted;
4. Plaintiff's costs – if the plaintiff wins, then the defendant will pay his costs; should the plaintiff lose, each party will pay its own costs; and if the plaintiff loses, then each party will pay their own costs;
5. Costs of the day – when one step in the action, for example, a motion, is adjourned at the request of one party, then he will be required to pay the other party those costs which he has incurred by preparing for that particular step;
6. Costs reserved – the question of costs is reserved for the decision of the trial judge.

Q. What is meant by taxation of costs?

Though the other party may be ordered to pay your costs, you will be entitled to receive that part of your costs which has been both assessed and approved by the court's taxing officer, who will be guided by the appropriate fixed scale of allowable costs and also upon which basis the court has ordered the taxation to be made.

There are two basis of taxation; these are:

1. The standard basis – which is a reasonable amount in respect of all costs reasonably incurred and any doubts as to questions of reasonableness will be resolved in favour of the paying party;
2. The indemnity basis – which is all costs except in so far as they are of an unreasonable amount or have been unreasonably incurred and any doubts as to questions of reasonableness shall be resolved in favour of the receiving party; generally the indemnity basis will only be awarded where the party who is paying has acted in a way which is either unmeritorious, oppressive or in contempt of court.

Q. How can I make the other party pay when judgment has been given in my favour?

The way in which a judgment may be enforced depends upon what asset is to be used to satisfy a judgment debt. The following methods, among others, are available:

1. Asset   Goods, chattels, leases and cheques.
   Method   Writ of *fieri facias* in the High Court (or a warrant of execution in the county court).
             The writ allows the sheriff or other court

A cautionary tale about claiming damages for economic loss

There is no general rule that claims in negligence might succeed on proof of foreseeable economic loss caused by a defendant, even where no damage to property and no proprietary or possessory interest are shown.

A new building in Abu Dhabi was owned by Sheikh Al-Oteiba. The main contractors were Simaan General Contracting. The supply and erection of curtain walling had been subcontracted to Industria Componenti per l'Architettura Feal SpA ('Feal'). Glass units for incorporation in the walling had been supplied by Pilkington Glass Ltd.

The alleged defects related to the colour of the units. They should have been a uniform shade of green. They were, it was said, in variable shades of green, and in places red. That discrepancy was unacceptable to the building owner. Green was the colour of peace in Islam, so the discrepancy was regarded as of some moment.

One might have expected a claim by the building owner against Simaan, by Simaan against Feal and by Feal against Pilkington's. The problem arose because Simaan's had chosen to sue Pilkington's in tort rather than Feal in contract. There was no meaningful sense in which Simaan could be said to have relied on Pilkington's. There had been no technical discussion of the product between them.

Where a specialist subcontractor was vetted, selected and nominated by a building owner, it might be possible to conclude that the nominated subcontractor had assumed a direct responsibility to the building owner. On that basis, it might have been said that Pilkington's owed a duty to the sheikh in tort, as well as to Feal in contract. But there was no basis on which they could be said to have assumed a direct responsibility for the quality of the goods to Simaan. That was inconsistent with the structure of the contract the parties had chosen to make.

There was no physical damage in the present case. The units were as good as ever they had been. The defects were failures to comply with conditions of correspondence with description or sample, merchantability or perhaps fitness for purpose. It would be an abuse of language to describe the units as damaged.

The authorities did not establish a general rule that claims in negligence might succeed on proof of economic loss caused by Pilkington's, even where no damage to property and no proprietary or possessory interest had been shown. Simaan's real complaint was that Pilkington's failure to supply goods in conformity with the specification had rendered their main contract less profitable. That was a type of claim against which the law had consistently set its face.

If the units could be regarded as damaged, the damage occurred at the time of manufacture. Simaan had failed to show any interest in them at the time when damage occurred. Foreseeability of harm or loss did not of itself lead to a duty of care. It was a necessary ingredient, but not the only ingredient.

The approach of the law to awarding damages for economic loss on the grounds of negligence where there had been no injury to the person or property had throughout been greatly affected by pragmatic considerations.

It was held that Pilkington's were not liable in tort to the main contractors, Simaan.

Simaan General Contracting Co. v. *Pilkington Glass Ltd.*, [1988] 1 All E.R. 791 C.A.

A cautionary tale about how much or how little may be recovered in damages

In 1983, Mr Dean purchased a property near Tenbury Wells, Herefordshire, from Mrs Ainley. At the rear of the house was a large, damp, vaulted cellar, some 74 ft long. Over part of that cellar was a flagstone terrace through which water could seep.

Before the purchase, Mr Dean was advised by his surveyor that water was penetrating the cellar both from the terrace above and laterally through the brickwork. Thus a specific term was included in the contract of sale, that 'The vendor will at her own expense prior to completion hereunder complete to the reasonable satisfaction of the purchaser or his surveyor the following works: . . . (c) prevention of leaking of water from the patio into the premises beneath'. Mr Dean wanted to use the cellar as a rifle-range. Shortly after the purchase it became apparent that Mrs Ainley was in breach of that term.

Evidence from surveyors for both parties showed that waterproofing of the terrace would prevent water entering the cellar vertically, but that water would still penetrate horizontally through the surrounding ground. The best solution to damp-proofing the cellar, the surveyors agreed, was the construction of a waterproof envelope around the cellar at a cost estimated by Mr Dean of £11 150. Both surveyors agreed that it would not be sensible to waterproof the terrace – a considerably cheaper operation.

At the hearing of the action the judge held that Mrs Ainley was in breach, but that Mr Dean had not proved that he had suffered more than nominal damage as a result. He gave judgment for him for £5 and made no order as to costs. Mr Dean appealed.

It was held that the approach of the judge at first instance was correct. It followed that if Mr Dean in the present case could show (1) that he had suffered some damage as a result of Mrs Ainley's breach, and (2) that if he was awarded substantial damages, he intended to use the money to pay for the work which was required by the covenant, then the proper measure of damages was the cost of that work.

The judge held that Mr Dean had not suffered any damage. In so concluding he appeared to have adopted Mrs Ainley's argument that what Mr Dean wanted was a dry cellar, that the prevention of water leaking from the terrace would not make it completely dry and thus he had suffered no damage. That argument was fallacious.

The covenant required Mrs Ainley to carry out work to prevent water leaking from the terrace into the cellar. The judge had accepted that if that were done, a substantial proportion – something less than 70% – of the total penetration of water would have been prevented. Mr Dean had suffered damage as a result of Mrs Ainley failing to carry out work.

Moreover, Mr Dean had given a firm undertaking that if damages were awarded, he would carry out the work of 'tanking' the cellar. He had satisfied the conditions entitling him to damages.

There remained a question as to the amount of damages; while 'tanking' the cellar would prevent seepage from the terrace, the water-proofing of the terrace would also achieve that objective. The latter would be less expensive than the former.

On general principle, Mr Dean was entitled only to damages equal to the cost of the less expensive solution. The cost of that work would be assessed at £7500.

Dean v. *Ainley*, [1987] 1 W.L.R. 1729.

officers to seize the property of the judgment debtor to the value of the judgment. The property is auctioned and the proceeds paid to you up to the sum which you have been awarded, plus interest from the date on which judgment was entered. Having deducted their own costs, the court officers return any money which remains from the auction to the judgment debtor.

2. Asset   Land, stocks and shares, i.e. securities.

   Method   Charging order

A charge is registered against the freehold or leasehold land in the ownership of the judgment debtor to provide security for the payment of the judgment debt. After a court order has been obtained, the land may be sold and the proceeds used to settle the debt. A similar process applies in the case of stocks and shares.

3. Asset   Bank accounts and debts owed to the judgment debtor.

   Method   Garnishee order

A garnishee order prevents a person who owes money to the judgment debtor from paying it to him. Instead that person is ordered to pay the sum of money which he owes directly to you.

4. Asset   Money which is due to the judgment debtor in the future, e.g. rent, legacies, reversionary interest under a trust fund, insurance policies, royalties on books, income from a partnership.

   Method   Receivership

A receiver is appointed after an application is made to the court. The receiver will collect any income which the judgment debtor would otherwise receive.

5. Asset   Salary

   Method   Instalment order and an attachment of earnings order

Where the judgment debtor receives a salary, he may satisfy the judgment debt by paying it off in regular weekly or monthly instalments upon the order of the court. If he defaults on one or more instalments, you may apply to the court for an attachment of earnings order. Under the order the judgment debtor's employer deducts from his salary whatever sum is ordered by the court. The employer then pays that sum into court.

6. Asset   Business run by the judgment debtor.

   Method   Bankruptcy notice and petition

You may present a petition to the court to wind up a company run by the judgment debtor if, for example, he has not satisfied the judgment debt either in whole or in part, or where the debt exceeds £750 it has not been paid within 3 weeks or has not been secured or compounded to your reasonable satisfaction. If the company is found to be bankrupt, then the judgment debtor cannot continue trading. A receiver will be appointed to take over the property of the judgment debtor and supervise the fair distribution of his assets among you and other creditors. The company will be dissolved if a winding-up order is made against it. Often the mere threat of bankruptcy proceedings will be a sufficient incentive for a judgment debtor to satisfy his debt to you.

THIRTEEN

What do words

mean?

Q. Sometimes our legal advisers use specialized words and phrases which they do not explain. Can you?

Acceptance   Upon an offer being accepted, a binding contract comes into existence. The following apply:

(a) The acceptance must be made while the offer is still open;
(b) The person to whom the offer is made must know of the offer;
(c) The person to whom the offer is made must conform to the terms of the offer;
(d) The acceptance must be communicated to the person making the offer or an act which has been specified must be done.

Approved inspector   A person who under the *Building Act 1984*, section 49, has been approved either by the secretary of state or by a body designated by him to consider Building Regulation applications.

ARCUK   The Architects' Registration Council of the United Kingdom under which all architects must register in order to use the word 'architect' to describe themselves.
Common Law   That part of the law which is not only unwritten, but has also been evolved from common customs.
Consideration   Consideration may be either:

(a) valuable consideration – a right, interest, profit or benefit accruing to one party, or a forbearance, detriment, loss or responsibility given, suffered or undertaken by the other;
(b) good consideration – based on natural love or relationship.

Counter-claim   A defendant may state in his defence that he himself has a claim against the plaintiff who is bringing an action against him.
Default summons   A debt or liquidated demand recovered by summary means in the County Court.
Discovery   List of documents served by each party to an action on the other after pleadings have been closed.

Equity   That which is fair or is derived from natural justice; it embraces a body of maxims which include the following:

(a) equity acts on the conscience;
(b) equity will not suffer a wrong to be without a remedy;
(c) equitable remedies are discretionary;
(d) he who comes into equity must come with clean hands;
     he who seeks equity must do equity.

Estoppel   A person cannot deny the truth of a statement which he has previously made.

Fee simple owner   A freehold estate in land which was originally held by free, rather than servile, services.

Indictable offence   Those serious crimes which are tried not before magistrates, but before judge and jury in the Crown Court.

Injunction   An order of the court whereby the party to whom it is addressed is required to do or refrain from doing a particular thing.

Interrogatories   An application made to the Master (*q.v.*) by one of the parties in an action for leave to serve a list of questions, interrogatories on the other party which the latter is obliged to answer by affidavit.

Master   An officer of the Supreme Court who has with certain exceptions similar powers to a Judge in Chambers to hear, among other matters, interlocutory applications – i.e. to decide certain matters which arise once an action has been started, but before it is heard in court.

Offer   When an offer is accepted, a binding agreement exists. The classic form of an offer is 'I promise [the offer], if you will in return make a certain promise or do a certain act'.

Restrictive covenants   A deed which sets out an agreed obligation forbidding the doing of some act which meets with the land and touches and concerns it. A restrictive covenant must be registered as a land charge.

RIBA   The Royal Institute of British Architects; the RIBA is the 'profesional' body to which an architect may if he wish belong. He is not obliged to be a member of the RIBA in order to practise architecture or to call himself an architect. However, he must be a member of ARCUK (*q.v.*) before he can describe himself as an architect.

Specific performance   A person may be compelled by the court to carry out or perform his obligations under a contract if damages would not be an adequate compensation.

Statute law   That part of the law which is written and contained in Acts of Parliament.

Strict liability   A person acts at his own peril and liability will arise without fault, it exists independently of negligence or wrongful intent.

Summary offence   Crimes which are less serious than an indictable offence and which are tried before magistrates in the Magistrates' Court.

Third parties to an action   A person who was not originally a party to a claim made by a plaintiff against the defendant, but against whom the defendant now claims an indemnity or contribution against any damages which the defendant has been ordered to pay the plaintiff.

Tort   An act which either intentionally or unintentionally causes harm to another and which is against the law but not a breach of duty arising out of a personal relation or contract.

Contracts

1. ACA form
   Association of Consultant Architects:
   Form of Building Agreement 1982 (Architectural Press, 2nd edn, 1984);

2. FAS contract
   Faculty of Architects and Surveyors:
   Building Contract (FAS, 1986);

3. FIDIC contract
   Fédération Internationale des Ingénieurs–Conseils:
   Conditions of Contract for Works of Civil Engineering Construction (FIDIC, 4th edn, 1987);

4. GC/Works/1
   HMSO: General Conditions of Government Contracts for Building and Civil Engineering Works. Form GC/Works/1 (HMSO, 2nd edn, 1977);

5. ICE contract
   Institution of Civil Engineers:
   Conditions of Contract and Forms of Tender, Agreement and Bond for Use in Connection with Works of Civil Engineering Construction (ICE, 5th rev. edn, 1979; reprinted, 1986);

6. J.C.T. 80
   Joint Contracts Tribunal for the Standard Form of Building Contract:
   Standard Form of Building Contract 1980 edition. Private with Approximate Quantities as amended (RIBA Publications, 1987).

Table of cases

Page entries in **bold** indicate citation of cases in text.

Table of statutes

Index